Date Due

NOV 3 0

SEP 1 6 1993

812
.54
Willi

Williams, Tennessee, 1911-1983.
    The theatre of Tennessee Williams. -- New York :
New Directions, c1971-1992.
    8 v. ; 22 cm.

    CONTENTS: v. 1. Battle of angels ; The glass menagerie ;
A streetcar named Desire -- v. 2. The eccentricities of
a nightingale ; Summer and smoke ; The rose tattoo ;
Camino Real -- v. 3. Cat on a hot tin roof ; Orpheus
descending ; Suddenly last summer -- v. 4. Sweet bird
of youth ; Period of adjustment ; The night of the
Iguana -- v. 5. The milk train doesn't stop here anymore
                    (SEE NEXT CARD)

1360   92JUL09   31/au   1-00942141

THE THEATRE OF TENNESSEE WILLIAMS

Volume VIII

By TENNESSEE WILLIAMS

THE THEATRE OF
TENNESSEE WILLIAMS

Volume VIII

Vieux Carré
A Lovely Sunday for Creve Coeur
Clothes for a Summer Hotel
The Red Devil Battery Sign

A NEW DIRECTIONS BOOK

Manufactured in the United States of America
New Directions Books are printed on acid-free paper.
First published clothbound by New Directions in 1992
Published simultaneously in Canada by Penguin Books Canada Limited

Library of Congress Cataloging-in-Publication Data
(Rev. for vol. 8)

Williams, Tennessee, 1911–1983.
    The theatre of Tennessee Williams.

    Contents: v. 1. Battle of angels. The glass menagerie. A streetcar named
Desire — [etc.] —
v. 7. In the bar of a Tokyo hotel and other plays —
v. 8. Vieux Carré. A lovely Sunday for Creve Coeur.
Clothes for a summer hotel. The red devil battery
sign.
    I. Title.
PS3545.I5365A19   1971   812'.54   78–159743
ISBN 0–8112–1201–7 (v.8)

New Directions Books are published for James Laughlin
by New Directions Publishing Corporation,
80 Eighth Avenue, New York 10011

Contents

VIEUX CARRÉ

IIIIIIIIIIIIIIIIIIIIIIIIIIIIIIIIIIIIIIIIIIIIIIIIIIIIIIIIIIIIIIIIIIIIIIIIIIIIIIIIIIIIIIIIIIIIIIIIIIIIIIIIIIIIIIIIIIIIIIIIIIIIIIIIIIIIIIIIIIIIIIIIIIIIIII

INSCRIBED TO KEITH HACK

The Nottingham Playhouse Production of *Vieux Carré* was presented at The Playhouse Theatre, Nottingham, on May 16, 1978 and at the Piccadilly Theatre, London, by Ian B. Albery for Calabash Productions Ltd., on August 9, 1978. It was directed by Keith Hack; stage design was by Voytek, lighting by Francis Reid, costumes by Maria Björnson, and music by Jeremy Nicholas; company stage manager, James Gill. The cast in order of appearance was as follows:

MRS. WIRE	SYLVIA MILES
NURSIE	NADIA CATTOUSE
THE WRITER	KARL JOHNSON
JANE	DI TREVIS
NIGHTINGALE	RICHARD KANE
MARY MAUDE	BETTY HARDY
MISS CARRIE	JUDITH FELLOWS
TYE	JONATHAN KENT
PHOTOGRAPHER	ROBIN MCDONALD
SKY	JACK ELLIOTT

TIME: The period between winter 1938 and spring 1939.

PLACE: A rooming house, No. 722 Toulouse Street, in the French Quarter of New Orleans.

THE SETTING OF THE PLAY: The stage seems bare. Various playing areas may be distinguished by sketchy partitions and doorframes. In the barrenness there should be a poetic evocation of all the cheap rooming houses of the world. This one is in the Vieux Carré of New Orleans, where it remains standing, at 722 Toulouse Street, now converted to an art gallery. I will describe the building as it was when I rented an attic room in the late thirties, not as it will be designed, or realized for the stage.

It is a three-story building. There are a pair of alcoves, facing Toulouse Street. These alcove cubicles are separated by plywood, which provides a minimal separation (spatially) between the writer (myself those many years ago) and an older painter, a terribly wasted man, dying of tuberculosis, but fiercely denying this circumstance to himself.

A curved staircase ascends from the rear of a dark narrow passageway from the street entrance to the kitchen area. From there it ascends to the third floor, or gabled attic with its mansard roof.

A narrow hall separates the gabled cubicles from the studio (with skylight) which is occupied by Jane and Tye.

Obviously the elevations of these acting areas can be only suggested by a few shallow steps: a realistic setting is impossible, and the solution lies mainly in very skillful lighting and minimal furnishings.

4

PART ONE

WRITER [*spotlighted downstage*]: Once this house was alive, it was occupied once. In my recollection it still is but by shadowy occupants like ghosts. Now they enter the lighter areas of my memory.

[*Fade in dimly visible characters of the play, turning about in a stylized manner. The spotlight fades on the writer and is brought up on Mrs. Wire, who assumes her active character in the play.*]

MRS. WIRE: Nursie! Nursie—where's my pillows?

[*Nursie is spotlighted on a slightly higher level, looking up fearfully at something. She screams.*]

Hey, what the hell is going on in there!

NURSIE [*running down in a sort of football crouch*]: A bat, a bat's in the kitchen!

MRS. WIRE: Bat? I never seen a bat nowhere on these premises, Nursie.

NURSIE: Why, Mizz Wire, I swear it was a bull bat up there in the kitchen. You tell me no bats, why, they's a pack of bats that hang upside down from that ole banana tree in the court-yard from dark till daybreak, when they all scream at once and fly up like a—explosion of—damned souls out of a graveyard.

MRS. WIRE: If such a thing was true—

NURSIE: As God's word is true!

5

MRS. WIRE: I repeat, if such a thing was true—which it isn't—an' you go tawkin' about it with you big black mouth, why it could ruin the reputation of this rooming house which is the only respectable rooming house in the Quarter. Now where's my pillows, Nursie?

NURSIE [sotto voce *as she arranges the pallet*]: Shit . . .

MRS. WIRE: What you say?

NURSIE: I said shoot . . . faw shit. You'd see they're on the cot if you had a light bulb in this hall. [*She is making up the cot.*] What you got against light? First thing God said on the first day of creation was, "Let there be light."

MRS. WIRE: You hear him say that?

NURSIE: You never read the scriptures.

MRS. WIRE: Why should I bother to read 'em with you quotin' 'em to me like a female preacher. Book say this, say that, makes me sick of the book. Where's my flashlight, Nursie?

NURSIE: 'Sunder the pillows. [*She stumbles on a heavy knapsack.*] Lawd! What that there?

MRS. WIRE: Some crazy young man come here wantin' a room. I told him I had no vacancies for Bourbon Street bums. He dropped that sack on the floor and said he'd pick it up tomorrow, which he won't unless he pays fifty cents for storage . . .

NURSIE: It's got something written on it that shines in the dark.

MRS. WIRE: "Sky"—say that's his name. Carry it on upstairs with you, Nursie.

NURSIE: Mizz Wire, I cain't hardly get myself up them steps no more, you know that.

MRS. WIRE: Shoot.

NURSIE: Mizz Wire, I think I oughta inform you I'm thinkin' of retirin'.

MRS. WIRE: *Retirin'* to what, Nursie? The banana tree in the courtyard with the bats you got in your head?

NURSIE: They's lots of folks my age, black an' white, that's called bag people. They just wander round with paper bags that hold ev'rything they possess or they can collect. Nights they sleep on doorsteps: spend days on boxes on corners of Canal Street with a tin cup. They get along: they live—long as intended to by the Lord.

MRS. WIRE: Yor place is with me, Nursie.

NURSIE: I can't please you no more. You keep callin' Nursie, Nursie, do this, do that, with all these stairs in the house and my failin' eyesight. No Ma'am, it's time for me to retire.

[*She crosses upstage. The kitchen area is dimly lighted. Nursie sits at the table with a cup of chicory coffee, eyes large and ominously dark as the continent of her race.*

[*A spot of light picks up the writer dimly at the entrance to the hall.*]

MRS. WIRE: Who? Who?

WRITER: It's—

MRS. WIRE: *You* . . .

7

WRITER: Mrs. Wire, you're blinding me with that light. [*He shields his left eye with a hand.*]

MRS. WIRE [*switching off the light*]: Git upstairs, boy. We'll talk in the mawnin' about your future plans.

WRITER: I have no plans for the future, Mrs. Wire.

MRS. WIRE: That's a situation you'd better correct right quick.

[*The writer, too, collides with the bizarre, colorfully decorated knapsack.*]

WRITER: What's—?

MRS. WIRE: Carry that sack upstairs with you. Nursie refused to.

[*With an effort the writer shoulders the sack and mounts a step or two to the kitchen level.*]

WRITER: Mrs. Wire told me to carry this sack up here.

NURSIE: Just put it somewhere it won't trip me up.

WRITER: Sky? Sky?

NURSIE: She say that's his name. Whose name? I think her mind is goin' on her again. Lately she calls out, "Timmy, Timmy," or she carries on conversations with her dead husband, Horace . . .

WRITER: A name—Sky? [*To himself.*] Shines like a prediction.

[*He drops the knapsack at the edge of the kitchen light and wanders musingly back to the table. Nursie automatically pours him a cup of chicory.*

[*Again the area serving as the entrance passage is lighted, and the sound of a key scraping at a resistant lock is heard.*]

MRS. WIRE [*starting up from her cot*]: Who? Who?

[*Jane enters exhaustedly.*]

JANE: Why, Mrs. Wire, you scared me! [*She has an elegance about her and a vulnerability.*]

MRS. WIRE: Miss Sparks, what're you doin' out so late on the streets of the Quarter?

JANE: Mrs. Wire, according to the luminous dial on my watch, it is only ten after twelve.

MRS. WIRE: When I give you a room here . . .

JANE: Gave me? I thought rented . . .

MRS. WIRE [*cutting through*]: I told you a single girl was expected in at midnight.

JANE: I'm afraid I didn't take that too seriously. Not since I lived with my parents in New Rochelle, New York, before I went to college, have I been told to be in at a certain hour, and even then I had my own key and disregarded the order more often than not. However! I *am* going to tell you why and where I've gone tonight. I have gone to the all-night drugstore, Waterbury's, on Canal Street, to buy a spray can of Black Flag, which is an insect repellent. I took a cab there tonight and made this purchase because, Mrs. Wire, when I opened the window without a screen in my room, a cockroach, a *flying* cockroach, flew

9

right into my face and was followed by a squadron of others. *Well!* I do *not* have an Oriental, a Buddhistic tolerance for certain insects, least of all a cockroach and even less a flying one. Oh, I've learned to live reluctantly with the ordinary pedestrian kind of cockroach, but to have one fly directly into my face almost gave me convulsions! Now as for the window without a screen, if a screen has not been put in that window by tomorrow, I will buy one for it myself and deduct the cost from next month's rent. [*She goes past Mrs. Wire toward the steps.*]

MRS. WIRE: Hold on a minute, young lady. When you took your room here, you gave your name as Miss Sparks. Now is that young fellow that's living up there with you Mr. Sparks, and if so why did you register as Miss instead of Mrs.?

JANE: I'm sure you've known for some time that I'm sharing my room with a young man, whose name is not Mr. Sparks, whose name is Tye McCool. And if that offends your moral scruples—well—sometimes it offends mine, too.

MRS. WIRE: If I had not been a young lady myself once! Oh yes, once, yaiss! I'd have evicted both so fast you'd think that . . .

JANE: No, I've stopped thinking. Just let things happen to me.

[*Jane is now at the stairs and starts up them weakly. Mrs. Wire grunts despairingly and falls back to her cot. Jane enters the kitchen.*]

NURSIE: Why, hello, Miss Sparks.

JANE: Good evening, Nursie—why is Mrs. Wire sleeping in the entrance hall?

NURSIE: Lawd, that woman, she got the idea that 722 Tou-

10

louse Street is the address of a jailhouse. And she's the keeper—have some hot chick'ry with me?

JANE: Do you know I still don't know what chicory is? A beverage of some kind?

NURSIE: Why chicory's South'n style coffee.

JANE: Oh, well, thank you, maybe I could try a bit of it to get me up that flight of stairs . . .

[*She sits at the table. Below, the door has opened a third time. The painter called Nightingale stands in the doorway with a pickup.*]

MRS. WIRE: Who? Ah!

NIGHTINGALE [*voice rising*]: Well, cousin, uh, Jake . . .

PICKUP [*uneasily*]: Blake.

NIGHTINGALE: Yes, we do have a lot of family news to exchange. Come on in. We'll talk a bit more in my room.

MRS. WIRE: In a pig's snout you will!

NIGHTINGALE: Why, Mrs. Wire! [*He chuckles, coughs.*] Are you sleeping in the hall now?

MRS. WIRE: I'm keeping watch on the comings and goings at night of tenants in my house.

NIGHTINGALE: Oh, yes, I know your aversion to visitors at night, but this is my first cousin. I just bumped into him at Gray Goose bus station. He is here for one day only, so I have taken the license of inviting him in for a little family talk since we'll have no other chance.

MRS. WIRE: If you had half the cousins you claim to have, you'd belong to the biggest family since Adam's.

PICKUP: Thanks, but I got to move on. Been nice seeing you—cousin . . .

NIGHTINGALE: Wait—here—take this five. Go to the America Hotel on Exchange Alley just off Canal Street, and I will drop in at noon tomorrow—cousin . . . [*He starts to cough.*]

PICKUP: Thanks, I'll see ya, cousin.

MRS. WIRE: Hah, cousin.

[*Nightingale coughs and spits near her cot.*]

Don't you spit by my bed!

NIGHTINGALE: Fuck off, you old witch!

MR. WIRE: What did you say to me?

NIGHTINGALE: Nothing not said to and about you before! [*He mounts the steps.*]

MRS. WIRE: Nursie! Nursie! [*Receiving no response she lowers herself with a groan onto the cot.*]

NIGHTINGALE [*starting up the stairs*]: Midnight staircase—still in—your [*coughs*] fatal position . . . [*He climbs slowly up.*]

[*The writer, Jane, and Nursie are in the kitchen. The crones enter, wild-eyed and panting with greasy paper bags. The kitchen area is lighted.*]

MARY MAUDE: Nursie? Miss Carrie and I ordered a little more dinner this evening than we could eat, so we had the waiter put the remains of the, the—

MISS CARRIE [*her wild eyes very wild*]: The steak "Diane," I had the steak Diane and Mary Maude had the chicken "bonne femme." But our eyes were a little bigger than our stomachs.

MARY MAUDE: The sight of too much on a table can kill your appetite! But this food is too good to waste.

MISS CARRIE: And we don't have ice to preserve it in our room, so would you kindly put it in Mrs. Wire's icebox, Nursie.

NURSIE: The last time I done that Miss Wire raised Cain about it, had me throw it right out. She said it didn' smell good.

JANE: I have an icebox in which I'd be glad to keep it for you ladies.

MARY MAUDE: Oh, that's very kind of you!

WRITER [*rising from the kitchen table*]: Let me carry it up.

[*He picks up the greasy bags and starts upstairs. Miss Carrie's asthmatic respiration has steadily increased. She staggers with a breathless laugh.*]

MARY MAUDE: Oh, Miss Carrie, you better get right to bed. She's having another attack of her awful asthma. Our room gets no sun, and the walls are so damp, so—dark . . .

[*They totter out of the light together.*]

NURSIE [*averting her face from the bag with a sniff of repugnance*]: They didn't go to no restaurant. They been to the garbage pail on the walk outside, don't bother with it, it's spoiled [*pointing upstage*] just put it over there, I'll throw it out.

JANE: I wonder if they'd be offended if I bought them a sack of groceries at Solari's tomorrow.

NURSIE: Offend 'em did you say?

JANE: I meant their pride.

NURSIE: Honey, they gone as far past pride as they gone past mistaking a buzzard for a bluebird.

[*She chuckles. Tye appears. Jane pretends not to notice.*]

JANE: I'm afraid pride's an easy thing to go past sometimes. I am living—I am sharing my studio with a, an addicted—delinquent, a barker at a—stripshow joint. [*She has pretended to ignore Tye's disheveled, drugged, but vulnerably boyish appearance at the edge of the light.*]

TYE [*in a slurred voice*]: You wouldn't be tawkin' about—nobody—present . . .

JANE: Why, hello, Tye. How'd you get back so early? How'd you get back at all, in this—condition?

TYE: Honey! If I didn't have my arms full of—packages.

JANE: The less you say out loud about the hot merchandise you've been accumulating here . . .

TYE: Babe, you're asking for a— [*He doubles his fist.*]

14

JANE: Which I'd return with a kick in the balls! [*She gasps.*] My Lord, did I say that?

MRS. WIRE: What's that shoutin' about?

[*Jane breaks into tears. She falls back into the chair and buries her head in her arms.*]

TYE: Hey, love, come here, I knocked off work early to be with you—do you think I'd really hit you?

JANE: I don't know . . .

TYE: Come to—bed . . .

JANE: Don't lean on me.

[*They cross out of the light. The writer looks after them wistfully as the light dims out.*]

The writer has undressed and is in bed. Nightingale coughs—a fiendish, racking cough. He is hacking and spitting up bloody phlegm. He enters his cubicle.

Then across the makeshift partition in the writer's cubicle, unlighted except by a faint glow in its alcove window, another sound commences—a sound of dry and desperate sobbing which sounds as though nothing in the world could ever appease the wound from which it comes: loneliness, inborn and inbred to the bone.

Slowly, as his coughing fit subsides, Nightingale, the quick-sketch artist, turns his head in profile to the sound of the sobbing. Then the writer, across the partition, is dimly lighted, too. He is also sitting up on his cot, staring at the partition between his cell and Nightingale's.

Nightingale clears his throat loudly and sings hoarsely and softly a pop song of the era such as "If I Didn't Care" or "Paper Doll." Slowly the audience of one whom he is serenading succeeds in completely stifling the dry sobbing with a pillow. Nightingale's voice rises a bit as he gets up and lights a cigarette; then he goes toward the upstage limit of the dim stage lighting and makes the gesture of opening a door.

He moves into the other gable room of the attic and stands, silent, for several beats of the song as the writer slowly, reluctantly, turns on his cot to face him.

NIGHTINGALE: . . . I want to ask you something.

WRITER: Huh?

NIGHTINGALE: The word "landlady" as applied to Mrs. Wire and to all landladies that I've encountered in my life—isn't it the biggest one-word contradiction in the English language? [*The writer is embarrassed by Nightingale's intrusion and steady scrutiny.*] She owns the land, yes, but is the witch a lady? Mind if I switch on your light?

16

WRITER: The bulb's burned out.

NIGHTINGALE [*chuckles and coughs*]: She hasn't replaced a burnt-out light bulb in this attic since I moved here last spring. I have to provide my own light bulbs by unscrewing them from the gentleman's lavatory at the City of the Two Parrots, where I ply my trade. Temporarily, you know. Doing portraits in pastel of the tourist clientele. [*His voice is curiously soft and intimate, more as if he were speaking of personal matters.*]

Of course I . . . [*He coughs and clears his throat.*] . . . have no shame about it, no guilt at all, since what I do there is a travesty of my talent, I mean a prostitution of it, I mean, painting these tourists at the Two Parrots, which are actually two very noisy macaws. Oh, they have a nice patio there, you know, palm trees and azaleas when in season, but the cuisine and the service . . . abominable. The menu sometimes includes cockroaches . . . (There are a lot of great eating places in New Orleans, like Galatoire's, Antoine's, Arnaud's in the Vieux Carré and . . . Commander's Palace and Plantation House in the Garden District . . . lovely old mansions, you know, converted to restaurants with a gracious style . . . haunted by dead residents, of course, but with charm . . .)

[*This monologue is like a soothing incantation, interspersed with hoarseness and coughing.*]

Like many writers, I know you're a writer, you're a young man of very few spoken words, compared to my garrulity.

WRITER: Yes, I . . .

NIGHTINGALE: So far, kid, you're practically . . . monosyllabic.

WRITER: I . . . don't feel well . . . tonight.

NIGHTINGALE: That's why I intruded. You have a candle on that box beside your cot.

17

WRITER: Yes, but no matches.

NIGHTINGALE: I have matches, I'll light it. Talk is easier . . . [*He strikes the match and advances to the writer's bedside.*] . . . between two people visible to each other, if . . . not too sharply . . . [*He lights the candle.*] Once I put up for a night in a flophouse without doors, and a gentleman entered my cubicle without invitation, came straight to my cot and struck a match, leaned over me peering directly into my face . . . and then said, "No," and walked out . . . as if he assumed that I would have said, "Yes." [*He laughs and coughs.*]

[*Pause*]

You're not a man of few words but a boy of no words. I'll just sit on the cot if you don't object.

WRITER: . . . I, uh . . . do need sleep.

NIGHTINGALE: You need some company first. I know the sound of loneliness, heard it through the partition. [*He has sat on the cot. The writer huddles away to the wall, acutely embarrassed.*] . . . Trying not to, but crying . . . why try not to? Think it's unmanly? Crying is a release for man or woman . . .

WRITER: I was taught not to cry because it's . . . humiliating . . .

NIGHTINGALE: You're a victim of conventional teaching, which you'd better forget. What were you crying about? Some particular sorrow or . . . for the human condition.

WRITER: Some . . . particular sorrow. My closest relative died last month.

NIGHTINGALE: Your mother?

WRITER: The mother of my mother, Grand. She died after a long illness just before I left home, and at night I remember . . .

NIGHTINGALE [*giving a comforting pat*]: Well, losses must be accepted and survived. How strange it is that we've occupied these adjoining rooms for about three weeks now and have just barely said hello to each other when passing on the stairs. You have interesting eyes.

WRITER: In what way do you mean?

NIGHTINGALE: Isn't the pupil of the left one a little bit lighter?

WRITER: . . . I'm afraid I'm . . . developing a—cataract in that eye.

NIGHTINGALE: That's not possible for a kid.

WRITER: I am twenty-eight.

NIGHTINGALE: What I meant is, your face is still youthful as your vulnerable nature, they go—together. Of course, I'd see an oculist if you suspect there's a cataract.

WRITER: I plan to when I . . . if I . . . can ever afford to . . . the vision in that eye's getting cloudy.

NIGHTINGALE: Don't wait till you can afford to. Go straight away and don't receive the bill.

WRITER: I couldn't do that.

NIGHTINGALE: Don't be so honest in this dishonest world. [*He pauses and coughs.*] Shit, the witch don't sleep in her bedroom you know.

19

WRITER: Yes, I noticed she is sleeping on a cot in the hall now.

NIGHTINGALE: When I came in now she sprang up and hollered out, "Who?" And I answered her with a hoot owl imitation, "Hoo, Hooo, Hooooo." Why, the lady is all three furies in one. A single man needs visitors at night. Necessary as bread, as blood in the body. Why, there's a saying, "Better to live with your worst enemy than to live alone."

WRITER: Yes, loneliness is an—affliction.

NIGHTINGALE: Well, now you have a friend here.

WRITER [*dryly*]: Thanks.

NIGHTINGALE: Of course we're in a madhouse. I wouldn't tolerate the conditions here if the season wasn't so slow that—my financial condition is difficult right now. I don't like insults and *la vie solitaire*—with bedbugs bleeding me like leeches . . . but now we know each other, the plywood partition between us has been dissolved, no more just hellos. So tonight you were crying in here alone. What of it? Don't we all? Have a cigarette.

WRITER: Thanks.

[*Nightingale holds the candle out.*]

I won't smoke it now, I'll save it till morning. I like a cigarette when I sit down to work.

[*Nightingale's steady scrutiny embarrasses him. They fall silent. After several beats, the writer resumes.*]

There's—a lot of human material—in the Quarter for a writer . . .

NIGHTINGALE: I used to hear you typing. Where's your type-writer?

WRITER: I, uh, hocked it.

NIGHTINGALE: That's what I figured. Wha'd you get for it?

WRITER: Ten dollars. It was a secondhand Underwood port-able. I'm worried about just how I'll redeem it. [*He is increasingly embarrassed.*]

NIGHTINGALE: Excuse my curiosity, I mean concern. It's sympathetic . . . smoke a cigarette now and have another for mawnin'. You're not managing right. Need advice and . . . company in this sad ole house. I'm happy to give both if accepted.

WRITER: . . . I appreciate . . . both.

NIGHTINGALE: You don't seem experienced yet . . . kid, are you . . . excuse my blunt approach . . . but are you . . . ? [*He completes the question by placing a shaky hand on the writer's crumpled, sheet-covered body.*]

WRITER [*in a stifled voice*]: Oh . . . I'm not sure I know . . . I . . .

NIGHTINGALE: Ain't come out completely, as we put it?

WRITER: Completely, no, just one—experience.

NIGHTINGALE: Tell me about that one experience.

WRITER: I'm not sure I want to discuss it.

NIGHTINGALE: That's no way to begin a confidential friend-ship.

WRITER: . . . Well, New Year's Eve, I was entertained by a married couple I had a letter of introduction to when I came down here, the . . . man's a painter, does popular bayou pictures displayed in shop windows in the Quarter, his name is . . .

NIGHTINGALE: Oh, I know him. He's got a good thing going, commercially speaking, tourists buy them calendar illustrations in dreamy rainbow colors that never existed but in the head of a hack like him.

WRITER: . . . The, uh, atmosphere is . . . effective.

NIGHTINGALE: Oh, they sell to people that don't know paint from art. Maybe you've never seen artistic paintings. [*His voice shakes with feverish pride.*] I could do it, in fact I've done good painting, serious work. But I got to live, and you can't live on good painting until you're dead, or nearly. So, I make it, temporarily, as a quick sketch artist. I flatter old bitches by makin' 'em ten pounds lighter and ten years younger and with some touches of—decent humanity in their eyes that God forgot to put there, or they've decided to dispense with, not always easy. But what is? So—you had an experience with the bayou painter? I didn't know he was, oh, inclined to boys, this is killing.

WRITER [*slowly with embarrassment*]: It wasn't with Mr. Block, it was with a . . . paratrooper.

NIGHTINGALE: Aha, a paratrooper dropped out of the sky for you, huh? You have such nice smooth skin . . . Would you like a bit of white port? I keep a half pint by my bed to wash down my sandman special when this touch of flu and the bedbugs keep me awake. Just a mo', I'll fetch it, we'll have a nightcap—now that we're acquainted! [*He goes out rapidly, coughing, then rushes back in with the bottle.*]

The witch has removed the glass, we'll have to drink from the bottle. I'll wash my pill down now, the rest is yours. [*He pops a*

22

capsule into his mouth and gulps from the bottle, immediately coughing and gagging. He extends the bottle to the writer.

[*Pause. The writer half extends his hand toward the bottle, then draws it back and shakes his head.*]

Oh yes, flu is contagious, how stupid of me, I'm sorry.

WRITER: Never mind, I don't care much for liquor.

NIGHTINGALE: Where you from?

WRITER: . . . St. Louis.

NIGHTINGALE: Christ, do people live there?

WRITER: It has a good art museum and a fine symphony orchestra and . . .

NIGHTINGALE: No decent gay life at all?

WRITER: You mean . . .

NIGHTINGALE: You know what I mean. I mean like the . . . paratrooper.

WRITER: Oh. No. There could be but . . . living at home . . .

NIGHTINGALE: Tell me, how did it go with the paratrooper who descended on you at Block's?

WRITER: Well at midnight we went out on the gallery and he, the paratrooper, was out on the lower gallery with a party of older men, antique dealers, they were all singing "Auld Lang Syne."

NIGHTINGALE: How imaginative and *appropriate* to them.

WRITER: —I noticed him down there and he noticed me.

NIGHTINGALE: Noticing him?

WRITER: . . . Yes. He grinned, and hollered to come down; he took me into the lower apartment. It was vacant, the others still on the gallery, you see I . . . couldn't understand his presence among the . . .

NIGHTINGALE: Screaming old faggots at that antique dealer's. Well, they're rich and they buy boys, but that's a scene that you haven't learned yet. So. What happened downstairs?

WRITER: He took me into a bedroom; he told me I looked pale and wouldn't I like a sunlamp treatment. I thought he meant my face so I—agreed—

NIGHTINGALE: Jesus, you've got to be joking.

WRITER: I was shaking violently like I was a victim of—St. Vitus's Dance, you know, when he said, "Undress"!

NIGHTINGALE: But you did.

WRITER: Yes. He helped me. And I stretched out on the bed under the sunlamp and suddenly he—

NIGHTINGALE: . . . turned it off and did you?

WRITER: Yes, that's what happened. I think that he was shocked by my reaction.

NIGHTINGALE: You did *him* or—?

24

WRITER: . . . I told him that I . . . loved . . . him. I'd been drinking.

NIGHTINGALE: Love can happen like that. For one night only.

WRITER: He said, he laughed and said, "Forget it. I'm flying out tomorrow for training base."

NIGHTINGALE: He said to you, "Forget it," but you didn't forget it.

WRITER: No . . . I don't even have his address and I've forgotten his name . . .

NIGHTINGALE: Still, I think you loved him.

WRITER: . . . Yes. I . . . I'd like to see some of your serious paintings sometime.

NIGHTINGALE: Yeah. You will. Soon. When I get them canvases shipped down from Baton Rouge next week. But meanwhile . . . [*His hand is sliding down the sheet.*] How about this?

WRITER [*with gathering panic*]: . . . I think I'd better get some sleep now. I didn't mean to tell you all that. Goodnight, I'm going to sleep.

NIGHTINGALE [*urgently*]: This would help you.

WRITER: I need to sleep nights—to work.

NIGHTINGALE: You are alone in the world, and I am, too. Listen. Rain!

[*They are silent. The sound of rain is heard on the roof.*]

Look. I'll give you two things for sleep. First, this. [*He draws back the sheet. The light dims.*] And then one of these pills I call my sandman special.

WRITER: I don't . . .

NIGHTINGALE: Shh, walls have ears! Lie back and imagine the paratrooper.

[*The dim light goes completely out. A passage of blues piano is heard. It is an hour later. There is a spotlight on the writer as narrator, smoking at the foot of the cot, the sheet drawn about him like a toga.*]

WRITER: When I was alone in the room, the visitor having retreated beyond the plywood partition between his cubicle and mine, which was chalk white that turned ash-gray at night, not just he but everything visible was gone except for the lighter gray of the alcove with its window over Toulouse Street. An apparition came to me with the hypnotic effect of the painter's sandman special. It was in the form of an elderly female saint, of course. She materialized soundlessly. Her eyes fixed on me with a gentle questioning look which I came to remember as having belonged to my grandmother during her sieges of illness, when I used to go to her room and sit by her bed and want, so much, to say something or to put my hand over hers, but could do neither, knowing that if I did, I'd betray my feelings with tears that would trouble her more than her illness . . . Now it was she who stood next to my bed for a while. And as I drifted toward sleep, I wondered if she'd witnessed the encounter between the painter and me and what her attitude was toward such—perversions? Of longing?

[*The sound of stifled coughing is heard across the plywood partition.*]

Nothing about her gave me any sign. The weightless hands clasping each other so loosely, the cool and believing gray eyes in the faint pearly face were as immobile as statuary. I felt that she neither blamed nor approved the encounter. No. Wait. She . . . seemed to lift one hand very, very slightly before my eyes closed with sleep. An almost invisible gesture of . . . forgiveness? . . . through understanding? . . . before she dissolved into sleep . . .

Tye is in a seminarcotized state on the bed in Jane's room. Jane is in the hall burdened with paper sacks of groceries; the writer appears behind her.

JANE [*brightly*]: Good morning.

WRITER [*shyly*]: Oh, good morning.

JANE: Such a difficult operation, opening a purse with one hand.

WRITER: Let me hold the sacks for you.

JANE: Oh, thanks; now then, come in, put the sacks on one of those chairs. Over the weekend we run out of everything. Ice isn't delivered on Sundays, milk spoils. Everything of a perishable kind has got to be replaced. Oh, don't go out. Have you had a coffee?

WRITER [*looking at Tye*]: I was about to but . . .

JANE: Stay and have some with me. Sorry it's instant, can you stand instant coffee?

WRITER: I beg your pardon?

JANE: Don't mind him, when his eyes are half open it doesn't mean he is conscious.

TYE: Bullshit, you picked up a kid on the street?

JANE [*suppressing anger*]: This is the young man from across the hall—I'm Jane Sparks, my friend is Tye McCool, and you are—

WRITER [*pretending to observe a chess board to cover his embarrassment*]: What a beautiful chess board!

JANE: Oh, that, yes!

WRITER: Ivory and ebony? Figures?

JANE: The white squares are mother-of-pearl. Do you play chess?

WRITER: Used to. You play together, you and Mr.—McCool?

TYE: Aw, yeh, we play together but not chess. [*He rubs his crotch. Jane and the writer nervously study the chess board.*]

JANE: I play alone, a solitary game, to keep in practice in case I meet a partner.

WRITER: Look. Black is in check.

JANE: My imaginary opponent. I choose sides you see, although I play for both.

WRITER: I'd be happy to—I mean sometimes when you—

TYE [*touching the saucepan on the burner*]: OW!

JANE: I set it to boil before I went to the store.

[*Jane sets a cup and doughnuts on the table.*]

TYE: Hey, kid, why don't you take your cup across the hall to your own room?

JANE: Because I've just now—you heard me—invited him to have it here in this room with me.

29

TYE: I didn't invite him in, and I want you to git something straight: I live here. And if I live in a place I got equal rights in this place, and it just so happens I don't entertain no stranger to look at me undressed.

WRITER [*gulping down his coffee*]: Please. Uh, please, I think I'd rather go in my room because I, I've got some work to do there. I always work immediately after my coffee.

JANE: I will not have this young grifter who has established squatter's rights here telling me that I can't enjoy a little society in a place where—frankly I am frantic with loneliness!

[*The writer does not know what to do. Tye suddenly grins. He pulls out a chair for the writer at the table as if it were for a lady.*]

TYE: Have a seat kid, you like one lump or two? Where's the cat? Can I invite the goddam cat to breakfast?

JANE: Tye, you said you were pleased with the robe I gave you for your birthday, but you never wear it.

TYE: I don't dress for breakfast.

JANE: Putting on a silk robe isn't dressing.

[*She removes the robe from a hook and throws it about Tye's shoulders. Automatically he circles her hips with an arm.*]

TYE: Mmm. Good. Feels good.

JANE [*shyly disengaging herself from his embrace*]: It ought to. Shantung silk.

TYE: I didn't mean the robe, babe.

30

JANE: Tye, behave yourself. [*She turns to the writer.*] I've cherished the hope that by introducing Tye to certain little improvements in wearing apparel and language, I may gradually, despite his resistance—

TYE: Ain't that lovely? That classy langwidge she uses?

JANE: Inspire him to—seek out some higher level of employment. [*Ignoring Tye, she speaks.*] I heard that you are a writer?

WRITER: I, uh—write, but—

JANE: What form of writing? I mean fiction or poetry or . . .

TYE: Faggots, they all do something artistic, all of 'em.

JANE [*quickly*]: Do you know, I find myself drinking twice as much coffee here as I did in New York. For me the climate here is debilitating. Perhaps because of the dampness and the, and the—very low altitude, really there's no altitude at all, it's slightly under sea level. Have another cup with me?

[*The writer doesn't answer: Jane prepares two more cups of the instant coffee. Tye is staring steadily, challengingly at the writer, who appears to be hypnotized.*]

Of course, Manhattan hasn't much altitude either. But I grew up in the Adirondacks really. We lived on high ground, good elevation.

TYE: I met one of 'em once by accident on the street. You see, I was out of a job, and he came up to me on a corner in the Quarter an' invited me to his place for supper with him. I seen right off what he was an' what he wanted, but I didn't have the price of a poor boy sandwich so I accepted, I went. The place was all Japanese-like, everything very artistic. He said to me,

"Cross over that little bridge that crosses my little lake which I made myself and sit on the bench under my willow tree while I make supper for us and bathe an' change my clo'se. I won't be long." So I crossed over the bridge over the lake, and I stretched out under the weepin' willow tree: fell right asleep. I was woke up by what looked like a female but was him in drag. "Supper ready," he—she—said. Then this freak, put her hand on my—I said, "It's gonna cost you more than supper . . ."

JANE: Tye.

TYE: Huh, baby?

JANE: You will *not* continue that story.

TYE: It's a damn good story. What's your objection to it? I ain't got to the part that's really funny. [*He speaks to the writer, who is crossing out of the light.*] Don't you like the story?

[*The writer exits.*]

JANE: Why did you do that?

TYE: Do what?

JANE: You know what, and the boy knew what you meant by it. Why did you want to hurt him with the implication that he was in a class with a common, a predatory transvestite?

TYE: Look Jane . . . You say you was brought up on high ground, good elevation, but you come in here, you bring in here and expose me to a little queer, and . . .

JANE: Does everyone with civilized behavior, good manners, seem to be a queer to you?

32

TYE: . . . Was it good manners the way he looked at me, Babe?

JANE [*voice rising*]: Was it good manners for you to stand in front of him rubbing your—groin the way you did?

TYE: I wanted you to notice his reaction.

JANE: He was just embarrassed.

TYE: You got a lot to learn about life in the Quarter.

JANE: I think that he's a serious person that I can talk to, and I need some one to talk to!

[*Pause*]

TYE: You can't talk to *me* huh?

JANE: With you working all night at a Bourbon Street strip-joint, and sleeping nearly all day? Involving yourself with all the underworld elements of this corrupt city . . .

TYE: 'Sthat all I do? Just that? I never pleasure you, Babe?

[*Fade in piano blues. She draws a breath and moves as if half asleep behind Tye's chair.*]

JANE: Yes, you—pleasure me, Tye.

TYE: I try to do my best to, Babe. Sometimes I wonder why a girl—

JANE: Not a girl, Tye. A woman.

TYE: —How did—why did—you get yourself mixed up with me?

JANE: A sudden change of circumstances removed me from—how shall I put it so you'd understand?

TYE: Just—say.

JANE: What I'd thought was myself. So I quit my former connections, I came down here to—[*She stops short.*] Well, to make an adjustment to—[*Pause.*] We met by chance on Royal Street when a deluge of rain backed me into a doorway. Didn't know you were behind me until you put your hand on my hip and I turned to say, "Stop that!" but didn't because you were something I'd never encountered before—faintly innocent—boy's eyes. Smiling. Said to myself, "Why not, with nothing to lose!" Of course you pleasure me, Tye!—I'd been alone so long . . .

[*She touches his throat with trembling fingers. He leans sensually back against her. She runs her hand down his chest.*]

Silk on silk is—lovely . . . regardless of the danger.

[*As the light on this area dims, typing begins offstage. The dim-out is completed.*]

A lighted area represents Mrs. Wire's kitchen, in which she is preparing a big pot of gumbo despite the hour, which is midnight. She could be mistaken for a witch from Macbeth in vaguely modern but not new costume.

The writer's footsteps catch her attention. He appears at the edge of the light in all that remains of his wardrobe: riding boots and britches, a faded red flannel shirt.

MRS. WIRE: Who, who?—Aw, you, dressed up like a jockey in a donkey race!

WRITER: —My, uh, clothes are at the cleaners.

MRS. WIRE: Do they clean clothes at the pawnshop, yeah, I reckon they do clean clothes not redeemed. Oh. Don't go upstairs. Your room is forfeited, too.

WRITER: . . . You mean I'm . . . ?

MRS. WIRE: A loser, boy. Possibly you could git a cot at the Salvation Army.

WRITER [*averting his eyes*]: May I sit down a moment?

MRS. WIRE: Why, for what?

WRITER: Eviction presents . . . a problem.

MRS. WIRE: I thought you was gittin' on the WPA Writers' Project? That's what you tole me when I inquired about your prospects for employment, you said, "Oh, I've applied for work on the WPA for writers."

WRITER: I couldn't prove that my father was destitute, and the

35

fact he contributes nothing to my support seemed—immaterial to them.

MRS. WIRE: Why're you shifty-eyed? I never seen a more shifty-eyed boy.

WRITER: I, uh, have had a little eye trouble, lately.

MRS. WIRE: You're gettin' a cataract on your left eye, boy, face it!—Cataracts don't usually hit at your age.

WRITER: I've noticed a lot of things have hit me—prematurely . . .

MRS. WIRE [*stirring gumbo*]: Hungry? I bet. I eat at irregular hours. I suddenly got a notion to cook up a gumbo, and when I do, the smell of it is an attraction, draws company in the kitchen. Oh ho—footsteps fast. Here comes the ladies.

WRITER: Mrs. Wire, those old ladies are starving, dying of malnutrition.

[*Miss Carrie and Mary Maude appear at the edge of the lighted area with queer, high-pitched laughter or some bizarre relation to laughter.*]

MRS. WIRE: Set back down there, boy. [*Pause.*] Why, Mizz Wayne an' Miss Carrie, you girls still up at this hour!

MISS CARRIE: We heard you moving about and wondered if we could . . .

MARY MAUDE: Be of some assistance.

MRS. WIRE: Shoot, Mrs. Wayne, do you imagine that rusty ole saucepan of yours is invisible to me? Why, I know when I put this gumbo on the stove and lit the fire, it would smoke you ladies out of your locked room. What do you all do in that locked room so much?

MARY MAUDE: We keep ourselves occupied.

MISS CARRIE: We are compiling a cookbook which we hope to have published. A Creole cookbook, recipes we remember from our childhood.

MRS. WIRE: A recipe is a poor substitute for food.

MARY MAUDE [*with a slight breathless pause*]: We ought to go out more regularly for meals but our . . . our light bulbs have burned out, so we can't distinguish night from day anymore. Only shadows come in.

MISS CARRIE: Sshh! [*Pause.*] Y'know, I turned down an invitation to dinner this evening at my cousin Mathilde Devereau Pathet's in the Garden District.

MRS. WIRE: Objected to the menu?

MISS CARRIE: No, but you know, very rich people are so inconsiderate sometimes. With four limousines and drivers at their constant disposal, they wouldn't send one to fetch me.

MRS. WIRE: Four? Limousines? Four drivers?

[*A delicate, evanescent music steals in as the scene acquires a touch of the bizarre. At moments the players seem bewildered as if caught in a dream.*]

MISS CARRIE: Oh, yes, four, four . . . spanking new Cadillacs with uniformed chauffeurs!

37

MRS. WIRE: Now, that's very impressive.

MISS CARRIE: They call Mr. Pathet the "Southern Planter."

MRS. WIRE: Has a plantation, in the Garden District?

MISS CARRIE [*gasping*]: Oh, no, no, no, no. He's a mortician, most prominent mortician, buries all the best families in the parish.

MRS. WIRE: And poor relations, too? I hope.

MARY MAUDE: Miss Carrie goes into a family vault when she goes.

MRS. WIRE: When?

MARY MAUDE: Yes, above ground, has a vault reserved in . . .

MISS CARRIE: Let's not speak of that! . . . now.

MRS. WIRE: Why not speak of that? You got to consider the advantage of this connection. Because of the expenses of "The Inevitable" someday soon, 'specially with your asthma? No light? And bad nutrition?

MISS CARRIE: The dampness of the old walls in the Quarter— you know how they hold damp. This city is actually eight feet below sea level. Niggers are buried under the ground, and their caskets fill immediately with water.

MRS. WIRE: But I reckon your family vault is above this nigger water level?

MISS CARRIE: Oh, yes, above water level, in fact, I'll be on top of my great-great-uncle, Jean Pierre Devereau, the third.

[*The writer laughs a bit, involuntarily. The ladies glare at him.*]

Mrs. Wire, who is this . . . transient? Young man?

MARY MAUDE: We did understand that this was a guesthouse, not a . . . refuge for delinquents.

MISS CARRIE [*turning her back on the writer*]: They do set an exquisite table at the Pathets, with excellent food, but it's not appetizing, you know, to be conducted on a tour of inspection of the business display room, you know, the latest model of caskets on display, and that's what René Pathet does, invariably escorts me, proud as a peacock, through the coffin display rooms before . . . we sit down to dinner. And all through dinner, he discusses his latest clients and . . . those expected shortly.

MRS. WIRE: Maybe he wants you to pick out your casket cause he's noticed your asthma from damp walls in the Quarter.

MISS CARRIE: I do, of course, understand that business is business with him, a night and day occupation.

MRS. WIRE: You know, I always spit in a pot of gumbo to give it special flavor, like a bootblack spits on a shoe. [*She pretends to spit in the pot. The crones try to laugh.*] Now help yourself, fill your saucepan full, and I'll loan you a couple of spoons, but let it cool a while, don't blister your gums . . . [*She hands them spoons.*] . . . and Mrs. Wayne, I'll be watching the mailbox for Buster's army paycheck.

MARY MAUDE: That boy has never let me down, he's the most devoted son a mother could hope for.

MRS. WIRE: Yais, if she had no hope.

MARY MAUDE: I got a postcard from him . . .

MRS. WIRE: A postcard can't be cashed.

MARY MAUDE [*diverting Mrs. Wire's attention, she hopes, as Miss Carrie ladles out gumbo*]: Of course, I wasn't prepared for the circumstance that struck me when I discovered that Mr. Wayne had not kept up his insurance payments, *that* I was not prepared for, that it was *lapsed.*

MRS. WIRE [*amused*]: I bet you wasn't prepared for a little surprise like that.

MARY MAUDE: No, not for that nor for the discovery that secretly for years he'd been providing cash and real estate to that little redheaded doxy he'd kept in Bay St. Louie.

MISS CARRIE: Owwwww!

[*Mrs. Wire whirls about, and Miss Carrie is forced to swallow the scalding mouthful.*]

MRS. WIRE: I bet that mouthful scorched your throat, Miss Carrie. Didn't I tell you to wait?

MARY MAUDE: Carrie, give me that saucepan before you spill it, your hand's so shaky. Thank you, Mrs. Wire. Carrie, thank Mrs. Wire for her being so concerned always about our— circumstances here. Now let's go and see what can be done for that throat. [*They move toward the stairs but do not exit.*]

MRS. WIRE: Cut it, if all else fails.

[*Something crashes on the stairs. All turn that way. Tye appears dimly, bearing two heavy cartons; he speaks to the writer, who is nearest to him.*]

40

TYE: Hey, you, boy?

WRITER: —Me?

TYE: Yeh, yeh, you, I dropped one of these packages on th' steps, so goddam dark I dropped it. And I'd appreciate it if you'd pick it up fo' me an' help me git it upstairs.

WRITER: I'll be—glad to try to . . .

[*Tye focuses dimly on Miss Carrie. He blinks several times in disbelief.*]

TYE: Am I . . . in the right place?

MRS. WIRE [*shouting*]: Not in your present condition. Go on back out. Sleep it off in the gutter.

MISS CARRIE [*to Mrs. Wire*]: Tragic for such a nice-looking young man to return to his wife in that condition at night.

MRS. WIRE: Practically every night.

[*Miss Carrie and Mary Maude exit.*

[*Tye has almost miraculously managed to collect his dropped packages, and he staggers to stage right where the lower steps to the attic are dimly seen. The writer follows.*]

TYE [*stumbling back against the writer*]: Can you make it? Can you make it, kid?

[*They slowly mount the steps. The lighted kitchen is dimmed out. There is a brief pause. A soft light is cast on the attic hall.*]

TYE: Now, kid, can you locate my room key in my pocket?

WRITER: Which, uh—pocket?

TYE: Pan's pocket.

WRITER: Left pocket or—

TYE: —Head—spinnin'—money in hip pocket, key in—right-lef' side. Shit—key befo' I—fall . . .

[*The writer's hand starts to enter a pocket when Tye collapses, spilling the boxes on the floor and sprawling across them.*]

WRITER: You're right outside my cubbyhole. I suggest you rest in there before you—wake up your wife . . .

TYE: M'ole lady, she chews my ass off if I come home this ways . . . [*He struggles heroically to near standing position as the writer guides him into his cubicle.*] . . . This—bed?

[*There is a soft, ghostly laugh from the adjoining cubicle. A match strikes briefly.*]

WRITER: Swing your legs the other way, that way's the pillow—would you, uh, like your wet shoes off?

TYE: Shoes? Yes, but nothin' else. Once I—passed out on—Bourbon Street—late night—in a dark doorway—woke up—this guy, was takin' liberties with me and I don't go for that stuff—

WRITER: I don't take advantages of that kind, I am—going back downstairs, if you're comfortable now . . .

TYE: I said to this guy, "Okay, if you wanto blow me, you can pay me one hunnerd dollars—before, not after."

[*Tye's voice dies out. Nightingale becomes visible, rising stealthily in his cubicle and slipping on a robe, as Tye begins to snore.*]

[*The attic lights dim out. The lights on the kitchen come up as the writer re-enters.*]

MRS. WIRE: Got that bum to bed? Set down, son. Ha! Notice I called you, son. Where do you go nights?

WRITER: Oh, I walk, I take long solitary walks. Sometimes I . . . I . . .

MRS. WIRE: Sometimes you what? You can say it's none of my business, but I, well, I have a sort of a, well you could say I have a sort of a—maternal—concern. You see, I do have a son that I never see no more, but I worry about him so I reckon it's natural for me to worry about you a little. And get things straight in my head about you—you've changed since you've been in this house. You know that?

WRITER: Yes, I know that.

MRS. WIRE: This I'll tell you, when you first come to my door, I swear I seen and I recognized a young gentleman in you—shy. Shaky, but . . .

WRITER: Panicky! Yes! Gentleman? My folks say so. I wonder.

[*The light narrows and focuses on the writer alone; the speech becomes an interior reflection.*]

I've noticed I do have some troublesome little scruples in my nature that may cause difficulties in my . . . [*He rises and rests his foot on the chair.*] . . . negotiated—truce with—life. Oh—there's a price for things, that's something I've learned in the

43

Vieux Carré. For everything that you purchase in this market-place you pay out of *here!* [*He thumps his chest.*] And the cash which is the stuff you use in your work can be overdrawn, depleted, like a reservoir going dry in a long season of drought . . .

[*The scene is resumed on a realistic level with a change in the lighting.*]

MRS. WIRE [*passing a bowl of gumbo to the writer*]: Here, son, have some gumbo. Let it cool a while. I just pretended to spit in it, you know.

WRITER: I know.

MRS. WIRE: I make the best gumbo, I do the best Creole cookin' in Louisiana. It's God's truth, and now I'll tell you what I'm plannin' to do while your gumbo's coolin'. I'll tell you because it involves a way you could pay your room and board here.

WRITER: Oh?

MRS. WIRE: Uh huh, I'm plannin' to open a lunchroom.

WRITER: On the premises? Here?

MRS. WIRE: On the premises, in my bedroom, which I'm gonna convert into a small dinin' room. So I'm gonna git printed up some bus'ness cards. At twelve noon ev'ry day except Sundays you can hit the streets with these little bus'ness cards announcin' that lunch is bein' served for twenty-five cents, a cheaper lunch than you could git in a greasy spoon on Chartres . . . and no better cooking in the Garden District or the Vieux Carré.

44

WRITER: Meals for a quarter in the Quarter.

MRS. WIRE: Hey! That's the slogan! I'll print it on those cards that you'll pass out.

WRITER [*dreamily*]: Wonderful gumbo.

MRS. WIRE: Why this "Meals for a quarter in the Quarter" is going to put me back in the black, yeah! Boy! . . . [*She throws him the key to his attic rooms. The lights dim out briefly.*]

TYE'S VOICE: Hey! Whatcha doin'? Git yuh fuckin' hands off me!

[*The writer appears dimly in the attic hall outside his room. He stops.*]

NIGHTINGALE'S VOICE: I thought that I was visiting a friend.

TYE'S VOICE: 'Sthat how you visit a friend, unzippin' his pants an' pullin' out his dick?

NIGHTINGALE'S VOICE: I assure you it was a mistake of—identity . . .

TYE [*becoming visible on the side of the bed in the writer's cubicle*]: This ain't my room. Where is my ole lady? Hey, *hey, Jane!*

WRITER: You collapsed in the hall outside your door so I helped you in here.

TYE: Both of you git this straight. No goddam faggot messes with me, never! For less'n a hundred dollars!

[*Jane becomes visible in the hall before this line.*]

45

A hunnerd dollars, yes, maybe, but not a dime less.

NIGHTINGALE [*emerging from the cubicle in his robe*]: I am afraid that you have priced yourself out of the market.

JANE: Tye, come out of there.

TYE: I been interfered with 'cause you'd locked me out.

WRITER: Miss, uh, Sparks, I didn't touch your friend except to, to . . . offer him my bed till you let him in.

JANE: Tye, stand up—if you can stand! Stand. Walk.

[*Tye stumbles against her, and she cries out as she is pushed against the wall.*]

TYE'S VOICE: Locked out, bolted outa my room, to be— molested.

JANE: I heard you name a price, with you everything has a price. Thanks, good night.

[*During this exchange Nightingale in his purple robe has leaned, smoking with a somewhat sardonic look, against the partition between the two cubicles. The writer reappears.*]

NIGHTINGALE: Back so quick?—*Tant pis* . . .

WRITER: I think if I were you, I'd go in your own room and get to bed.

[*The writer enters his cubicle. Nightingale's face slowly turns to a mask of sorrow past expression. There is music. Nightingale puts out his cigarette and enters his cubicle.*]

[*Jane undresses Tye. The writer undresses. Nightingale sits on his cot. Tye and Jane begin to make love. Downstairs, Nursie mops the floor, singing to herself. The writer moves slowly to his bed and places his hand on the warm sheets that Tye has left. The light dims.*

[*There is a passage of time.*]

The attic rooms are dimly lit. Nightingale is adjusting a necker-chief about his wasted throat. He enters the writer's cubicle without knocking.

NIGHTINGALE: May I intrude once more? It's embarrassing—this incident. Not of any importance, nothing worth a second thought. [*He coughs.*] Oh Christ. You know my mattress is full of bedbugs. Last night I smashed one at least the size of my thumbnail, it left a big blood spot on the pillow. [*He coughs and gasps for breath.*] I showed it to the colored woman that the witch calls Nursie, and Nursie told her about it, and she came charging up here and demanded that I exhibit the bug, which I naturally . . . [*A note of uncertainty and fear enters his voice.*]

WRITER: . . . removed from the pillow.

NIGHTINGALE: Who in hell wouldn't remove the remains of a squashed bedbug from his pillow? Nobody I'd want social or any acquaintance with . . . she even . . . intimated that I coughed up the blood, as if I had . . . [*coughs*] consumption.

WRITER [*stripped to his shorts and about to go to bed*]: I think with that persistent cough of yours you should get more rest.

NIGHTINGALE: Restlessness. Insomnia. I can't imagine a worse affliction, and I've suffered from it nearly all my life. I consulted a doctor about it once, and he said, "You don't sleep because it reminds you of death." A ludicrous assumption—the only true regret I'd have over leaving this world is that I'd leave so much of my serious work unfinished.

WRITER [*holding the bedsheet up to his chin*]: Do show me your serious work.

48

NIGHTINGALE: I know why you're taking this tone.

WRITER: I am not taking any tone.

NIGHTINGALE: Oh yes you are, you're very annoyed with me because my restlessness, my loneliness, made me so indiscreet as to—offer my attentions to that stupid but—physically appealing young man you'd put on that cot with the idea of reserving him for yourself. And so I do think your tone is a bit hypocritical, don't you?

WRITER: All right, I do admit I find him attractive, too, but I did *not* make a pass at him.

NIGHTINGALE: I heard him warn you.

WRITER: I simply removed his wet shoes.

NIGHTINGALE: Little man, you are sensual, but I, I—am rapacious.

WRITER: And I am tired.

NIGHTINGALE: Too tired to return my visits? Not very appreciative of you, but lack of appreciation is something I've come to expect and almost to accept as if God—the alleged—had stamped on me a sign at birth—"This man will offer himself and not be accepted, not by anyone ever!"

WRITER: Please don't light that candle.

NIGHTINGALE: I shall, the candle is lit.

WRITER: I do wish that you'd return to your side of the wall—well, now I am taking a tone, but it's . . . justified. Now do

49

please get out, get out, I mean it, when I blow out the candle I want to be alone.

NIGHTINGALE: You know, you're going to grow into a selfish, callous man. Returning no visits, reciprocating no . . . caring.

WRITER: . . . Why do you predict that?

NIGHTINGALE: That little opacity on your left eye pupil could mean a like thing happening to your heart. [*He sits on the cot.*]

WRITER: You have to protect your heart.

NIGHTINGALE: With a shell of calcium? Would that improve your work?

WRITER: You talk like you have a fever, I . . .

NIGHTINGALE: I have a fever you'd be lucky to catch, a fever to hold and be held! [*He throws off his tattered silk robe.*] Hold me! Please, please hold me.

WRITER: I'm afraid I'm tired, I need to sleep and . . . I don't want to catch your cold.

[*Slowly with dignity, Nightingale rises from the cot and puts his silk robe on.*]

NIGHTINGALE: And I don't want to catch yours, which is a cold in the heart, that's a hell of a lot more fatal to a boy with literary pretensions.

[*This releases in the writer a cold rage which he has never felt before. He springs up and glares at Nightingale, who is coughing.*]

WRITER [*in a voice quick and hard as a knife*]: I think there has been some deterioration in your condition and you ought to face it! A man has got to face everything sometime and call it by its true name, not to try to escape it by—cowardly!—evasion— go have your lungs x-rayed and don't receive the doctor's bill when it's sent! But go there quick, have the disease stated clearly! Don't, don't call it a cold anymore or a touch of the flu!

NIGHTINGALE [*turning with a gasp*]: You've gone mad, you've gone out of your mind here, you little one-eyed bitch! [*He coughs again and staggers out of the light.*]

MRS. WIRE'S VOICE: I heard you from the kitchen, boy! Was he molesting you in here? I heard him. Was he molesting you in here? Speak up! [*Her tone loses its note of concern as she shouts to Nightingale.*] You watch out, I'll get the goods on you yet!

NIGHTINGALE'S VOICE: The persecution continues.

Daylight appears in the alcove window—daylight tinged with rain. The room of Jane and Tye is lighted. Tye is sprawled, apparently sleeping, in shorts on the studio bed. Jane has just completed a fashion design. She stares at it with disgust, then crumples it and throws it to the floor with a sob of frustration.

JANE: Yes? Who's there?

WRITER: Uh, me, from across the hall, I brought in a letter for you—it was getting rained on.

JANE: Oh, one moment, please. [*She throws a robe over her panties and bra and opens the door.*] A letter for me?

WRITER: The mail gets wet when it rains since the lid's come off the mailbox.

[*His look irresistibly takes in the figure of Tye. Jane tears the letter open and gasps softly. She looks slowly up, with a stunned expression, at the young writer.*]

JANE: Would you care for some coffee?

WRITER: Thanks, no, I just take it in the morning.

JANE: Then please have a drink with me. I need a drink. Please, please come in. [*Jane is speaking hysterically but abruptly controls it.*] Excuse me—would you pour the drinks—I can't. I . . .

WRITER [*crossing to the cabinet*]: Will you have . . .

JANE: Bourbon. Three fingers.

52

WRITER: With?

JANE: Nothing, nothing.

[*The writer glances again at Tye as he pours the bourbon.*]

Nothing . . . [*The writer crosses to her with the drink.*] Nothing. And you?

WRITER: Nothing, thanks. I have to retype the manuscripts soaked in the rain.

JANE: *Manuscripts,* you said? Oh, yes, you're a writer. I knew, it just slipped my mind. The manuscripts were returned? Does that mean rejection? —Rejection is always so painful.

WRITER [*with shy pride*]: This time instead of a printed slip there was this personal signed note . . .

JANE: Encouraging—that. Oh, my glass is weeping—an Italian expression. Would you play barman again? Please? [*She doesn't know where to put the letter, which he keeps glancing at.*]

WRITER: Yes, I am encouraged. He says, "This one doesn't quite make it but try us again." *Story* magazine—they print William Saroyan, you know!

JANE: It takes a good while to get established in a creative field.

WRITER: And meanwhile you've got to survive.

JANE: I was lucky, but the luck didn't hold. [*She is taking little sips of the straight bourbon.*]

WRITER: You're—upset by that—letter? I noticed it came from—isn't Ochsner's a clinic?

JANE: Yes, actually. I am, I was. It concerns a relative rather—critically ill there.

WRITER: Someone close to you?

JANE: Yes. Quite close, although lately I hardly recognize the lady at all anymore . . .

[*Tye stirs on the bed; the writer irresistibly glances at him.*]

Pull the sheet over him. I think he unconsciously displays himself like that as if posing for a painter of sensual inclinations. Wasted on me. I just illustrate fashions for ladies.

TYE [*stirring*]: Beret? Beret?

[*The writer starts off, pausing at the edge of the light.*]

WRITER: Jane, what was the letter, wasn't it about you?

JANE: Let's just say it was a sort of a personal, signed rejection slip, too.

[*The writer exits with a backward glance.*]

TYE: Where's Beret, where's the goddam cat?

[*Jane is fiercely tearing the letter to bits. The lights dim out.*]

A dim light comes up on the writer, stage front, as narrator.

WRITER: The basement of the building had been leased by Mrs. Wire to a fashionable youngish photographer, one T. Hamilton Biggs, a very effete man he was, who had somehow acquired a perfect Oxford accent in Baton Rouge, Louisiana. He made a good living in New Orleans out of artfully lighted photos of debutantes and society matrons in the Garden District, but for his personal amusement—he also photographed, more realistically, some of the many young drifters to be found along the streets of the Vieux Carré.

[*The lights go up on the kitchen. Mrs. Wire is seen at the stove, which bears steaming pots of water.*]

MRS. WIRE [*to the writer*]: Aw, it's you sneakin' in at two A.M. like a thief.

WRITER: Yes, uh, good night.

MRS. WIRE: Hold on, don't go up yet. He's at it again down there, he's throwin' one of his orgies, and this'll be the last one he throws down there. By God an' by Jesus, the society folk in this city may tolerate vice but not me. Take one of them pots off the stove.

WRITER: You're, uh . . . cooking at this hour?

MRS. WIRE: Not cooking . . . I'm boiling water! I take this pot and you take the other one, we'll pour this water through the hole in this kitchen floor, which is directly over that studio of his!

WRITER: Mrs. Wire, I can't be involved in . . .

MRS. WIRE: Boy, you're employed by me, you're fed and housed here, and you do like I tell you or you'll go on the street. [*She lifts a great kettle off the stove.*] Take that pot off the stove! [*She empties the steaming water on the floor. Almost instant screams are heard below.*] Hahh, down there, what's the disturbance over?!

WRITER: Mrs. Wire, that man has taken out a peace warrant against you, you know that.

MRS. WIRE: Git out of my way, you shifty-eyed little— [*With demonical energy she seizes the other pot and empties it onto the floor, and the screams continue. She looks and runs to the proscenium as if peering out a window.*] Two of 'em run out naked. Got two of you, I'm not done with you yet! . . . you perverts!

WRITER: Mrs. Wire, he'll call the police.

MRS. WIRE: Let him, just let him, my nephew is a lieutenant on the police force! But these Quarter police, why anybody can buy 'em, and that Biggs, he's got big money. Best we be quiet, sit tight. Act real casual-like. If they git in that door, you seen a, you seen a—

WRITER: What?

MRS. WIRE: A drunk spillin' water in here.

WRITER: . . . that much water?

MRS. WIRE: *Hush up!* One contradictory word out of you and I'll brain you with this saucepan here.

[*Nightingale enters in his robe.*]

56

NIGHTINGALE: May I inquire what this bedlam is about? [*He pants for breath.*] I had just finally managed to . . . [*He gasps.*] This hellish disturbance . . .

MRS. WIRE: May you inquire, yeah, you may inquire. Look. Here's the story! You're in a doped-up condition. Drunk and doped-up you staggered against the stove and accidentally knocked a kettle of boiling water off it. Now that's the story you'll tell in payment of back rent and your habits! . . . disgracing my house!

NIGHTINGALE [*to writer*]: *What* is she talking about?

MRS. WIRE: And *you . . . one eye!* [*She turns to the writer.*] You say you witnessed it, you back up the story, you heah?

WRITER [*grinning*]: Mrs. Wire, the story wouldn't . . . hold water.

MRS. WIRE: I said accidental. In his condition who'd doubt it?

NIGHTINGALE: Hoo, hoo, hoo!

MRS. WIRE: That night court buzzard on the bench, he'd throw the book at me for no reason but the fight that I've put up against the corruption and evil that this Quarter is built on! All I'm asking is . . .

[*Abruptly Miss Carrie and Mary Maude in outrageous negligees burst into the kitchen. At the sight of them, Mrs. Wire starts to scream wordlessly as a peacock at a pitch that stuns the writer but not Nightingale and the crones. Just as abruptly she falls silent and flops into a chair.*]

MISS CARRIE: Oh, Mrs. Wire!

MARY MAUDE: We thought the house had caught fire!

NIGHTINGALE [*loftily*]: . . . What a remarkable . . . *tableau vivant* . . . The paddy wagon's approaching. Means night court, you know.

WRITER: . . . I think I'll . . . go to bed now . . .

MRS. WIRE: Like shoot you will!

[*Jane appears, stage right, in a robe. She speaks to the writer, who is nearest to her.*]

JANE: Can you tell me what is going on down here?

WRITER: Miss Sparks, why don't you stay in your room right now?

JANE: Why?

WRITER: There's been a terrible incident down here, I think the police are coming.

[*Mary Maude screams, wringing her hands.*]

MARY MAUDE: Police!

MISS CARRIE: Oh, Mary Maude, this is not time for hysterics. You're not involved, nor am I! We simply came in to see what the disturbance was about.

JANE [*to the writer*]: Was Tye here? Was Tye involved in this . . .

WRITER [*in a low voice to Jane*]: Nobody was involved but Mrs. Wire. She poured boiling water through a hole in the floor.

mrs. wire [*like a field marshal*]: Everybody in here stay here and sit tight till the facts are reported.

[*Nursie enters with black majesty. She is humming a church hymn softly, "He walks with me and he talks with me." She remains at the edge of the action, calm as if unaware.*]

I meant ev'ry goddam one of you except Nursie. Nursie! Don't stand there singin' gospel, barefoot, in that old dirty nightgown!

writer [*to Jane*]: She wants us to support a totally false story.

mrs. wire: I tell you—the Vieux Carré is the new Babylon destroyed by evil in Scriptures!!

jane: It's like a dream . . .

nightingale: The photographer downstairs belongs to the Chateau family, one of the finest and most important families in the Garden District.

mrs. wire: Oh, do you write the social register now?

nightingale: I know he is New Orleans's most prominent society photographer!

mrs. wire: I know he's the city's most notorious *pervert* and is occupying space in my building!

miss carrie: Mary Maude and I can't afford the notoriety of a thing like this.

[*Mary Maude cries out and leans against the table.*]

mary maude: Mrs. Wire, Miss Carrie and I have—positions to maintain!

59

JANE: Mrs. Wire, surely there's no need for these ladies to be involved in this.

MRS. WIRE: Deadbeats, all, all! Will stay right here and—

JANE: Do what?

MRS. WIRE: —testify to what happened!

NIGHTINGALE: She wishes you all to corroborate her lie! That I, that I! Oh, yes, I'm appointed to assume responsibility for—

PHOTOGRAPHER [*off stage*]: Right up there! Burns like this could disfigure me for life!

[*Mrs. Wire rushes to slam and bolt the door.*]

MISS CARRIE [*to Mary Maude*]: Honey? Can you move now?

MRS. WIRE: No, she cain't, she stays—which applies to you all!

PHOTOGRAPHER: The fact that she is insane and allowed to remain at large . . . doesn't excuse it.

[*A patrolman bangs at the door.*]

MRS. WIRE: Shh! Nobody make a sound!

PHOTOGRAPHER: Not only she but her tenants; why, the place is a psycho ward.

[*More banging is heard.*]

MRS. WIRE: What's this banging about?

PATROLMAN: Open this door.

PHOTOGRAPHER: One of my guests was the nephew of the District Attorney!

PATROLMAN: Open or I'll force it.

PHOTOGRAPHER: Break it in! Kick it open!

MRS. WIRE [*galvanized*]: You ain't comin' in here, you got no warrant to enter, you filthy—morphodite, you!

WRITER: Mrs. Wire, you said not to make a sound.

MRS. WIRE: Make no sound when they're breakin' in my house, you one-eyed Jack? [*The banging continues.*] What's the, meaning of this, wakin' me up at two A.M. in the mawnin'?

PHOTOGRAPHER: Scalded! Five guests, including two art models!

MRS. WIRE [*overlapping*]: You broken the terms of your lease, and it's now broke. I rented you that downstair space for legitimate business, you turned it into a—continual awgy!

PATROLMAN: Open that door, ma'am, people have been seriously injured.

MRS. WIRE: That's no concern of mine! I open no door till I phone my nephew, a lieutenant on the police force, Jim Flynn, who knows the situation I've put up with here, and then we'll see who calls the law on who!

WRITER: I hear more police sirens comin'.

[*The pounding and shouting continue. A patrolman forces entry, followed by another. All during the bit just preceding, Miss Carie and Mary Maude have clung together, their terri-*]

fied whispers maintaining a low-pitched threnody to the shouting and banging. Now as the two patrolmen enter, their hysteria erupts in shrill screams. The screams are so intense that the patrolmen's attention is directed upon them.]

PATROLMAN 1: Christ! Is this a fuckin' madhouse?

[*Still clinging together, the emaciated crones sink to their knees as if at the feet of an implacable deity.*]

MRS. WIRE [*inspired*]: Officers, remove these demented, old horrors. Why, you know what they done? Poured water on the floor of my kitchen, boiling water!

NIGHTINGALE: She's lying. These unfortunate old ladies just came in, they thought the house was on fire.

PHOTOGRAPHER: This woman is the notorious Mrs. Wire, and it was she who screamed out the window. Why, these old women should be hospitalized, naturally, but it's her, her! [*He points at Mrs. Wire from the door.*] that poured the scalding water into my studio, and screamed with delight when my art models and guests ran naked into the street!

MRS. WIRE: There, now, AWGY CONFESSED!!

PATROLMAN 2: All out to the wagon!

[*The scene is dimmed out fast. A spot comes up on the writer in the witness box at night court.*]

OLD JUDGE'S VOICE: Let's not have no more beatin' aroun' the bush in this court, young fellow. The question is plain. You're under oath to give an honest answer. Now for the last time, at risk of being held in contempt of court, "Did you or did you not see the proprietor of the rooming house . . ."

MRS. WIRE'S VOICE [*shrilly*]: Restaurant and roomin' house respectfully run!

[*The judge pounds his gavel.*]

OLD JUDGE'S VOICE: Defendant will keep silent during the witness' testimony. To repeat the question: "Did you or did you not see this lady here pour boiling water through the floor of her kitchen down into the studio of Mr. T. Hamilton Biggs?"

WRITER [*swallows, then in a low voice*]: I, uh . . . think it's unlikely . . . a lady would do such a thing.

OLD JUDGE'S VOICE: Speak up so I can heah you! What's that you said?

WRITER: . . . I said I thought it very unlikely a lady would do such a thing.

[*Laughter is heard in the night court. The judge gavels, then pronounces the verdict.*]

OLD JUDGE'S VOICE: This court finds the defendant, Mrs. Hortense Wire, guilty as charged and imposes a fine of fifty dollars plus damages and releases her on probation in the custody of her nephew, Police Lieutenant James Flynn of New Orleans Parish, for a period of . . .

[*His voice fades out as does the scene. A spotlight comes up on Mrs. Wire in a flannel robe, drinking at the kitchen table. The writer appears hesitantly at the edge of the kitchen light.*]

MRS. WIRE [*without turning*]: I know you're standing there, but I don't wanta see you. It sure does surprise me that you'd dare to enter this house again after double-crossing me in court tonight.

WRITER: —I—just came back to pick up my things.

MRS. WIRE: You ain't gonna remove nothing from this place till you paid off what you owe me.

WRITER: You know I'm—destitute.

MRS. WIRE: You get tips from the customers.

WRITER: Nickels and dimes. [*Pause. The sound of rain is heard.*] —Mrs. Wire? [*She turns slowly to look at him.*] Do you think I really intended to lose you that case? Other witnesses had testified I was in the kitchen when you poured those kettles of water through the floor. And the judge knew I could see with at least one eye. I was on the witness stand under oath, couldn't perjure myself. I did try not to answer directly. I *didn't* answer directly. All I said was—

MRS. WIRE: You said what lost me the case, goddam it! Did you expect that old buzzard on the bench to mistake me for a lady, my hair in curlers, me wearin' the late, long ago Mr. Wire's old ragged bathrobe. Shoot! All of you witnesses betrayed me in night court because you live off me an' can't forgive me for it.

WRITER: —I guess you want me to go . . .

MRS. WIRE: To where would you go? How far could you get on your nickels and dimes? You're shiverin' like a wet dog. Set down. Have a drink with me befo' you go up to bed.

WRITER: You mean I can stay? [*She nods slightly. He sits down at the kitchen table; she pours him a drink.*] I don't think I ever saw you drink before, Mrs. Wire.

64

MRS. WIRE: I only touch this bottle, which also belonged to the late Mr. Wire before he descended to hell between two crooked lawyers, I touch it only when forced to by such a shocking experience as I had tonight, the discovery that I was completely alone in the world, a solitary ole woman cared for by no one. You know, I heard some doctor say on the radio that people die of loneliness, specially at my age. They do. Die of it, it kills 'em. Oh, that's not the cause that's put on the death warrant, but that's the *true* cause. I tell you, there's so much loneliness in this house that you can hear it. Set still and you can hear it: a sort of awful—soft—groaning in all the walls.

WRITER: All I hear is rain on the roof.

MRS. WIRE: You're still too young to hear it, but I hear it and I feel it, too, like a—ache in ev'ry bone of my body. It makes me want to scream, but I got to keep still. A landlady ain't permitted to scream. It would disturb the tenants. But some time I will, I'll scream, I'll scream loud enough to bring the roof down on us all.

WRITER: This house is full of people.

MRS. WIRE: People I let rooms to. Less than strangers to me.

WRITER: There's—me. I'm not.

MRS. WIRE: You—just endure my company 'cause you're employed here, boy.

WRITER: Miss Sparks isn't employed here.

MRS. WIRE: That woman is close to no one but the bum she keeps here. I'll show you. [*She rises and knocks her chair over, then bawls out as if to Tye.*] More boxes! Take 'em out an' stay out with 'em, sleep it off on the streets!

[*Jane rises in her dim spot of light. She crosses to the door.*]

JANE [*offstage*]: Tye! Tye! I thought I heard Tye down there.

MRS. WIRE: Miss Sparks—don't you know that bum don't quit work till daybreak and rarely shows here before noon?

JANE: Sorry. Excuse me.

WRITER [*his speech slurred by drink*]: God, but I was ignorant when I came here! This place has been a—I ought to pay you— tuition . . .

MRS. WIRE: One drink has made you drunk, boy. Go up to bed. We're goin' on tomorrow like nothing happened. [*He rises and crosses unsteadily from the kitchen light.*] Be careful on the steps.

WRITER [*pausing to look back at her*]: Good night, Mrs. Wire. [*He disappears.*]

MRS. WIRE: —It's true, people die of it . . .

[*On the hall stairs the writer meets Nightingale, who speaks before the writer enters his own cubicle.*]

NIGHTINGALE [*imitating the writer's testimony in night court*]: "I, uh, think it's unlikely a lady would do such a thing." [*He coughs.*] —A statement belonging in a glossary of deathless quotations. [*He coughs again.*] —Completely convinced me you really do have a future in the—literary—profession.

[*The light builds on Mrs. Wire, and she rises from the kitchen table and utters a piercing cry. Nursie appears.*]

NURSIE: Mizz Wire, what on earth is it? A bat?

MRS. WIRE: I just felt like screaming, and so I screamed! That's all . . .

[*The lights dim out.*]

INTERVAL

PART TWO

A spotlight focuses on the writer working at his dilapidated typewriter in his gabled room in the attic.

WRITER: Instinct, it must have been[*He starts typing.*] directed me here, to the Vieux Carré of New Orleans, down country as a—river flows no plan. I couldn't have consciously, deliberately, selected a better place than here to discover—to encounter—my true nature. *Exposition! Shit!*

[*He springs up and kicks at the worn, wobbly table. A lean, gangling young man, whose charming but irresponsible nature is apparent in his genial grin, appears at the entrance of the writer's cubicle.*]

SKY: Having trouble?

WRITER: Even the typewriter objected to those goddamn lines. The ribbon's stuck, won't reverse.

SKY: Let me look at it. [*He enters the cubicle.*] Oh, my name is Schuyler but they call me Sky.

WRITER: The owner of the knapsack with "SKY" printed on it, that was—that was deposited here last winter sometime?

SKY [*working on the typewriter*]: Right. Landlady won't surrender it to me for less than twenty-five bucks, which is more than I can pay. Yeah, you see—I'm a fugitive from—from legal wedlock in Tampa, Florida, with the prettiest little bitsy piece of it you ever did see. There, now the ribbon's reversing, it slipped out of the slots like I slipped out of matrimony in Tampa—couldn't you see that?

69

WRITER: I don't think there's a room in this building where you could be certain it was night or day, and I've . . .

SKY: Something wrong with that eye.

WRITER: Operation. For a cataract. Just waiting till it heals.—Are you staying here?

SKY: Just for a day or two while I look into spots for a jazz musician in the Quarter.

WRITER: There's several jazz combos just around the corner on Bourbon Street.

SKY: Yeah, I know, but they're black and not anxious to work with a honky. So, I'll probably drive on West.

WRITER: How far West?

SKY: The Coast. Is there a toilet up here? I gotta piss. Downstairs john's occupied.

WRITER: I know a girl across the hall with a bathroom, but she's probably sleeping.

SKY: With the angels wetting the roof, would it matter if I did, too?

WRITER: Go ahead.

[*Sky leaps onto the alcove and pisses upstage out of the window.*]

Why'd you decide not to marry?

SKY: Suddenly realized I wasn't ready to settle. The girl, she had a passion for pink, but she extended it out of bounds in the love nest she'd picked out for us. Pink, pink, pink. So I cut out before daybreak.

WRITER: Without a word to the girl?

SKY: A note, "Not ready. Be back." Wonder if she believed it, or if I did. That was Christmas week. I asked permission to leave my knapsack here with the landlady, overnight. She said, "For fifty cents." Extortionary, but I accepted the deal. However was unavoidably detained like they say. Returned last night for my gear and goddam, this landlady here refuses to surrender it to me except for twenty-five bucks. Crazy witch!

[*Mrs. Wire is at the cubicle entrance.*]

MRS. WIRE: What's he doin' up there?

SKY: Admiring the view.

MRS. WIRE: You was urinating out of the window! Jailbird! You ain't been in a hospital four months, you been in the House of Detention for resistin' arrest and assaultin' an officer of the law. I know. You admire the view in the bathroom. I don't allow no trashy behavior here. [*She turns to the writer.*] Why ain't you on the streets with those business cards?

WRITER: Because I'm at the last paragraph of a story.

MRS. WIRE: Knock it off this minute! Why, the streets are swarming this Sunday with the Azalea Festival trade.

WRITER: The time I give to "Meals for a Quarter in the Quarter" has begun to exceed the time originally agreed on, Mrs. Wire.

71

MRS. WIRE: It's decent, healthy work that can keep you off bad habits, bad company that I know you been drifting into.

WRITER: How would you know anything outside of this moldy, old—

MRS. WIRE: Don't talk that way about this—*historical* old building. Why, 722 Toulouse Street is one of the oldest buildings in the Vieux Carré, and the courtyard, why, that courtyard out there is on the tourist list of attractions!

WRITER: The tourists don't hear you shoutin' orders and insults to your, your—prisoners here!

MRS. WIRE: Two worthless dependents on me, that pair of scavenger crones that creep about after dark.

[*Nightingale coughs in his cubicle. Mrs. Wire raises her voice.*]

And I got that TB case spitting contagion wherever he goes, leaves a track of blood behind him like a chicken that's had it's head chopped off.

NIGHTINGALE: 'sa goddam libelous lie!

MRS. WIRE [*crossing to the entrance of the adjoining cubicle*]: Been discharged from the Two Parrots, they told you to fold up your easel and git out!

NIGHTINGALE [*hoarsely*]: I'm making notes on these lies, and my friend, the writer, is witness to them!

MRS. WIRE: You is been discharged from the Two Parrots. It's God's truth, I got it from the cashier!

72

[*Sky chuckles, fascinated. He sits on the edge of the table or cot, taking a cigarette and offering one to the writer. Their casual friendly talk is contrapuntal to the violent altercation in progress outside.*]

She told me they had to scrub the pavement around your easel with a bucket of lye each night, that customers had left without payin' because you'd hawked an' spit by their tables!

NIGHTINGALE: Bucket of lies, not lye, that's what she told you!

MRS. WIRE: They only kept you there out of human pity!

NIGHTINGALE: Pity!

MRS. WIRE: Yais, pity! But finally pity and patience was exhausted, it run out there and it's run out here! Unlock that door! NURSIE!

NURSIE [*off stage*]: Now what?

MRS. WIRE: Bring up my keys! Mr. Nightingale's locked himself in! You're gonna find you'self mighty quicker than you expected in a charity ward on your way to a pauper's grave!

WRITER: Mrs. Wire, be easy on him . . .

MRS. WIRE: You ain't heard what he calls me? Why, things he's said to me I hate to repeat. He's called me a fuckin' ole witch, yes, because I stop him from bringin' pickups in here at midnight that might stick a knife in the heart of anyone in the buildin' after they done it to him.

NIGHTINGALE [*in a wheezing voice as he drops onto the cot in his cubicle*]: It's you that'll get a knife stuck in you, between your—dried up old—dugs . . .

73

WRITER [sotto voce, *near tears*]: Be easy on him, he's dying.

MRS. WIRE: Not here. He's defamed this place as infested with bedbugs to try to explain away the blood he coughs on his pillow.

WRITER: That's—his last defense against—

MRS. WIRE: The truth, there's no defense against truth. Ev'rything in that room is contaminated, has got to be removed to the incinerator an' burned. Start with the mattress, Nursie!

[*Nursie has entered the lighted area with a bunch of musty keys.*]

NIGHTINGALE: I warn you, if you attempt to enter my room, I'll strike you down with this easel!

MRS. WIRE: You do that, just try, the effort of the exertion would finish you right here! Oh, shoot, here's the master key, opens all doors!

NIGHTINGALE: At your own risk—I'll brain you, you bitch.

MRS. WIRE: Go on in there, Nursie!

NURSIE: Aw, no, not me! I told you I would never go in that room!

MRS. WIRE: We're coming in!

NIGHTINGALE: WATCH OUT!

[*He is backed into the alcove, the easel held over his head like a crucifix to exorcise a demon. A spasm of coughing wracks him. He bends double, dropping the easel, collapses to his knees, and then falls flat upon the floor.*]

NURSIE [*awed*]: Is he daid, Mizz Wire?

MRS. WIRE: Don't touch him. Leave him there until the coroner gets here.

NIGHTINGALE [*gasping*]: Coroner, your ass—I'll outlive you.

MRS. WIRE: If I dropped dead this second! Nursie, haul out that filthy mattress of his, pour kerosene on it.

NURSIE: Wouldn't touch that mattress with a pole . . .

MRS. WIRE: And burn it. Git a nigger to help you haul everything in here out, it's all contaminated. Why, this whole place could be quarantined!

NURSIE: Furniture?

MRS. WIRE: All! Then wash off your hands in alcohol to prevent infection, Nursie.

NURSIE: Mizz Wire, the courtyard is full of them Azalea Festival ladies that paid admission to enter! You want me to smoke 'em out?

MRS. WIRE: Collect the stuff you can move.

NURSIE: Move where?

MRS. WIRE: Pile it under the banana tree in the courtyard, cover it with tarpaulin, we can burn it later.

NIGHTINGALE: If anyone lays a hand on my personal effects,

75

I'll [*His voice chokes with sobs.*]—I will be back in the Two Parrots tonight. I wasn't fired. I was given a leave of absence till I recovered from . . . asthma . . .

MRS. WIRE [*with an abrupt compassion*]: Mr. Nightingale.

NIGHTINGALE: Rossignol!—of the Baton Rouge Rossignols, as any dog could tell you . . .

MRS. WIRE: I won't consult a dawg on this subject. However, the place for you is not here but in the charity ward at St. Vincent's. Rest there till I've made arrangements to remove you.

SKY: The altercation's subsided.

WRITER [*to Sky, who has begun to play his clarinet*]: What kind of horn is that?

[*Mrs. Wire appears at the entrance to the writer's cubicle. Sky plays entrance music—"Ta-ta-taaaa!"*]

SKY: It's not a horn, kid, horns are brass. A clarinet's a wood-wind instrument, not a horn.

MRS. WIRE: Yais, now about you all.

SKY: Never mind about us. We're leaving for the West Coast.

[*Mrs. Wire and the writer are equally stunned in opposite ways.*]

MRS. WIRE: —What's he mean, son? You're leavin' with this jailbird?

WRITER: —I—

MRS. WIRE: You won't if I can prevent it, and I know how. In my register book, when you signed in here, you wrote St. Louis. We got your home address, street and number. I'm gonna inform your folks of the vicious ways and companions you been slipping into. They's a shockin' diff'rence between your looks an' manners since when you arrived here an' now, mockin' me with that grin an' that shifty-eyed indifference, evidence you're setting out on a future life of corruption. Address and phone number, I'll write, I'll phone! —You're not leavin' here with a piece of trash like *that* that pissed out the window! —Son, son, don't do it! [*She covers her face, unraveled with emotion. Exchanging a look with Sky, the writer places an arm gingerly about her shoulder.*] You know I've sort of adopted you like the son took away from me by the late Mr. Wire and a—and a crooked lawyer, they got me declared to be—mentally incompetent.

WRITER: Mrs. Wire, I didn't escape from one mother to look for another.

[*Nursie returns, huffing, to the lighted area.*]

NURSIE: Mizz Wire, those tourists ladies, I can't control them, they're pickin' the azaleas off the bushes, and—

MRS. WIRE: That's what I told you to stay in the courtyard to stop.

NURSIE: Oh, I try, but one of 'em jus' called me a impudent ole nigger, and I won't take it. I come here to tell you I QUIT!

MRS. WIRE: AGAIN! COME BACK OUT THERE WITH ME! [*She turns to the writer.*] We'll continue this later. [*She exits with Nursie.*]

WRITER [*to Sky*]: —Were you serious about the West Coast offer?

SKY: You're welcome to come along with me. I don't like to travel a long distance like that by myself.

WRITER: How do you travel?

SKY: I've got a beat-up old '32 Ford across the street with a little oil and about half a tank of gas in it. If you want to go, we could share the expense. Have you got any cash?

WRITER: I guess I've accumulated a capital of about thirty-five dollars.

SKY: We'll siphon gas on the way.

WRITER: Siphon?

SKY: I travel with a little rubber tube, and at night I unscrew the top of somebody's gas tank and suck the gas out through the tube and spit it into a bucket and empty it into my car. Is it a deal?

WRITER [*with suppressed excitement*]: How would we live on the road?

SKY [*rolling a cigarette with obvious practice*]: We'd have to exercise our wits. And our personal charm. And, well, if that don't suffice, I have a blanket in the car, and there's plenty of wide open spaces between here and the Coast. [*He pauses for a beat.*] Scared? Of the undertaking?

WRITER [*smiling slowly*]: No—the Coast—starting when?

SKY: Why not this evening? The landlady won't admit me to the house again, but I'll call you. Just keep your window open. I'll blow my clarinet in the courtyard. Let's say about six.

[*The conversation may continue in undertones as the area is dimmed out.*]

SCENE NINE

The lights come up on Jane's studio area. The shuttered doors to the windows overlooking the courtyard below are ajar. Jane is trying to rouse Tye from an unnaturally deep sleep. It is evident that she has been engaged in packing her effects and his.

JANE: Tye, Tye, oh—Christ . . .

[*He drops a bare arm off the disordered bed and moans slightly. She bends over to examine a needle mark on his arm.*]

TYE: —Wh—?

[*Jane crosses to the sink and wets a towel, then returns to slap Tye's face with it. He begins to wake slowly.*]

Some men would beat a chick up for less'n that, y'know.

JANE: All right, get out of bed and beat me up, but get *up*.

TYE [*stroking a promontory beneath the bed sheet*]: —Can't you see I *am* up?

JANE: I don't mean that kind of up, and don't bring stripshow lewdness in here this—Sunday afternoon.

TYE: Babe, don't mention the show to me t'day.

JANE: I'd like to remind you that when we first stumbled into this—crazy—co-habitation, you promised me you'd quit the show in a week.

TYE: For what? Tight as work is for a dude with five grades of school and no skill training from the Mississippi sticks?

79

JANE: You could find something less—publicly embarrassing, like a—filling station attendant.

TYE: Ha!

JANE: But of course your choice of employment is no concern of mine now.

TYE: Why not, Babe?

JANE: I'm not "Babe" and not "Chick"!

TYE: You say you're not my chick?

JANE: I say I'm nobody's chick.

TYE: Any chick who shacks with me's my chick.

JANE: This is my place. You just—moved in and stayed.

TYE: I paid the rent this month.

JANE: Half of it, for the first time, my savings being as close to exhaustion as me.

[*There is the sound of a funky piano and a voice on the Bourbon Street corner: "I've stayed around and played around this old town too long." Jane's mood softens under its influence.*]

Lord, I don't know how I managed to haul you to bed.

TYE: Hey, you put me to bed last night?

JANE: It was much too much exertion for someone in my— condition.

TYE [*focusing on her more closely*]: —Honey, are you pregnant?

JANE: No, Lord, now who'd be fool enough to get pregnant by a Bourbon Street stripshow barker?

TYE: When a chick talks about her condition, don't it mean she's pregnant?

JANE: All female conditions are not pregnancy, Tye. [*She staggers, then finishes her coffee.*] Mine is that of a desperate young woman living with a young bum employed by gangsters and using her place as a depository for hot merchandise. Well, they're all packed. You're packed too.

TYE: —Come to bed.

JANE: No, thank you. Your face is smeared with lipstick; also other parts of you. I didn't know lip rouge ever covered so much—territory.

TYE: I honestly don't remember a fuckin' thing after midnight.

JANE: That I do believe. Now have some coffee, I've warmed it. It isn't instant, it's percolated.

TYE: Who's birthday is it?

JANE: It's percolated in honor of our day of parting.

TYE: Aw, be sweet, Babe, please come back to bed. I need comfort, not coffee.

JANE: You broke a promise to me.

TYE: Which?

81

JANE: Among the many? You used a needle last night. I saw the mark of it on you.

TYE: No shit. Where?

JANE [*returning to the bedside*]: There, right there on your— [*He circles her with his arm and pulls her onto the bed.*] I've been betrayed by a—sensual streak in my nature. Susceptibility to touch. And you have skin like a child. I'd gladly support you if I believed you'd—if I had the means to and the time to. Time. Means. Luck. Things that expire, run out. And all at once you're stranded.

TYE: Jane you—lie down with me and hold me.

JANE: I'm afraid, Tye, we'll just have to hold each other in our memories from now on.

TYE [*childishly*]: Don't talk that way. I never had a rougher night in my life. Do I have to think and remember?

JANE: Tye, we've had a long spell of dreaming, but now we suddenly have to.

TYE: Got any aspirin, Babe?

JANE: You're past aspirin, Tye. I think you've gone past all legal—analgesics.

TYE: You say words to me I've never heard before.

JANE: Tye, I've been forced to make an urgent phone call to someone I never wanted to call.

TYE: Call?

JANE: And then I packed your personal belongings and all that loot you've been holding here. Exertion of packing nearly blacked me out. Trembling, sweating—had to bathe and change.

TYE: Babe?

JANE: You're vacating the premises, "Babe." It's *afternoon.*

TYE: Look, if you're knocked up, have the kid. I'm against abortion.

JANE: On moral principles?

TYE: Have the kid, Babe. I'd pull myself together for a kid.

JANE: You didn't for me.

TYE: A baby would be a livin' thing between us, with both our blood.

JANE: Never mind.

[*Voices in the courtyard are heard.*]

NURSIE: Any donations t'keep the cou'tyard up, just drop it in my apron as you go out, ladies! . . .

JANE: Those tourists down there in the courtyard! If I'd known when I took this room it was over a tourist attraction—

TYE: It's the Festival, Babe. It ain't always Festival . . . gimme my cigarettes, ought to be some left in a pocket.

JANE [*throwing his pants and a fancy sport shirt on the bed*]: Here, your clothes, get in them.

83

TYE [*putting on his shorts*]: Not yet. It's Sunday, Babe . . . Where's Beret? I like Beret to be here when I wake up.

JANE: Not even a cat will wait ten, twelve hours for you to sleep off whatever you shot last night. How did a girl well educated and reasonably well brought up get involved in this . . . Oh, I'm talking to myself.

TYE: I hear you, Babe, and I see you.

JANE: Then . . . get up and dressed.

TYE: It's not dark yet, Babe. Y'know I never get dressed till after dark on Sundays.

JANE: Today has to be an exception. I'm . . . expecting a caller, very important to me.

TYE: Fashion designer?

JANE: No. Buyer . . . to look at my illustrations. They're no good, I'm no good. I just had a flair, not a talent, and the flair flared out, I'm . . . finished. These sketches are evidence of it! [*She starts tearing fashion sketches off the wall.*] Look at me! Bangles, jangles! All taste gone! [*She tears off her costume jewelry.*]

TYE: Babe, you're in no shape to meet a buyer.

JANE [*slowly and bitterly*]: He's no buyer of anything but me.

TYE: —Buyer of *you?* Look. You said that you were expecting a buyer to look at your drawin's here.

JANE: I know what I said, I said a buyer to look at my illustrations, but what I said was a lie. Among other things, many other undreamed of before, you've taught me to practice deception.

VOICES OFFSTAGE: Edwina, Edwina, come see this dream of a little courtyard. Oh, my, yaiss, like a dream.

JANE: I know what I said, but let's say, Tye, that I experienced last week a somewhat less than triumphant encounter with the buyer of fashion illustrations at *Vogue Moderne.* In fact, it left me too shattered to carry my portfolio home without a shot of Metaxas brandy at the Blue Lantern, which was on the street level of the building. It was there that I met a gentleman from Brazil. He had observed my entrance, the Brazilian, and apparently took me for a hooker, sprang up with surprising agility for a gentleman of his corpulence, hauled me to his table, and introduced me to his *camaradas,* "Señorita, this is Señor and Señor and Señor," declared me, "*Bonita, muy, muy, bonita*"— tried to press a hundred-dollar bill in my hand. Well, some atavistic bit of propriety surfaced and I, like a fool, rejected it—but did accept his business card, just in case. This morning, Tye, I called him. "Señorita Bonita of the Blue Lantern awaits you, top floor of seven-two-two Toulouse," that was the invitation that I phoned in to the message desk. He must have received it by now at the Hotel Royal Orleans, where the Presidential Suite somehow contains him.

TYE: Who're you talkin' about?

JANE: My expected caller, a responsible businessman from Brazil. Sincerely interested in my bankrupt state . . .

TYE: Forget it, come back to bed and I'll undress you, Babe, you need rest.

JANE: The bed bit is finished between us. You're moving out today.

85

[*He slowly stumbles up, crosses to the table, and gulps coffee, then grasps her arm and draws her to bed.*]

No, no, no, no, no, no!

TYE: Yes, yes, yes, yes, yes!

[*He throws her onto the bed and starts to strip her; she resists; he prevails. As the lights very gradually dim, a Negro singer-pianist at a nearby bar fades in, "Fly a-way! Sweet Kentucky baby-bay, fly, away . . ."*]

MRS. WIRE [*from a few steps below the writer*]: What's paralyzed you there? Son?

WRITER: Miss Sparks is crying.

[*Mrs. Wire appears behind the writer in the lighted spot.*]

MRS. WIRE: That woman's moanin' in there don't mean she's in pain. Son, I got a suspicion you never had close relations with wimmen in your life.

JANE: Ohhh!

WRITER: I never heard sounds like that.

[*Jane utters a wild cry. It impresses even Mrs. Wire.*]

TYE'S VOICE: Babe, I don't wanna force you . . .

JANE'S VOICE: Plee-ase! I'm not a thing, I'm not—a—thing!

MRS. WIRE [*shouting*]: You all quit that loud fornication in there!

TYE'S VOICE [*shouting back*]: Get the fuck downstairs, goddam ole witch!

MRS. WIRE: Howlin' insults at me in my own house, won't tolerate it! [*She bursts into the room.*] Never seen such a disgustin' exhibition!

[*Tye starts to rise from the bed. Jane clings desperately to him.*]

JANE: As! You see!—Mrs. Wire!—Everything is!—packed, he's —moving—today . . .

TYE: The rent is paid in full! So get the fuck outa here!

JANE: Tye, please.

MRS. WIRE: What's in them boxes?

TYE: None of your—

JANE: Our personal—belongings, Mrs. Wire.

MRS. WIRE: That I doubt! The contents of these boxes will be inspected before removed from this place and in the presence of my nephew on the police force!

[*Tye charges toward Mrs. Wire.*]

Don't you expose yourself naykid in my presence! Nursie!

JANE: Mrs. Wire, for once I do agree with you! Can you get him out, please, please get him out!

MRS. WIRE [*averting her face with an air of shocked propriety*]: Dress at once and—

NURSIE: Mizz Wire, I got the hospital on the phone.

MRS. WIRE: They sendin' an ambulance for Nightingale?

NURSIE: Soon's they got a bed for him, but they want you to call 'em back and—

MRS. WIRE: St. Vincent's is run by taxpayers' money, I'll remind 'em of that. [*She crosses off stage. Tye slams the door.*]

[*Jane is sobbing on the bed.*]

TYE: Now, Babe.

JANE: If you approach this bed—

TYE: Just want to comfort you, honey. Can't we just rest together? Can't we? Rest and comfort each other?

[*The area dims as the black pianist sings "Kentucky Baby."*]

MRS. WIRE: Cut out that obscene talking up there, I'm on the phone. Emergency call is from here at 722 Toulouse. Christ Almighty, you drive me to profane language. You mean to admit you don't know the location of the most historical street in the Vieux Carré? You're not talking to no . . . no nobody, but a personage. Responsible. Reputable. Known to the authorities on the list of attractions. God damn it, you twist my tongue up with your . . . Nursie! Nursie! Will you talk to this incompetent . . . Nursie! Nursie!

[*Nursie appears.*]

Got some idiot on the phone at the hospital. Will you inform this idiot who I am in the Quarter. Phone. Talk.

[*Nursie takes the phone.*]

NURSIE: Stairs . . . took my breath . . .

MRS. WIRE [*snatching back the phone*]: Now I want you to know, this here Nightingale case . . . I don't lack sympathy for the dying or the hopelessly inflicted . . . [*She kicks at Nursie beside her.*] Git! But I've got responsibilities to my tenants. Valuable paying tenants, distinguished society ladies, will quit my premises this day, I swear they will, if this Nightingale remains. Why, the State Board of Health will clap a suit on me unless . . . at once . . . ambulance. When? At what time? Don't say approximate to me. Emergency means immediate. Not when you drag your arse around to it. And just you remember I'm a taxpayer . . . No, no, you not me. I pay, you collect. Now get the ambulance here immediately, 722 Toulouse, with a stretcher with straps, the Nightingale is violent with fever. [*She slams down the phone.*] Shit!

NURSIE: My guess is they're going to remove you, too.

[*Mrs. Wire leans on Nursie.*]

There is a spotlight on the writer, stage front, as narrator.

WRITER: That Sunday I served my last meal for a quarter in the Quarter, then I returned to the attic. From Nightingale's cage there was silence so complete I thought, "He's dead." Then he cried out softly—

NIGHTINGALE: Christ, how long do I have to go on like this?

WRITER: Then, for the first time, I returned his visits. [*He makes the gesture of knocking at Nightingale's door.*]—Mr. Rossignol . . .

[*There is a sound of staggering and wheezing. Nightingale opens the door; the writer catches him as he nearly falls and assists him back to his cot.*]

—You shouldn't try to dress.

NIGHTINGALE: Got to—escape! She wants to commit me to a charnal house on false charges . . .

WRITER: It's raining out.

NIGHTINGALE: A Rossignol will not be hauled away to a charity hospital.

WRITER: Let me call a private doctor. He wouldn't allow them to move you in your—condition . . .

NIGHTINGALE: My faith's in Christ—not doctors . . . .

WRITER: Lie down.

NIGHTINGALE: Can't breathe lying—down . . .

WRITER: I've brought you this pillow. I'll put it back of your head. [*He places the pillow gently in back of Nightingale.*] Two plilows help you breathe.

NIGHTINGALE [*leaning weakly back*]: Ah—thanks—better . . . Sit down.

[*A dim light comes up on the studio area as Tye, sitting on the table, lights a joint.*]

WRITER: Theren' nowhere to sit.

NIGHTINGALE: You mean nowhere not contaminated? [*The writer sits.*] —God's got to give me time for serious work! Even God has moral obligations, don't He? —Well, *don't* He?

WRITER: I think that morals are a human invention that He ignores as successfully as we do.

NIGHTINGALE: Christ, that's evil, that is infidel talk. [*He crosses himself.*] I'm a Cath'lic believer. A priest would say that you have fallen from Grace, boy.

WRITER: What's that you're holding?

NIGHTINGALE: Articles left me by my sainted mother. Her tortoise-shell comb with a mother-of-pearl handle and her silver framed mirror.

[*He sits up with difficulty and starts combing his hair before the mirror as if preparing for a social appearance.*]

Precious heirlooms, been in the Rossignol family three generations. I look pale from confinement with asthma. Bottom of box is—toiletries, cosmetics—please!

WRITER: You're planning to make a public appearance, intend-ing to go on the streets with this—advanced case of asthma?

NIGHTINGALE: Would you kindly hand me my Max Factor, my makeup kit?!

WRITER: I have a friend who wears cosmetics at night—they dissolve in the rain.

NIGHTINGALE: If necessary, I'll go into *Sanctuary!*

[*The writer utters a startled, helpless laugh; he shakes with it and leans against the stippled wall.*]

Joke, is it, is it a joke?! Foxes have holes, but the Son of Man hath nowhere to hide His head!

WRITER: Don't you know you're delirious with fever?

NIGHTINGALE: You used to be kind—gentle. In less than four months you've turned your back on that side of your nature, turned rock-hard as the world.

WRITER: I had to survive in the world. Now where's your pills for sleep, you need to rest.

NIGHTINGALE: On the chair by the bed.

[*Pause.*]

WRITER [*softly*]: Maybe this time you ought to take more than one.

NIGHTINGALE: Why, you're suggesting suicide to me which is a cardinal sin, would put me in unhallowed ground in—potter's

92

field. I believe in God the Father, God the Son, and God the Holy Ghost . . . you've turned into a killer?

WRITER [*compulsively, with difficulty*]: Stop calling it asthma —the flu, a bad cold. Face the facts, deal with them. [*He opens the pillbox.*] Press tab to open, push down, unscrew the top. Here it is where you can reach it.

NIGHTINGALE: —Boy with soft skin and stone heart . . .

[*Pause. The writer blows the candle out and takes Nightingale's hand.*]

WRITER: Hear the rain, let the rain talk to you, I can't.

NIGHTINGALE: Light the candle.

WRITER: The candle's not necessary. You've got an alcove, too, with a window and bench. Keep your eyes on it, she might come in here before you fall asleep.

[*A strain of music is heard. The angel enters from her dark passage and seats herself, just visible faintly, on Nightingale's alcove bench.*]

Do you see her in the alcove?

NIGHTINGALE: Who?

WRITER: Do you feel a comforting presence?

NIGHTINGALE: None.

WRITER: Remember my mother's mother? Grand?

NIGHTINGALE: I don't receive apparitions. They're only seen by the mad.

[*The writer returns to his cubicle and continues as narrator.*]

WRITER: In my own cubicle, I wasn't sure if Grand had entered with me or not. I couldn't distinguish her from a—diffusion of light through the low running clouds. I thought I saw her, but her image was much fainter than it had ever been before, and I suspected that it would fade more and more as the storm of my father's blood obliterated the tenderness of Grand's. I began to pack my belongings. I was about to make a panicky departure to nowhere I could imagine . . . The West Coast? With Sky?

[*He is throwing things into a cardboard suitcase. Nursie appears at the edge of his light with a coffee tray.*]

NURSIE: Mizz Wire knows you're packin' to leave an' she tole me to bring you up this hot coffee and cold biscuits.

WRITER: Thank her. Thank you both.

NURSIE: She says don't make no mistakes.

WRITER [*harshly*]: None, never?

NURSIE: None if you can help, and I agree with her about that. She's phoned your folks about you. They're coming down here tomorrow.

WRITER: If she's not bluffing . . .

NURSIE: She ain't bluffin', I heard her on the phone myself. Mizz Wire is gettin' you confused with her son Timmy. Her mind is slippin' again. Been through that before. Can't do it again.

WRITER: We all have our confusions . . . [*He gulps down the coffee as Nursie crosses out of the light.*]

NURSIE [*singing softly*]: "My home is on Jordan."

WRITER: Then I started to write. I worked the longest I'd ever worked in my life, nearly all that Sunday. I wrote about Jane and Tye, I could hear them across the narrow hall. —Writers are shameless spies . . .

SCENE · ELEVEN

The studio light builds. Jane is sobbing on the bed. Tye is rolling a joint, seated on the table. The clearing sky has faded toward early blue dusk. Tye regards Jane with a puzzled look. Faintly we hear the black singer-pianist. "Bye, bye, blues. Don't cry blues," etc.

TYE: Want a hit, Babe? [*She ignores the question.*] How long have I been asleep? Christ, what are you crying about. Didn't I just give you one helluva Sunday afternoon ball, and you're cryin' about it like your mother died.

JANE: You forced me, you little pig, you did, you forced me.

TYE: You wanted it.

JANE: I didn't.

TYE: Sure you did. [*Jane is dressing again.*] Honey, you got shadows under your eyes.

JANE: Blackbirds kissed me last night. Isn't that what they say about shadows under the eyes, that blackbirds kissed her last night. The Brazilian must have been blind drunk when he took a fancy to me in the Blue Lantern, mistook me for a hundred-dollar girl. —Tye, I'm not a whore! I'm the Northern equivalent of a lady, fallen, yes, but a lady, not a whore.

TYE: Whores get paid for it, Babe. I never had to.

JANE: You little—prick! Now I'm talkin' your jive, how do you like it? Does she talk like that when she's smearing you with lipstick, when you ball her, which I know you do, repeatedly, between shows.

TYE: —Who're you talkin' about?

JANE: That headliner at the strip show, the Champagne Girl.

TYE [*gravely*]: She's—not with the show no more.

JANE: The headliner's quit the show?

TYE: Yeah, honey, the Champagne Girl is dead an' so she's not in the show.

JANE: You mean—not such a hot attraction any more?

TYE: Don't be funny about it, it ain't funny.

JANE: You mean she's actually—

TYE: Yes. Ackshally. Dead. Real dead, about as dead as dead, which is totally dead— So now you know why I needed a needle to get me through last night.

JANE: —Well, of course that's—

TYE: You was jealous of her . . . [*Jane looks away.*] I never touched the Champagne Girl. She was strictly the property of the Man. Nobody else dared t' touch her.

JANE: The Man—what man?

TYE: The Man—no other name known by. —Well—he wasted her.

JANE: —Killed her? —Why?

TYE: 'Cause she quit sleeping with him. She was offered a deal on the West Coast, Babe. The Man said, "No." The Champagne

97

Girl said, "Yes." So the Man . . . you don't say no to the Man—
so if she's going to the West Coast it'll be packed in ice—

[*Voices are heard from the courtyard.*]

TOURIST 1: My slippers are wet through.

[*Piano music is heard.*]

TOURIST 2: What's next on the tour, or is it nearly finished?

TYE: When the Man is annoyed by something, he piles his
lupos in the back seat of his bulletproof limo and he let's 'em
loose on the source of his annoyance.

JANE: —Lupos?

TYE: Lupos are those big black dawgs that're used for attack.
The Man has three of 'em, and when he patrols his territory at
night, they sit in the back seat of his Lincoln, set up there,
mouths wide open on their dagger teeth and their black eyes
rollin' like dice in a nigger crapshooter's hands. And night before
last, Jesus! he let 'em into the Champagne Girl's apartment, and
they—well, they ate her. Gnawed her tits off her ribs, gnawed
her sweet little ass off. Of course the story is that the Champagne
Girl entertained a pervert who killed her and ate her like that,
but it's pretty well known it was them lupos that devoured that
girl, under those ceiling mirrors and crystal chandeliers in her
all white satin bedroom. —Yep—gone—the headliner— Y'know
what you say when the Man wastes somebody? You got to say
that he or she has "Gone to Spain." So they tole me last night,
when people ask you where's the Champagne Girl, answer 'em
that the Champagne Girl's gone to Spain. —Sweet kid from
Pascagoula.

JANE: Please don't—continue—the story.

TYE: All champagne colored without face or body makeup on her, light gold like pale champagne and not a line, not a pore to be seen on her body! Was she meant for dawg food? I said, was she meant for dawg food? Those lupos ate that kid like she was their—last—supper . . .

JANE [*who has now managed to get round the table*]: Tye, Tye, open the shutters!

TYE: Why? You goin' out naked?

JANE: I'm going to vomit and die—in clean air . . . [*She has moved slowly upstage to the gallery with its closed shutters, moving from one piece of furniture to another for support. Now she opens the shutter doors and staggers out onto the gallery, and the tourist ladies' voices are raised in thrilled shock and dismay.*]

TOURIST 1: Look at that!

TOURIST 2: What at?

TOURIST 1: There's a whore at the gallery window! Practically naked!

[*All gallery speeches should overlap.*]

JANE [*wildly*]: Out, out, out, out, out!

NURSIE: Miss, Miss Sparks! These are Festival ladies who've paid admission.

JANE: Can't endure any more! Please, please, I'm sick!

TYE: Fawgit it, Babe, come back in.

JANE: It isn't real, it couldn't be—

[*The writer shakes his head with a sad smile.*]

But it was—it is . . . like a dream . . .

TYE: What did you say, Babe?

JANE: Close the gallery door—please?

TYE: Sure, Babe. [*He shuts the door on the voices below.*]

JANE: And—the hall door—bolt it. Why do you bring home nightmare stories to me?!

TYE [*gently*]: Babe, you brought up the subject, you asked me about the Champagne Girl, I wasn't planning to tell you. Chair?

JANE: Bed.

TYE: Weed?

JANE: —Coffee.

TYE: Cold.

JANE: —Cold—coffee.

[*Tye pours her a cup and puts it in her trembling hand. He holds the hand and lifts the cup to her lips, standing behind her. He lets his hand fall to her breasts; she sobs and removes the hand.*

[*The singer-pianist is heard again.*]

JANE: . . . Why do you want to stay on here?

100

TYE: Here's where you are, Babe.

JANE [*shaking her head*]: No more. I . . . have to dress . . . [*She dresses awkwardly, frantically. He watches in silence.*] You have to get dressed, too. I told you I was expecting a very important visitor. Tye, the situation's turned impossible on us, face it.

TYE: You're not walkin' out on me.

JANE: Who have I got to appeal to except God, whose phone's disconnected, or this . . . providential . . . protector.

TYE: From the banana republic, a greaseball. And you'd quit me for that?

JANE: You've got to be mature and understanding. At least for once, now dress. The Brazilian is past due . . . I realized your defects, but you touched me like nobody else in my life had ever before or ever could again. But, Tye, I counted on you to grow up, and you refused to. I took you for someone gentle caught in violence and degradation that he'd escape from . . .

TYE: Whatever you took me for, I took you for honest, for decent, for . . .

JANE: Don't be so . . . "Decent"? You ridiculous little . . . sorry, no. Let's not go into . . . abuse . . . Tye? When we went into this it wasn't with any long-term thing in mind. That's him on the steps. Go in the bathroom quiet!

TYE: You go in the bathroom quiet. I'll explain without words.

[*She thrusts his clothes at him. He throws them savagely about the stage.*]

101

. . . Well?

[*There is a sound on the stairs.*]

Sounds like the footsteps of a responsible man.

[*Tye opens the door. We see hospital interns with a stretcher. Jane stares out. The interns pass again with Nightingale's dying body on the stretcher. The writer is with them. Jane gasps and covers her face with her arm. The writer turns to her.*]

WRITER: It's just—they're removing the painter.

JANE: —*Just!*

TYE: No Brazilian, no buyer?

JANE: No. No sale . . .

WRITER [*standing in the open doorway, as narrator*]: It was getting dim in the room.

TYE: It's almost getting dark.

WRITER: They didn't talk. He smoked his reefer. He looked at her steady in the room getting dark and said . . .

TYE: I see you clear.

WRITER: She turned her face away. He walked around that way and looked at her from that side. She turned her face the other way. She was crying without a sound, and a black man

102

was playing piano at the Four Deuces round the corner, an oldie, right for the atmosphere . . . something like . . .

[*The piano fades in, "Seem like Old Times." Tye begins to sing softly with the piano.*]

JANE: Don't.

[*Tye stops the soft singing but continues to stare at Jane.*]

DON'T

[*Pause.*]

TYE: Jane. You've gotten sort of—skinny. How much weight you lost?

JANE: I . . . don't know . . .

TYE: Sometimes you walk a block and can't go no further.

[*Pause.*]

JANE: I guess I'm a yellow-cab girl. With limousine aspirations.

TYE: Cut the smart talk, Babe. Let's level.

[*Pause. She extends her hand.*]

Want a drag? Well?

[*Jane nods and takes a drag off his cigarette.*]

Huh?

JANE: Well, after all, why not, if you're interested in it. It hasn't been just lately I've lost weight and energy but for more than a year in New York. Some—blood thing—progressing rather fast at my age . . . I think I had a remission when I met you. A definite remission . . . here . . . like the world stopped and turned backward, or like it entered another universe— *months!* [*She moves convulsively; Tye grips her shoulders.*] . . . Then . . . it . . . I . . .

TYE: Us?

JANE: No, no, that unnatural tiredness started in again. I went to Ochsners. Don't you remember when the doctor's letter was delivered? No, I guess you don't, being half conscious all the time. It was from Ochsners. It informed me that my blood count had changed for the worse. It was close to . . . collapse . . . [*Pause.*] . . . Those are the clinical details. Are you satisfied with them? Have you any more questions to ask?

[*She stares at him; he averts his face. She moves around him to look at his face; he averts it again. She claps it between her hands and compels him to look at her. He looks down. A scratching sound is heard at the shutter doors.*]

JANE: That's Beret, let her in. Isn't it nice how cats go away and come back and—you don't have to worry about them. So unlike human beings.

[*Tye opens the door. He opens a can of cat food and sets it on the floor, then crosses to his clothes, collecting them from the floor.*]

TYE [*gently*]: Jane, it's getting dark and I—I better get dressed now.

104

JANE [*with a touch of harshness*]: Yes, dress—dress . . . [*But he is lost in reflection, lighting a joint. She snatches it from his lips.*]

And leave me alone as always in a room that smells, that reeks of marijuana!

SCENE TWELVE

WRITER [as narrator]: She was watching him with an unspoken question in her eyes, a little resentful now.

MRS. WIRE'S VOICE [from off stage, curiously altered]: Why are those stairs so dark?

[The light in the studio area is dimmed to half during the brief scene that follows. The writer rises and stands apprehensively alert as Mrs. Wire becomes visible in a yellowed silk robe with torn lace, a reliquary garment. Her hair is loose, her steps unsteady, her eyes hallucinated.]

WRITER [crossing from the studio, dismayed]: Is that you, Mrs. Wire?

MRS. WIRE: Now, Timmy, Timmy, you mustn't cry every time Daddy gets home from the road and naturally wants to be in bed just with Mommy. It's Daddy's privilege, Mommy's— obligation. You'll understand when you're older—you see, Daddy finds Mommy attractive.

WRITER [backing away from the cubicle entrance]: Mrs. Wire, you're dreaming.

MRS. WIRE: Things between grownups in love and marriage can't be told to a child. [She sits on the writer's cot.] Now lie down and Mommy will sing you a little sleepy-time song. [She is staring into space. He moves to the cubicle entrance; the candle is turned over and snuffed out.]

MRS. WIRE: "Rock-a-bye, baby, in a tree top, If the wind blows, the cradle will rock . . ."

WRITER: Mrs. Wire, I'm not Timothy, I'm not Tim, I'm not Timmy. [He touches her.]

MRS. WIRE: Dear child given to me of love . . .

WRITER: Mrs. Wire, I'm not your child. I am nobody's child. Was maybe, but not now. I've grown into a man, about to take his first step out of this waiting station into the world.

MRS. WIRE: Mummy knows you're scared sleeping alone in the dark. But the Lord gave us dark for sleep, and Daddy don't like to find you took his rightful place . . .

WRITER: Mrs. Wire, I'm no relation to you, none but a tenant that earned his keep a while . . . Nursie! Nursie!

NURSIE [*approaching*]: She gone up there? [*Nursie appears.*] She gets these spells, goes back in time. I think it musta been all that Azalea Festival excitement done it.

MRS. WIRE: "If the bough breaks, the cradle will fall . . ."

NURSIE [*at the cubicle entrance*]: Mizz Wire, it's Nursie. I'll take you back downstairs.

MRS. WIRE [*rousing a bit*]: It all seemed so real. —I even remember lovemaking . . .

NURSIE: Get up, Mizz Wire, come down with Nursie.

MRS. WIRE [*accepting Nursie's support*]: Now I'm—old.

[*They withdraw from the light.*]

MRS. WIRE'S VOICE: Ahhhhhhhh . . . Ahhhhhhhh . . . Ahhhh . . . Ahhhhh . . .

[*This expression of despair is lost in the murmur of the wind. The writer sinks onto his cot; the angel of the alcove appears in the dusk.*]

WRITER: Grand! [*She lifts her hand in a valedictory gesture.*] I guess angels warn you to leave a place by leaving before you.

[*The light dims in the cubicle as the writer begins to pack and builds back up in the studio. The writer returns to the edge of the studio light.*]

JANE: You said you were going to get dressed and go back to your place of employment and resume the pitch for the ladies.

TYE: What did you say, Babe?

[*He has finished dressing and is now at the mirror, absorbed in combing his hair. Jane utters a soft, involuntary laugh.*]

JANE: A hundred dollars, the price, and worth it, certainly worth it. I must be much in your debt, way over my means to pay off!

TYE: Well, I ain't paid to make a bad appearance at work. [*He puts on a sport shirt with girls in grass skirts printed on it.*]

JANE: I hate that shirt.

TYE: I know you think it's tacky. Well, I'm tacky, and it's the only clean one I got.

JANE: It isn't clean, not really. And does it express much grief over the Champagne Girl's violent departure to Spain?

TYE: Do you have to hit me with that? What reason . . . ?

JANE: I've really got no reason to hit a goddamn soul but myself that lacked pride to keep my secrets. You know I shouldn't have told you about my—intentions, I should have just slipped away. The Brazilian was far from attractive but—my circumstances required some drastic—compromises.

TYE [*crouching beside her*]: You're talking no sense, Jane. The Brazilian's out of the picture; those steps on the stairs were steps of hospital workers coming to take a—pick a dying fruit outa the place.

JANE: *Do you think I expect you back here again?* You'll say yes, assure me now as if forever—but—reconsider—the moment of impulse . . .

TYE: Cut some slack for me, Babe. We all gotta cut some slack for each other in this fucking world. Lissen. You don't have to sweat it.

JANE: Give me another remission; one that lasts!

TYE: Gotta go now, it's late, after dark and I'm dressed.

JANE: Well, zip your fly up unless you're now in the show. [*She rises and zips up his fly, touches his face and throat with trembling fingers.*]

TYE: Jane, we got love between us! Don't ya know that?

JANE [*not harshly*]: Lovely old word, love, it's travelled a long way, Tye.

TYE: And still's a long way to go. Hate to leave you alone, but—

JANE: I'm not alone. I've got Beret. An animal is a comforting presence sometimes. I wonder if they'd admit her to St. Vincent's?

109

TYE: St. Vincent's?

JANE: That charity hospital where they took the painter called Nightingale.

TYE: You ain't going there, honey.

JANE: It strikes me as being a likely destination.

TYE: Why?

JANE: I watched you dress. I didn't exist for you. Nothing existed for you but your image in the mirror. Understandably so. [*With her last strength she draws herself up.*]

TYE: What's understandable, Jane? —You got a fever? [*He rises, too, and stretches out a hand to touch her forehead. She knocks it away.*]

JANE: What's understandable is that your present convenience is about to become an encumbrance. An invalid, of no use, financial or sexual. Sickness is repellent, Tye, demands more care and gives less and less in return. The person you loved—assuming that you *did* love when she was still useful—is now, is now as absorbed in preparing herself for oblivion as you were absorbed in your—your image in the—mirror!

TYE [*frightened by her vehemence*]: Hey, Jane!

[*Again she strikes away his extended hand.*]

JANE: Readies herself for it as you do for the street! [*She continues as to herself.*] —Withdraws into another dimension. Is indifferent to you except as—caretaker! Is less aware of you than of—[*Panting, she looks up slowly through the skylight.*]—sky that's visible to her from her bed under the skylight—at night, these—filmy white clouds, they move, they drift over the roofs of the Vieux Carré so close that if you have fever you feel as if you could touch them, and bits would come off on your fingers, soft as—cotton candy—

TYE: Rest, Babe. I'll be back early. I'll get Smokey to take over for me at midnight, and I'll come back with tamales and a bottle of vino! [*He crosses out of the light. She rushes to the door.*]

JANE: *No, no, not before daybreak and with a new needle mark on your arm.* Beret? Beret!

[*She staggers wildly out of the light, calling the cat again and again.*]

WRITER: I lifted her from the floor where she'd fallen . . .

[*Various voices are heard exclaiming around the house.*

[*The writer reappears in the studio area supporting Jane, who appears half conscious.*]

Jane? Jane?

JANE: —My cat, I scared it away . . .

NURSIE [*offstage*]: What is goin' on up there?

WRITER: She was frightened by something.

JANE: I lost my cat, that's all. —They don't understand . . . [*The writer places her on the bed.*] Alone. I'm alone.

WRITER: She'll be back. [*He continues as narrator.*] Jane didn't seem to hear me. She was looking up at the skylight.

JANE: It isn't blue any more, it's suddenly turned quite dark.

WRITER: It was dark as the question in her eyes. [*The blues piano fades in.*]

JANE: It's black as the piano man playing around the corner.

WRITER [*to Jane*]: It must be after six. What's the time now?

JANE: Time? What? Oh. Time. My sight is blurred. [*She shows him her wristwatch.*] Can't make out the luminous dial, can you?

WRITER: It says five of twelve.

JANE: An improbable hour. Must have run down.

WRITER: I'll take it off. To wind it. [*He puts the watch to his ear.*] I'm afraid it's broken.

JANE [*vaguely*]: I hadn't noticed. —Lately— I tell time by the sky.

WRITER: His name was Sky.

JANE: Tye . . .

WRITER: No, not Tye. Sky was the name of someone who offered me a ride West.

JANE: —I've had fever all day. Did you ask me a question?

WRITER: I said I'd planned a trip to the West Coast with this young vagrant, a musician.

JANE: Young vagrants are irresponsible. I'm not at all surprised—he let you down? Well. I have travel plans, too.

112

WRITER: With Tye?

JANE: No, I was going alone, not with Tye. What are you doing there?

WRITER: Setting up the chess board. Want to play?

JANE: Oh, yes, you said you play. I'd have a partner for once. But my concentration's—I warn you—it's likely to be—impaired.

WRITER: Want to play white or black?

JANE: You choose.

[*The piano fades in. Jane looks about in a confused way.*]

WRITER: Black. In honor of the musician around the corner.

JANE: —He's playing something appropriate to the occasion as if I'd phoned in a request. How's it go, so familiar?

WRITER: "Makes no difference how things break,
                 I'll still get by somehow
                 I'm not sorry, cause it makes no difference now."

JANE: Each of us abandoned to the other. You know this is almost our first private conversation. [*She nearly falls to the floor. He catches her and supports her to the chair at the upstage side of the table.*] Shall we play, let's do. With no distractions at all. [*She seems unable to move; she has a frozen attitude.*]

[*There is a distant sustained high note from Sky's clarinet. They both hear it. Jane tries to distract the writer's attention from the sound and continues quickly with feverish animation. The sound of the clarinet becomes more urgent.*]

113

Vagrants, I can tell you about them. From experience. Incor-
irgibly delinquent. Purposeless. Addictive. Grab at you for support when support's what *you* need—gone? Whistling down the
last flight, such a lively popular tune. Well, I have travel plans,
but in the company of no charming young vagrant. Love Mediterranean countries but somehow missed Spain. I plan to go.
Now! Madrid, to visit the Prado, most celebrated museum of all.
Admire the Goyas, El Grecos. Hire a car to cross the—gold
plains of Toledo.

WRITER: Jane, you don't have to make up stories, I heard your
talk with Tye—all of it.

JANE: Then you must have heard his leaving. How his steps
picked up speed on the second flight down—started whistling . . .

WRITER: He always whistles down stairs—it's habitual to him—
you mustn't attach a special meaning to it.

[*The clarinet music is closer; the sound penetrates the shut
windows.*]

JANE: At night the Quarter's so full of jazz music, so many
entertainers. Isn't it now your move?

WRITER [*embarrassed*]: It's your move, Jane.

JANE [*relinquishing her game*]: No yours—your vagrant musician is late but you're not forgotten.

WRITER: I'll call down, ask him to wait till midnight when
Tye said he'll be back.

JANE: With tamales and vino to celebrate—[*She staggers to*

114

the window, shatters a pane of glass, and shouts.] —Your friend's coming right down, just picking up his luggage!

[*She leans against the wall, panting, her bleeding hand behind her.*]

Now go, quick. He might not wait, you'd regret it.

WRITER: Can't I do something for you?

JANE: Pour me three fingers of bourbon.

[*She has returned to the table. He pours the shot.*]

Now hurry, hurry. I know that Tye will be back early tonight.

WRITER: Yes, of course he will . . . [*He crosses from the studio light.*]

JANE [*smiling somewhat bitterly*]: Naturally, yes, how could I possibly doubt it. With tamales and vino . . . [*She uncloses her fist; the blood is running from palm to wrist. The writer picks up a cardboard laundry box and the typewriter case.*]

WRITER: As I left, I glanced in Jane's door. She seemed to be or was pretending to be—absorbed in her solitary chess game. I went down the second flight and on the cot in the dark passageway was—[*He calls out.*] Beret?

[*For the first time the cat is visible, white and fluffy as a piece of cloud. Nursie looms dimly behind him, a dark solemn fact, lamplit.*]

NURSIE: It's the cat Miss Sparks come runnin' after.

WRITER: Take it to her, Nursie. She's alone up there.

115

MRS. WIRE: Now watch out, boy. Be careful of the future. It's a long ways for the young. Some makes it and others git lost.

WRITER: I know . . . [*He turns to the audience.*] I stood by the door uncertainly for a moment or two. I must have been frightened of it . . .

MRS. WIRE: Can you see the door?

WRITER: Yes—but to open it is a desperate undertaking . . . !

[*He does, hesitantly. Transparencies close from either wing. Dim spots of light touch each character of the play in a characteristic position.*

[*As he first draws the door open, he is forced back a few steps by a cacophony of sound: the waiting storm of his future—mechanical racking cries of pain and pleasure, snatches of song. It fades out. Again there is the urgent call of the clarinet. He crosses to the open door.*]

They're disappearing behind me. Going. People you've known in places do that: they go when you go. The earth seems to swallow them up, the walls absorb them like moisture, remain with you only as ghosts; their voices are echoes, fading but remembered.

[*The clarinet calls again. He turns for a moment at the door.*]

This house is empty now.

THE END

A LOVELY SUNDAY FOR CREVE COEUR

The New York premiere of *A Lovely Sunday for Creve Coeur* took place at the Hudson Guild Theatre on January 10, 1979. It was directed by Keith Hack; set design by John Conklin; lighting design by Craig Miller; costume design by Linda Fisher; producing director, Craig Anderson. The cast in order of appearance was as follows:

DOROTHEA	SHIRLEY KNIGHT
BODEY	PEG MURRAY
HELENA	CHARLOTTE MOORE
MISS GLUCK	JANE LOWRY

SCENE ONE

It is late on a Sunday morning, early June, in St. Louis.

   The interior is what was called an efficiency apartment in the period of this play, the middle or late thirties. It is in the West End of St. Louis. Attempts to give the apartment brightness and cheer have gone brilliantly and disastrously wrong, and this wrongness is emphasized by the fiercely yellow glare of light through the oversize windows which look out upon vistas of surrounding apartment buildings, vistas that suggest the paintings of Ben Shahn: the dried-blood horror of lower middle-class American urban neighborhoods. The second thing which assails our senses is a combination of counting and panting from the bedroom, to the left, where a marginally youthful but attractive woman, Dorothea, is taking "setting-up exercises" with fearful effort.

   SOUND: Ninety-one, *ha!* —ninety-two, *ha!* —ninety-three, *ha!* —ninety-four, *ha!*

This breathless counting continues till one hundred is achieved with a great gasp of deliverance. At some point during the counting, a rather short, plumpish woman, early middle-aged, has entered from the opposite doorway with a copy of the big Sunday St. Louis Post-Dispatch.

   The phone rings just as Bodey, who is hard-of-hearing, sits down on a sofa in the middle of the room. Bodey, absorbed in the paper, ignores the ringing phone, but it has caused Dorothea to gasp with emotion so strong that she is physically frozen except for her voice. She catches hold of something for a moment, as if reeling in a storm, then plunges to the bedroom door and rushes out into the living room with a dramatic door-bang.

DOROTHEA: WHY DIDN'T YOU GET THAT PHONE?

119

BODEY [*rising and going to the kitchenette at the right*]: Where, where, what, what phone?

DOROTHEA: Is there more than one phone here? Are there several other phones I haven't discovered as yet?

BODEY: —Dotty, I think these setting-up exercises get you overexcited, emotional, I mean.

DOROTHEA [*continuing*]: That phone was ringing and I told you when I woke up that I was expecting a phone call from Ralph Ellis who told me he had something very important to tell me and would phone me today before noon.

BODEY: Sure, he had something to tell you but he didn't.

DOROTHEA: Bodey, you are not hearing, or comprehending, what I'm saying at all. Your face is a dead giveaway. I said Ralph Ellis—you've heard me speak of Ralph?

BODEY: Oh, yes, Ralph, you speak continuously of him, that name Ralph Ellis is one I got fixed in my head so I could never forget it.

DOROTHEA: Oh, you mean I'm not permitted to mention the name Ralph Ellis to you?

BODEY [*preparing fried chicken in the kitchenette*]: Dotty, when two girls are sharing a small apartment, naturally each of the girls should feel perfectly free to speak of whatever concerns her. I don't think it's possible for two girls sharing a small apartment *not* to speak of whatever concerns her whenever—whatever—*concerns* her, but, Dotty, I know that I'm not your older sister. However, if I was, I would have a suspicion that you have got a crush on this Ralph Ellis, and as an older sister, I'd feel obliged to advise you to, well, look before you

120

leap in that direction. I mean just don't put all your eggs in one basket till you are one hundred percent convinced that the basket is the right one, that's all I mean. . . . Well, this is a lovely Sunday for a picnic at Creve Coeur. . . . Didn't you notice out at Creve Coeur last Sunday how Buddy's slimmed down round the middle?

DOROTHEA: No, I didn't.

BODEY: Huh?

DOROTHEA: Notice.

BODEY: Well, it was noticeable, Dotty.

DOROTHEA: Bodey, why should I be interested in whatever fractional—fluctuations—occur in your twin brother's waist-line—as if it was the Wall Street market and I was a heavy investor?

BODEY: You mean you don't care if Buddy shapes up or not?

DOROTHEA: Shapes up for what?

BODEY: Nacherly for you, Dotty.

DOROTHEA: Does he regard me as an athletic event, the high jump or pole vault? Please, please, Bodey, convince him his shape does not concern me at all.

BODEY: Buddy don't discuss his work with me often, but lately he said his boss at Anheuser-Busch has got an eye on him.

DOROTHEA: How could his boss ignore such a sizeable object? —Bodey, what are you up to in that cute little kitchenette?

BODEY: Honey, I stopped by Piggly-Wiggly's yesterday noon

121

when I got off the streetcar on the way home from the office, and I picked up three beautiful fryers, you know, nice and plump fryers.

DOROTHEA: I'd better remain out here till Ralph calls back, so I can catch it myself. [*She lies on the purple carpet and begins another series of formalized exercises.*]

BODEY: The fryers are sizzling so loud I didn't catch that, Dotty. You know, now that the office lets out at noon Saturday, it's easier to lay in supplies for Sunday. I think that Roosevelt did something for the country when he got us half Saturdays off because it used to be that by the time I got off the street-car from International Shoe, Piggly-Wiggly's on the corner would be closed, but now it's still wide open. So I went in Piggly-Wiggly's, I went to the meat department and I said to the nice old man, Mr. Butts, the butcher, "Mr. Butts, have you got any real nice fryers?" —"You bet your life!" he said, "I must of been expectin' you to drop in. Feel these nice plump fryers." Mr. Butts always lets me feel his meat. The feel of a piece of meat is the way to test it, but there's very few modern butchers will allow you to feel it. It's the German in me. I got to feel the meat to know it's good. A piece of meat can look good over the counter but to know for sure I always want to feel it. Mr. Butts, being German, he understands that, always says to me, "Feel it, go on, feel it." So I felt the fryers. "Don't they feel good and fresh?" I said, "Yes, Mr. Butts, but will they keep till tomorrow?" "Haven't you got any ice in your ice-box?" he asked me. I said to him, "I hope so, but ice goes fast in hot weather. I told the girl that shares my apartment with me to put up the card for a twenty-five pound lump of ice but sometimes she forgets to." Well, thank goodness, this time you didn't forget to. You always got so much on your mind in the morning, civics and—other things at the high school. —What are you laughin' at, Dotty? [*She turns around to glance at Dorothea who is covering her mouth to stifle breathless sounds of laughter.*]

122

DOROTHEA: Honestly, Bodey, I think you missed your calling. You should be in Congress to deliver a filibuster. I never knew it was possible to talk at such length about ice and a butcher.

BODEY: Well, Dotty, you know we agreed when you moved in here with me that I would take care of the shopping. We've kept good books on expenses. Haven't we kept good books? We've never had any argument over expense or disagreements between us over what I should shop for. —OW!

DOROTHEA: Now what?

BODEY: The skillet spit at me. Some hot grease flew in my face. I'll put bakin' soda on it.

DOROTHEA: So you are really and truly frying chickens in this terrible heat?

BODEY: And boiling eggs, I'm going to make deviled eggs, too. Dotty, what is it? You sound hysterical, Dotty!

DOROTHEA [*half strangled with laughter*]: Which came first, fried chicken or deviled eggs? —I swear to goodness, you do the funniest things. Honestly, Bodey, you are a source of continual astonishment and amusement to me. Now, Bodey, please suspend this culinary frenzy until the phone rings again so you can hear it this time before it stops ringing for me.

BODEY: Dotty, I was right here and that phone was not ringin'. I give you my word that phone was not makin' a sound. It was quiet as a mouse.

DOROTHEA: Why, it was ringing its head off!

BODEY: Dotty, about some things everyone is mistaken, and this is something you are mistaken about. I think your exercises give you a ringing noise in your head. I think they're too

123

strenuous for you, 'specially on Sunday, a day of rest, recreation . . .

DOROTHEA: We are both entitled to separate opinions, Bodey, but I assure you I do not suffer from ringing in my head. That phone was RINGING. And why you did not hear it is simply because you don't have your hearing aid on!

[*The shouting is congruent with the fiercely bright colors of the interior.*]

BODEY: I honestly ain't that deaf. I swear I ain't that deaf, Dotty. The ear specialist says I just got this little calcification, this calcium in my—eardrums. But I do hear a telephone ring, a sharp, loud sound like that, I hear it, I hear it clearly.

DOROTHEA: Well, let's hope Ralph won't imagine I'm out and will call back in a while. But do put your hearing aid in. I don't share your confidence in your hearing a phone ring or a dynamite blast without it, and anyway, Bodey, you must adjust to it, you must get used to it, and after a while, when you're accustomed to it, you won't feel complete without it.

BODEY: —Yes, well— This is the best Sunday yet for a picnic at Creve Coeur . . .

DOROTHEA: That we'll talk about later. Jut put your hearing aid in before I continue with my exercises. Put it in right now so I can see you.

BODEY: You still ain't finished with those exercises?

DOROTHEA: I've done one hundred bends and I did my floor exercises. I just have these bust development exercises and my swivels and—BODEY! PUT YOUR HEARING AID IN!

BODEY: I hear you, honey, I will. I'll put it on right now.

[*She comes into the living room from the kitchenette and picks up the hearing aid and several large artificial flowers from a table. She hastily moves the newspaper from the sofa to a chair behind her, then inserts the device in an ear with an agonized look.*]

DOROTHEA: It can't be that difficult to insert it. Why, from your expression, you could be performing major surgery on yourself! . . . without anesthesia . . .

BODEY: I'm just—not used to it yet. [*She covers the defective ear with an artificial chrysanthemum.*]

DOROTHEA [*in the doorway*]: You keep reminding yourself of it by covering it up with those enormous artificial flowers. Now if you feel you have to do that, why don't you pick out a flower that's suitable to the season? Chrysanthemums are for autumn and this is June.

BODEY: Yes. June. How about this poppy?

DOROTHEA: Well, frankly, dear, that big poppy is tacky.

BODEY: —The tiger lily?

DOROTHEA [*despairing*]: Yes, the tiger lily! Of course, Bodey, the truth of the matter is that your idea of concealing your hearing aid with a big artificial flower is ever so slightly fantastic.

BODEY: —Everybody is sensitive about something . . .

DOROTHEA: But complexes, obsessions must not be cultivated. Well. Back to my exercises. Be sure not to miss the phone.

125

Ralph is going to call me any minute now. [*She starts to close the bedroom door.*]

BODEY: Dotty?

DOROTHEA: Yes?

BODEY: Dotty, I'm gonna ask Buddy to go to Creve Coeur with us again today for the picnic. That's okay with you, huh?

DOROTHEA [*pausing in the doorway*]: Bodey, Buddy is your brother and I fully understand your attachment to him. He's got many fine things about him. A really solid character and all that. But, Bodey, I think it's unfair to Buddy for you to go on attempting to bring us together because—well, everyone has a type she is attracted to and in the case of Buddy, no matter how much—I appreciate his sterling qualities and all, he simply isn't—[*She has gone into the bedroom and started swiveling her hips.*]

BODEY: Isn't what, Dotty?

DOROTHEA: A type that I can respond to. You know what I mean. In a romantic fashion, honey. And to me—romance is—essential.

BODEY: Oh—but—well, there's other things to consider besides—romance . . .

DOROTHEA [*swiveling her hips as she talks*]: Bodey, can you honestly feel that Buddy and I are exactly right for each other? Somehow I suspect that Buddy would do better looking about for a steady, German-type girl in South St. Louis—a girl to drink beer with and eat Wiener schnitzel and get fat along with him, not a girl—well, a girl already romantically—pour me a little more coffee? —Thanks. —Why do you keep forgetting the understanding between me and Mr. Ellis? Is that fair to Buddy? To build up his hopes for an inevitable letdown?

[*Dorothea stops her swivels and returns to the living room to get the coffee Bodey has poured for her.*]

BODEY: This Mr. T. Ralph Ellis, well . . .

DOROTHEA: Well, *what?*

BODEY: Nothing except . . .

DOROTHEA: *What?*

BODEY: He might not be as reliable as Buddy—in the long run.

DOROTHEA: What is "the long run," honey?

BODEY: The long run is—*life.*

DOROTHEA: Oh, so that is the long run, the long run is life! With Buddy? Well, then give me the short run, I'm sorry, but I'll take the short run, much less exhausting in the heat of the day and the night!

BODEY: Dotty, I tell you, Dotty, in the long run or the short run I'd place my bet on Buddy, not on a—fly-by-night sort of proposition like this, this—romantic idea you got about a man that mostly you see wrote up in—society pages . . .

DOROTHEA: *That is your misconception!* —Of something about which you are in total ignorance, because I rarely step out of the civics classroom at Blewett without seeing Ralph Ellis a few steps down the corridor, pretending to take a drink at the water cooler on my floor which is two floors up from his office!

127

BODEY: Not really taking a drink but just pretending? Not a good sign, Dotty—pretending . . .

DOROTHEA: What I mean is—we have to arrange secret little encounters of this sort to avoid gossip at Blewett.

BODEY: —Well—

DOROTHEA: *WHAT?*

BODEY: I never trusted pretending.

DOROTHEA: Then why the paper flowers over the hearing aid, dear?

BODEY: That's—just—a little—sensitivity, there . . .

DOROTHEA: Look, you've got to live with it so take off the concealment, the paper tiger lily, and turn the hearing aid up or I will be obliged to finish my hip swivels out here to catch Ralph's telephone call.

BODEY [*as she is turning up the hearing aid, it makes a shrill sound*]: See? See?

DOROTHEA: I think you mean hear, hear! —Turn it down just a bit, find the right level for it!

BODEY: Yes, yes, I—[*She fumbles with the hearing aid, dislodging the paper flower.*]

DOROTHEA: For heaven's sake, let me adjust it for you! [*She rushes over to Bodey and fiddles with the hearing aid.*] Now! —Not shrieking. —But can you hear me? I said can you hear me! At this level!?

128

BODEY: Yes. Where's my tiger lily?

DOROTHEA: Dropped on the fierce purple carpet. Here. [*She picks it up and hands it to Bodey.*] What's wrong with you?

BODEY: I'm—upset. Over this maybe—dangerous—trust you've got in Ralph Ellis's—intentions . . .

DOROTHEA [*dreamily, eyes going soft*]: I don't like discussing an intimate thing like this but—the last time I went out in Ralph Ellis's Reo, that new sedan he's got called the Flying Cloud . . .

BODEY: Cloud? Flying?

DOROTHEA [*raising her voice to a shout*]: The Reo is advertised as "The Flying Cloud."

BODEY: Oh. Yes. He'd be attracted to that.

DOROTHEA: It was pouring down rain and Art Hill was deserted, no other cars on it but Ralph and I in his Reo. The windows curtained with rain that glistened in the lamplight.

BODEY: Dotty, I hope you're not leading up to something that shouldn't of happened in this Flying Cloud on Art Hill. It really scares me, Dotty . . .

DOROTHEA: Frankly, I was a little frightened myself because— we've never had this kind of discussion before, it's rather—difficult for me but you must understand. I've always drawn a strict line with a man till this occasion.

BODEY: Dotty, do you mean—?

DOROTHEA: It was so magical to me, the windows curtained

129

with rain, the soft look in his eyes, the warmth of his breath that's always scented with clove, his fingers touching so gently as he—

BODEY: Dotty, I don't think I want to know any more about this—experience on Art Hill because, because—I got a suspicion, Dotty, that you didn't hold the line with him.

DOROTHEA: The line just—didn't exist when he parked the car and turned and looked at me and I turned and looked at him. Our eyes, our eyes—

BODEY: Your eyes?

DOROTHEA: Burned the line out of existence, like it had never existed!

BODEY: —I'm not gonna tell this to Buddy!

DOROTHEA: You know, I wasn't aware until then that the Reo was equipped with adjustable seats.

BODEY: Seats that—?

DOROTHEA: Adjusted to pressure, yes, reclined beneath me when he pushed a lever.

BODEY [*distracted from the phonebook which she had begun to leaf through*]: —How far did this seat recline beneath you, Dotty?

DOROTHEA: Horizontally, nearly. So gradually though that I didn't know till later, later. Later, not then—the earth whirling beneath me and the sky was spinning above.

BODEY: Oh-ho, he got you drunk, did he, with a flask of liquor in that Flying Cloud on—

130

DOROTHEA: Drunk on a single Pink Lady?

BODEY: Pink?

DOROTHEA: Lady. —The mildest sort of cocktail! Made with sloe gin and grenadine.

BODEY: The gin was slow, maybe, but that man is a fast one, seducing a girl with adjustable seats and a flask of liquor in that Flying Cloud on—

DOROTHEA: Not a flask, a cocktail, and not in the Reo but in a small private club called The Onyx, a club so exclusive he had to present an engraved card at the entrance.

BODEY: Oh yes, I know such places!

DOROTHEA: How would you know such places?

BODEY: I seen one at the movies and so did you, at the West End Lyric, the last time you was all broke up from expectin' a call from this Ellis which never came in, so we seen Roy D'Arcy take poor Janet Gaynor to one of them—private clubs to—!

[*Bodey has not found the Blewett number in the phone-book. She dials the operator.*]

Blewett, Blewett, get me the high school named Blewett.

DOROTHEA: Bodey, what are you doing at the phone which I begged you not to use till Ralph has called?

BODEY: Reporting him to Blewett!

DOROTHEA: Bodey, that takes the cake, reporting on the principal of Blewett to Blewett that's closed on Sundays. What a remarkable—

131

BODEY [*darting about*]: Paper, pen!

DOROTHEA: Now what?

BODEY: A written report to the Board of Education of St. Louis. I tell you, that Board will be interested in all details of how that principal of the school system got you lying down drunk and defenseless in his Flying Cloud in a storm on Art Hill, every advantage taken with Valentino sheik tricks on a innocent teacher of civics just up from Memphis.

DOROTHEA: YOU WILL NOT—

BODEY: DON'T TELL ME NOT!

DOROTHEA: LIBEL THE REPUTATION OF A MAN THAT I LOVE, GAVE MYSELF TO NOT JUST FREELY BUT WITH ABANDON, WITH JOY!

BODEY [*aloud as she writes*]: Board of Education of St. Louis, Missouri. I think you should know that your principal at Blewett used his position to take disgusting advantage of a young teacher employed there by him for that purpose. I know, I got the facts, including the date and—

[*Dorothea snatches up and crumples the letter.*]

My letter, you tore up my—!

DOROTHEA: Bodey, if you had written and mailed that letter, do you know what you'd have obliged me to do? I would be morally obliged to go personally down to the Board of Education and tell them an *opposite* story which happens to be the *true* one: that I *desired* Ralph Ellis, possibly even more than he did me!

[*Bodey huffs and puffs wordlessly till she can speak.*]

BODEY: —Well, God help you, Dotty. —But I give you my word I won't repeat this to Buddy.

DOROTHEA: How does it concern Buddy?

BODEY: It concerns Buddy and me because Buddy's got deep feelings and respect for you, Dotty. He would respect you too much to cross the proper line before you had stood up together in the First Lutheran Church on South Grand.

DOROTHEA: *Now* you *admit* it!

BODEY: It's you that's makin' admissions of a terrible kind that might shock Buddy out of his serious intentions.

DOROTHEA: You are admitting that—

[*As she had threatened, Dorothea has begun doing her hip swivels in the living room, but now she stops and stares indignantly at Bodey.*]

—you've been deliberately planning and plotting to marry me off to your twin brother so that my life would be just one long Creve Coeur picnic, interspersed with knockwurst, sauerkraut—hot potato salad dinners. —Would I be asked to prepare them? Even in summer? I know what you Germans regard as the limits, the boundaries of a woman's life—*Kirche, Küche, und Kinder*—while being asphyxiated gradually by cheap cigars. I'm sorry but the life I design for myself is not along those lines or in those limits. My life must include romance. Without romance in my life, I could no more live than I could without breath. I've got to find a partner in life, or my life will have no meaning. But what I must have and finally do have is an affair of the heart, two hearts, a true consummated romance —yes consummated, I'm not ashamed! [*She gasps and sways.*]

BODEY: Dotty, Dotty, set down and catch your breath!

133

DOROTHEA: In this breathless efficiency apartment? —I've got to have space in my life.

BODEY: —Did I tell you that Buddy has made a down payment on a Buick?

DOROTHEA: No, you didn't and why should you, as it does not concern— Oh, my God, Blessed Savior!

BODEY: Dotty, what Dotty? D'you want your, your whatamacallit tablets?

DOROTHEA: Mebaral? No, I have not collapsed yet, but you've just about driven me to it.

BODEY: Take a breather, take a seventh inning stretch while I—

DOROTHEA: Bodey, this room is GLARING; it's not cheerful but GLARING!

BODEY: Stretch out on the sofa and look up, the ceiling is white!

DOROTHEA: I don't know why I'm so out of breath today.

BODEY: Don't do no more exercises. You drink too much coffee an' Cokes. That's stimulants for a girl high-strung like you. With a nervous heart condition.

DOROTHEA: It's functional—not nervous.

BODEY: Lie down a minute.

DOROTHEA: I will rest a little—but not because you say so. [*Between gasps she sinks into a chair.*] You're very bossy— and very inquisitive, too.

134

BODEY: I'm older'n you, and I got your interests at heart.

DOROTHEA: Whew!

BODEY: Think how cool it will be on the open-air streetcar to Creve Coeur.

DOROTHEA: You must have had your hearing aid off when I said I had other plans.

BODEY: Buddy, I been telling Buddy to cut down on his beer, and Buddy is listening to me. He's cut down to eight a day—from a dozen and will cut down more . . .

DOROTHEA: Bodey, could you stop talking about Buddy this hot Sunday morning? It's not a suitable subject for hot weather. I know brother-sister relationships are deep, but it's not just the beer, it's the almost total lack of interests in common, no topics of conversations, of—of mutual—interest.

BODEY: They could develop. I know Buddy just feels embarrassed. He hasn't opened up yet. Give him time and he will.

DOROTHEA: Bodey, this discussion is embarrassingly pointless in view of the fact that I'm already committed to Ralph Ellis. I still have to do my hip swivels . . .

[Sipping coffee as she goes, Dorothea returns to the bedroom and resumes her exercises.]

BODEY [rushing to the phone]: Olive 2697, Olive 2697! Buddy? Me! Grosser Gott! I can't talk now, but you absolutley got to go to Creve Coeur with us this Sunday. —Dress good! Don't smoke cigars! And laugh at her witty remarks. —Well, they are, they're witty! She teaches civics.

135

[*The doorbell rings*].

Now be at the Creve Coeur station at 1:30, huh? —Please!—
Somebody's at the door, I can't talk now. [*Leaving the phone
off the hook, she rushes to the door and opens it.*] Oh. Hello.

HELENA: Good morning.

BODEY: Are you a friend of Dotty's?

[*A stylishly dressed woman with the eyes of a predatory
bird appears.*]

HELENA: Of Dorothea's? —Yes.

BODEY: Well, then come on in. Any friend of Dotty's is a
friend of mine.

HELENA: Is that so?

BODEY [*discomfited*]: Yes, I—got grease on my hand. I was
fryin' up some chickens for a picnic.

HELENA: —Well! This is a surprise! [*She makes several turns
in a mechanical, rigid fashion, eyes staring.*]

BODEY: Excuse me, I should of—interduced myself.

HELENA: You are Miss Bodenheifer.

BODEY: Hafer, not heifer. [*She laughs nervously.*] Heifer
meaning a cow.

HELENA: No conscious association whatsoever. [*She advances
forward a step.*] So this is Schlogger Haven?

136

BODEY: Oh, Schlogger Haven, that's just a joke of Dotty's. The landlord's name is Schlogger, that's all—that's all . . .

HELENA: Dorothea was joking, was she?

BODEY: Yeh, she jokes a lot, full of humor. We have lots of laughs. [*Bodey extends her hand.*]

HELENA: I can imagine you might, Miss Bodenheifer.

BODEY: You can forget the Miss. —Everyone at the office calls me Bodey.

HELENA: But we are not at the office—we are here in Schlogger Haven. [*She continues enigmatically.*] Hmmm . . . I've never ventured this side of Blewett before.

BODEY: Never gone downtown?

HELENA: I do nearly all my shopping in the West End, so naturally it amazed me to discover street after street without a shade tree on it, and the glare, the glare, and the heat refracted by all the brick, concrete, asphalt—was so overpowering that I nearly collapsed. I think I must be afflicted with a combination of photo- and heliophobia, both.

BODEY [*unconsciously retreating a step as if fearing contagion*]: I never heard of neither—but you got *both?*

HELENA: An exceptional sensitivity to both heat and strong light.

BODEY: Aw.

HELENA: Yes. Now would you please let Dorothea know I'm here to see her?

137

BODEY: Does Dotty expect you, Miss, uh—

HELENA: Helena Brookmire, no, she doesn't expect me, but a very urgent business matter has obliged me to drop by this early.

BODEY: She won't have no one in there with her. She's exercising.

HELENA: But Dorothea and I are well acquainted.

BODEY: Well acquainted or not acquainted at all, makes no difference. I think that modern girls emphasize too much these advertised treatments and keep their weight down too much for their health.

HELENA: The preservation of youth requires some sacrifices.

[*She continues to stare about her, blinking her birdlike eyes as if dazzled.*]

BODEY: —I guess you and Dotty teach together at Blewett High?

HELENA: —Separately.

BODEY: You mean you're not at Blewett where Dotty teaches civics?

HELENA [*as if addressing a backward child*]: I teach there, too. When I said separately, I meant we teach separate classes.

BODEY: Oh, naturally, yes. [*She tries to laugh.*] I been to high school.

HELENA: Have you?

BODEY: Yes. I know that two teachers don't teach in the same class at the same time, on two different subjects.

HELENA [*opening her eyes very wide*]: Wouldn't *that* be peculiar.

BODEY: Yes. That would be peculiar.

HELENA [*chuckling unpleasantly*]: It might create some confusion among the students.

BODEY: Yes, I reckon it would.

HELENA: Especially if the subjects were as different as civics and the history of *art*.

[*Bodey attempts to laugh again; Helena imitates the laugh almost exactly.*

[*Pause*]

This *is*, it really *is!*

BODEY: Is *what?*

HELENA: The most remarkable room that I've ever stepped into! Especially the combination of colors! Such a *vivid* contrast! May I sit down?

BODEY: Yeh, yeh, excuse me, I'm not myself today. It's the heat and the—

HELENA: Colors? —The vivid contrast of colors? [*She removes a pair of round, white-rimmed dark glasses from her purse and puts them on.*] Did Dorothea assist you, Miss Bodenheifer, in decorating this room?

139

BODEY: No, when Dotty moved in, it was just like it is now.

HELENA: Then you are solely responsible for this inspired selection of colors?

[*There is a loud sputter of hot fat from the kitchenette.*]

BODEY: Excuse me a moment, I got to turn over the fryers in the skillet.

HELENA: Don't let me interrupt your preparations for a picnic.

BODEY: Didn't catch that. I don't hear good sometimes.

HELENA: Oh?

BODEY: You see, I got this calcium deposit in my ears . . . and they advised me to have an operation, but it's very expensive for me and sometimes it don't work.

PHONE VOICE: Booow-deeee!

[*Helena notices but doesn't comment on the unhooked phone.*]

HELENA: I would advise you against it. I had an elderly acquaintance who had this calcification problem and she had a hole bored in her skull to correct it. The operation is called fenestration—it involves a good deal of danger and whether or not it was successful could not be determined since she never recovered consciousness.

BODEY: Never recovered?

HELENA: Consciousness.

140

BODEY: Yeh, well, I think maybe I'd better learn to live with it.

PHONE VOICE [*shouting again*]: Bodeyyyyy—Bodeyyyy—

BODEY: What's that?

HELENA: I was wondering, too. Very strange barking sounds are coming out of the phone.

BODEY [*laughing*]: Oh, God, I left it unhooked. [*She snatches it up.*] Buddy, sorry, somebody just dropped in, forgot you was still on the line. Buddy, call me back in a few minutes, huh, Buddy, it's, uh, very important. [*She hangs up the phone.*] That was my brother. Buddy. He says he drunk two beers and made him a liverwurst sandwich before I got back to the phone. Thank God he is so good-natured. . . . He and me are going out on a picnic at Creve Coeur with Dotty this afternoon. My brother is very interested in Dotty.

HELENA: Interested? Romantically?

BODEY: Oh, yes, Buddy's a very serious person.

HELENA [*rising*]: —I am very impressed!

BODEY: By what, what by?

HELENA [*with disguised fury*]: The ingenuity with which you've fitted yourself into this limited space. Every inch seems to be utilized by some appliance or—*decoration?* [*She picks up a large painted china frog.*] —A frahg?

BODEY: Yes, frawg.

HELENA: So realistically colored and designed you'd almost

141

expect it to croak. —Oh, and you have a canary . . . stuffed!

BODEY: Little Hilda . . . she lived ten years. That's the limit for a canary.

HELENA: Limit of longevity for the species?

BODEY: She broke it by three months.

HELENA: Establishing a record. It's quite heroic, enduring more than ten years in such confinement. What tenacity to existence some creatures do have!

BODEY: I got so attached to it, I took it to a, a—

HELENA: Taxidermist.

BODEY: Excuse me a moment. [*She rushes to the stove in the alcove.*] OW! —Got burnt again.

HELENA [*following curiously*]: You were burnt before?

[*Bodey profusely powders her arms with baking soda. Helena backs away.*]

Miss Bodenheifer, *please!* You've sprinkled my clothes with that powder!

BODEY: Sorry, I didn't mean to.

HELENA: Intentional or not, I'm afraid you have! May I have a clothes brush?

BODEY: Look at that, I spilt it on the carpet. [*She rushes to fetch a broom.*]

HELENA: Miss Bodenheifer, I WOULD LIKE A CLOTHES BRUSH, IF YOU HAVE A *CLOTHES* BRUSH! Not a broom. I am not a carpet.

BODEY: AW. SURE. Dotty's got a clothes brush. Oh. Help yourself to some coffee. [*She drops the broom and enters the bedroom.*]

[*Through the open door, Dorothea can be heard counting as she swivels.*]

DOROTHEA'S VOICE: Sixty, *ha!* Sixty-one, *ha!* [*She continues counting but stops when she notices Bodey.*] —The PHONE? Is it the PHONE?

BODEY: Clothes brush. [*Bodey closes the bedroom door and begins opening and shutting drawers as she looks for the clothes brush.*]

DOROTHEA: DON'T, DON'T, DON'T—slam a drawer shut like that! I feel like screaming!

[*Helena opens a closet in the kitchenette; a box falls out.*]

HELENA: The hazards of this place almost equal the horrors.

DOROTHEA [*in the bedroom*]: I asked you if the phone rang.

BODEY: No, no, the doorbell.

HELENA [*who has moved to the icebox*]: Ah. Ice, mostly melted, what squalor!

[*This dual scene must be carefully timed.*]

DOROTHEA: I presume it's Miss Gluck from upstairs in boudoir

143

cap and wrapper. Bodey, get her out as quickly as possible. The sight of that woman destroys me for the whole day.

HELENA [*still in the kitchenette*]: This remnant of ice will not survive in this steaming glass of coffee.

[*A knock at the door is heard.*]

What's that?

[*Sophie Gluck opens the front door and sticks her head in. At the sight of Helena, she withdraws in alarm.*]

Another tenant. *Demented!*

[*Helena moves to the door and slams and bolts it with such force that Sophie, outside, utters a soft cry of confused panic.*]

BODEY: Don't do no more calisthenics if it affecks you this way.

DOROTHEA: Just, just—knock at the door when Miss Gluck has gone back upstairs, that's my—whew!—only—request . . .

BODEY: —Yes, well . . .

DOROTHEA: No coffee, no crullers or she—will stay—down here—forever—ha!

[*The phone rings; Helena picks it up. Bodey emerges from the bedroom with a whisk broom, closing the door behind her. Helena is at the phone.*]

HELENA: Oh, she seems engaged for the moment . . .

BODEY: Aw, the phone! Is it that principal, Ellis?

HELENA [*aside from the phone*]: I'm afraid not. It seems to be Dorothea's other admirer—*quel embarras de richesses* . . .

BODEY [*rushing to the phone*]: Must be Buddy. —Buddy? Well? —Yeh, good, what suit you got on? Well, take it off. It don't look good on you, Buddy. Put on the striped suit, Buddy an' the polka dot tie, and, Buddy, if you smoke a cigar at Creve Coeur, excuse yourself and smoke it in the bushes.

HELENA: This is—

BODEY: That's right, 'bye.

HELENA: —absolutely bizarre! You found a clothes brush? That's not a clothes brush. It's a whisk broom. Sorry. It doesn't look clean.

BODEY: Sorry. My nerves.

HELENA [*taking it and brushing herself delicately here and there*]: What was that counting I heard? Is Dorothea counting something in there?

BODEY: She's counting her swivels in there.

HELENA: Swivels of what?

BODEY: Hip swivels, that's what. She's counting. Every morning she does one hundred bends and one hundred set-ups and one hundred hip swivels.

HELENA: Regardless of weather?

BODEY: That's right, regardless of weather.

HELENA: And regardless of— Hmmm . . .

145

[*Bodey senses a touch of malice implicit in this unfinished sentence.*]

BODEY: —What else, huh?

HELENA: Dorothea has always impressed me as an emotionally fragile type of person who might collapse, just suddenly collapse, when confronted with the disappointing facts of a situation about which she'd allowed herself to have—romantic illusions.

[*It is now Bodey's turn to say, "Hmmm . . ."*]

—No matter how—well, I hate to say foolish but even intelligent girls can make mistakes of this nature . . . of course we all felt she was attaching too much importance to—

BODEY: "We all" is who?

HELENA: Our little group at Blewett.

BODEY: Yeh, there's always a gossipy little group, even down at International Shoe where I work there is a gossipy little group that feels superior to the rest of us. Well, personally, I don't want in with this gossipy little group because the gossip is malicious. Oh, they call it being concerned, but it's not the right kind of concern, naw, I'd hate for that gossipy little group to feel concerned about me, don't want that and don't need it.

HELENA: Understandably, yaiss. I will return this whisk broom to Dorothea.

BODEY: No, no, just return it to me.

HELENA: I have to speak to her and in order to do that I'll have to enter that room. So if you'll excuse me I'll—

146

[*She starts toward the bedroom. Bodey snatches the whisk broom from her with a force that makes Helena gasp.*]

BODEY: Miss Brooksit, you're a visitor here but the visit was not expected. Now you excuse me but I got to say you sort of act like this apartment was yours.

HELENA: —What a dismaying idea! I mean I—

BODEY: And excuse me or don't excuse me but I got a very strong feeling that you got something in mind. All right, your mind is your mind, what's in it is yours but keep it to yourself, huh?

HELENA [*cutting in*]: Miss Bodenheifer, you seem to be implying something that's a mystery to me.

BODEY: You know what I mean and I know what I mean so where's the mystery, huh?

DOROTHEA [*calling from the bedroom*]: Is somebody out there, Bodey?

BODEY: Just Sophie Gluck.

DOROTHEA: Oh, Lord!

HELENA: What was that you called me?

BODEY: I told Dotty that you was Miss Gluck from upstairs.

HELENA: —Gluck?

BODEY: Yeah, Miss Gluck is a lady upstairs that comes downstairs to visit.

147

HELENA: She comes down to see Dorothea?

BODEY: No, no, more to see me, and to drink coffee. She lost her mother, an' she's got a depression so bad she can't make coffee, so I save her a cup, keep her a cup in the pot. You know for a single girl to lose a mother is a terrible thing. What else can you do? She oughta be down. Weekdays she comes down at seven. Well, this is Sunday.

HELENA: Yes. This is Sunday.

BODEY: Sundays she comes down for coffee and a cruller at ten.

HELENA: Cruller? What is a cruller?

BODEY: Aw. You call it a doughnut, but me, bein' German, was raised to call it a cruller.

HELENA: Oh. A cruller is a doughnut but you call it a cruller. Now if you'll excuse me a moment, I will go in there and re- lieve Dorothea of the mistaken impression that I am Miss Gluck from upstairs who has come down for her coffee and—cruller.

BODEY: Oh, no, don't interrupt her calisthenics.

[*Helena ignores this admonition and opens the bedroom door.*]

DOROTHEA: Why, Helena Brookmire! —What a surprise. I— I—look a—*mess!*

HELENA: I heard this counting and gasping. Inquired what was going on. Your friend Miss—what?

DOROTHEA: You've met Miss Bodenhafer?

148

HELENA: Yes, she received me very cordially. We've dispensed with introductions. She says any friend of yours is a friend of hers and wants me to call her Bodey as they do at the office. Excuse me, Miss Bodenheifer, I must have a bit of private conversation—

[*Helena closes the bedroom door, shutting out Bodey.*]

DOROTHEA: Well, I wasn't expecting a visitor today, obviously not this early. You see, I—never receive a visitor here. . . . Is there something too urgent to hold off till Monday, Helena?

HELENA: Have our negotiations with the realty firm of Orthwein and Muller slipped your flighty mind?

DOROTHEA: Oh, the real estate people, but surely on Sunday—

HELENA: Mr. Orthwein called Cousin Dee-Dee last night and she called me this morning that now the news has leaked out and there's competitive bidding for the apartment on Westmoreland Place and the deal must be settled at once.

DOROTHEA: You mean by—?

HELENA: Immediate payment, yes, to pin it down.

DOROTHEA: *Today? Sunday?*

HELENA: The sanctity of a Sunday must sometimes be profaned by business transactions.

[*Bodey has now entered.*]

DOROTHEA: Helena, if you'll just have some coffee and wait in the living room, I will come out as soon as I've showered and dressed.

149

BODEY: Yeh, yeh, do that. You're embarrassing Dotty, so come back out and—

[*Bodey almost drags Helena out of the bedroom, kicking the bedroom door shut.*]

HELENA: Gracious!

BODEY: Yes, gracious, here! Set down, I'll get you some coffee.

HELENA [*with a sharp laugh*]: She said, "I look a mess," and I couldn't contradict her.

BODEY: Here! Your coffee! Your cruller!

HELENA [*haughtily*]: I don't care for the cruller, as you call it. Pastries are not included in my diet. However—I'd like a clean napkin. You've splashed coffee everywhere.

BODEY: Sure, we got plenty of napkins. You name it, we got it. [*She thrusts a paper napkin at Helena like a challenge.*]

HELENA: This paper napkin is stained. Would you please give me—

BODEY: Take 'em all. You stained that napkin yourself. [*She thrusts the entire pile of napkins at Helena.*]

HELENA: You shoved the cup at me so roughly the coffee splashed.

[*Helena fastidiously wipes the tabletop. There is a rap at the door.*]

BODEY: Aw, that's Sophie Gluck.

150

HELENA: I don't care to meet Miss Gluck.

BODEY: Will you set down so I can let in Sophie Gluck?

HELENA: So if you're going to admit her, I will take refuge again in Dorothea's bedroom. . . . There is another matter I've come here to . . .

BODEY [*seizing Helena's arm as she crosses toward the bed-room*]: I know what you're up to! —JUST A MINUTE, *BITTE*, SOPHIE! I can guess the other matter you just can't hold your tongue about, but you're gonna hold it. It's not gonna be mentioned to cloud over the day and spoil the Creve Coeur picnic for Dotty, Buddy, an' me! —COMIN', SOPHIE! [*Then, to Helena, fiercely.*] YOU SET BACK DOWN!

[*During this altercation, Dorothea has been standing in the bedroom paralyzed with embarrassment and dismay. Now she calls sweetly through the door, opened a crack.*]

DOROTHEA: Bodey, Bodey, what *is* going on out there? How could a phone be heard above that shouting? Oh, My Blessed Savior, I was bawn on a Sunday, and I am convinced that I shall die on a Sunday! Could you please tell me what is the cause of the nerve-shattering altercations going on out there?

HELENA: Dorothea, Miss Bodenheifer's about to receive Miss Gluck.

DOROTHEA: Oh, no, oh no, Bodey, entertain her upstairs! I'm not in shape for another visit today, especially not—Bodey!

BODEY: Sophie, Sophie, you had me worried about you.

HELENA: I'm afraid, Dorothea, your request has fallen upon a calcified eardrum.

151

BODEY: You come downstairs so late.

MISS GLUCK: *Sie hat die Tür in mein Kopf zugeschlagen!*

BODEY [*to Helena*]: You done that to Sophie!

HELENA: An unknown creature of demented appearance entering like a sneak thief!

BODEY: My best friend in the building!

HELENA: What a pitiful admission!

BODEY: You come here uninvited, not by Dotty or me, since I never heard of you, but got the nerve to call my best friend in the building . . .

MISS GLUCK: *Diese Frau ist ein Spion.*

BODEY: What did you call her?

HELENA: I called that woman demented. What I would call you is intolerably offensive.

MISS GLUCK: *Verstehen Sie?* Spy. *Vom Irrenhaus.*

BODEY: We live here, you don't. See the difference?

HELENA: Thank God for the difference. *Vive la différence.*

DOROTHEA [*coming just inside the living room*]: Helena, Bodey.

HELENA: Be calm Dorothea—don't get overexcited.

MISS GLUCK: *Zwei Jahre.* Two years.

DOROTHEA: Why is she coming at me like this?

MISS GLUCK: State asylum.

BODEY: You come here to scrounge money outta Dotty which she ain't got.

MISS GLUCK: *Sie ist hier—mich noch einmal—im Irrenhaus zu bringen.* To take back to hospital.

HELENA: Aside from the total inaccuracy of your assumption and the insulting manner in which you express it—. As you very well know, Dorothea and I are both employed at Blewett. We are both on salary there! And I have not come here to involve myself in your social group but to rescue my colleague from it.

BODEY: Awright, you put it your way, it adds up to the same thing. You want money from Dotty which she ain't got to give you. Dotty is broke, flat broke, and she's been on a big buying spree, so big that just last night I had to loan her the price of a medium bottle of Golden Glow Shampoo, and not only that, I had to go purchase it for her because she come home exhausted. Dotty was too exhausted to walk to the drugstore. Well, me, I was tired, too, after my work at International Shoe and shopping, but out I hoofed it to Liggett's and forked out the forty-nine cents for the medium size Golden Glow from my own pockets, money I set aside for incidentals at the Creve Coeur picnic. There's always—

HELENA [*cutting in*]: Miss Bodenheifer, you certainly have a gift for the felicitous phrase such as "out you hoofed it to Liggett's," sorry, sorry, but it does evoke an image.

BODEY: I know what you mean by "hoof it" since you keep repeating "heifer" for "hafer." I'm not too dumb like which

153

you regard me to know why you're struck so funny by "hoof it."

HELENA: You said you "hoofed it," not me.

BODEY: You keep saying "heifer" for "hafer." Me, I'm a sensitive person with feelings I feel, but sensitive to you I am not. Insults from you bounce off me. I just want you to know that you come here shaking your tin cup at the wrong door.

[*As a soft but vibrant counterpoint to this exchange, Sophie, sobbing and rolling her eyes like a* religieuse *in a state of sorrowful vision, continues her slow shuffle toward Dorothea as she repeats in German an account of her violent ejection by Helena.*]

DOROTHEA [*breathlessly*]: Bodey, what is she saying? Translate and explain to her I have no knowledge of German.

HELENA: Babbling, just lunatic babbling!

BODEY: One minute, one minute, Dotty. I got to explain to this woman she's wasting her time here and yours—and had the moxie to slam Sophie out of the door.

HELENA: Miss Bodenheifer, it's useless to attempt to intimidate me. . . . I would like the use of your phone for a moment. Then—

DOROTHEA: No calls on the phone!

BODEY: Dotty don't want this phone used; she's expecting a call to come in, but there is a pay phone at Liggett's three blocks east on West Pine and Pearl.

HELENA: Drugstores are shut on Sundays!

154

DOROTHEA: Quiet! Listen! All! This thing's getting out of hand!

HELENA: I want only to call a taxi for myself and for Dorothea. She's trapped here and should be removed at once. You may not know that just two weeks after she came to Blewett she collapsed on the staircase, and the staff doctor examined her and discovered that Dorothea's afflicted with neuro-circulatory asthenia.

[*Dorothea has disappeared behind the sofa. Miss Gluck is looking down at her with lamentations.*]

MISS GLUCK: BODEY.

BODEY: Moment, Sophie.

MISS GLUCK: Dotty, Dotty . . .

HELENA: What is she saying? Where's Dorothea?

BODEY: Dotty?

MISS GLUCK: *Hier, auf dem Fussboden. Ist fallen.*

HELENA: This Gluck creature has thrown Dorothea onto the floor.

BODEY: *Gott im*—! *Wo ist*—Dotty?

HELENA: The Gluck has flung her to the floor behind the sofa!

BODEY: Dotty!

HELENA: Dorothea, I'm calling us a cab. Is she conscious?

155

DOROTHEA: Mebaral—tablet—quick!

BODEY: Mebarals, where?

[*Sophie wails loudly.*]

DOROTHEA: My pocketbook!

BODEY: Hold on now, slowly, slowly—

DOROTHEA: Mebaral! Tablets!

HELENA: My physician told me those tablets are only pre-scribed for persons with—extreme nervous tension and asthenia.

BODEY: Will you goddam shut up? —Dotty, you just need to—

HELENA: What she needs is to stop these strenuous exercises and avoid all future confrontations with that lunatic from upstairs!

BODEY: Dotty, let me lift you.

DOROTHEA: Oh, oh, noooo, I—can't, I—I am *paralyzed, Bodey!*

BODEY: HEY, YOU BROOKS-IT, TAKE DOTTY'S OTHER ARM. HELP ME CARRY HER TO HER BED WILL YUH?

[*Sophie is moaning through clenched fists.*]

HELENA: All right, all right, but then I shall call my phy-sician!

[*Dorothea is carried into the bedroom and deposited on the bed. Sophie props pillows behind her.*]

156

DOROTHEA: Meb—my meb . . .

BODEY: Tablets. Bathroom. In your pocketbook.

[*Bodey rushes into the bathroom, then out with a small bottle. Dorothea raises a hand weakly and Bodey drops tablets in it.*]

Dotty, don't swallow, that's three tablets!

DOROTHEA: My sherry to wash it down with—

BODEY: Dotty, take out the *two extra tablets,* Dotty!

HELENA: Sherry? Did she say sherry? Where is it?

DOROTHEA: There, there.

BODEY: Dotty, open your mouth, I got to take out those extras!

HELENA: No glass, you must drink from the bottle.

BODEY: NO! NOOOO!

HELENA: STOP CLUTCHING AT ME!

[*Miss Gluck utters a terrified wail. Dorothea drinks from the bottle and falls back onto the pillows with a gasp.*]

BODEY [*so angry she speaks half in German*]: You *Schwein,* you bitch! *Alte böse Katze.* [*She then goes on in English.*] You washed three tablets down Dotty!

DOROTHEA: Now will you BOTH get out so I can breathe!

HELENA: The door's obstructed by Gluck.

157

BODEY: Sophie, go out, Sophie, go out of here with me for coffee and crullers!

[*Sobbing, Sophie retreats. Bodey grabs a strong hold of Helena's wrist.*]

HELENA: Let go of my wrist. Oh, my God, you have broken. . . . I heard a bone snap in my—!

BODEY: WALK! OUT! MOVE IT! . . .

HELENA [*turning quickly about and retreating behind the sofa*]: Miss Bodenheifer, you are a one-woman demonstration of the aptness of the term "Huns" for Germans. . . . And, incidentally, what you broke was not my wrist but my Cartier wristwatch, a birthday present from my Cousin Dee-Dee; you shattered the crystal, and you've broken the minute hand and bent the two others. I am afraid the repair bill will cost you considerably more than keeping Dorothea in Golden Glow Shampoo.

BODEY: It's all right, Sophie, set down right here and I'll. . . . Coffee's still hot for you. Have a coupla crullers. Blow your nose on this napkin and—

[*Helena laughs tonelessly.*]

What's funny, is something funny? You never been depressed, no sorrows in your life ever, yeh, and you call yourself a human.

HELENA: Really, this is fantastic as the—color scheme of this room or the—view through the windows.

[*In the bedroom, Dorothea has staggered from the bed and stumbled to the floor.*]

DOROTHEA: Bodey.

HELENA: Dorothea.

BODEY [*calling through*]: Dotty.

HELENA: You really must let me check on her condition.

DOROTHEA [*in the bedroom*]: Don't forget . . . phone call.

BODEY: No, Dotty.

DOROTHEA [*faintly, clinging to something*]: Tell Miss Brookmire I've retired for the day.

HELENA: *What?*

BODEY: She's not coming out. She's not coming out till you leave here—

[*Bodey bolts the bedroom door.*]

HELENA: I beg to differ. She *will* and I'll sit here till she does!

[*Miss Gluck has taken a bite of a cruller, dunked in coffee, and begins to blubber, the coffee-soaked cruller dribbling down her chin.*]

BODEY: Look, you upset Sophie!

MISS GLUCK: *Eine—Woche vor—Sonntag—meine Mutter—*

BODEY [*comfortingly*]: *Ich weiss*, Sophie, *ich weiss.*

MISS GLUCK: *Gestorben!*

BODEY: But she went *sudden*, huh, Sophie? [*She crouches be-*

side Miss Gluck, removing the dribblings of cruller and coffee from her mouth and chin.]

HELENA: I don't understand the language, and the scene appears to be private.

BODEY: Yeh, keep out of it. [*She turns to Miss Gluck.*]— Your mother, she didn't hang on like the doctor thought she would, Sophie. Now, face it, it was better sudden, no big hospital bill, just went and is waiting for you in Heaven.

HELENA: With open arms, I presume, and with coffee and crullers.

BODEY: So, Sophie, just be grateful that she went quick with no pain.

MISS GLUCK [*grotesquely tragic*]: *Nein, nein, sie hat geschrien!* I woke up runnin'!

BODEY: To her bed, you reached it and she was dead. Just one scream, it was over—wasn't that a mercy?

[*Helena laughs.*]

Sophie, honey, this woman here's not sympathetic. She laughs at sorrow, so maybe you better take the coffee, the cruller— here's another—upstairs, Sophie, and when we get back from the Creve Coeur picnic, I will bring you beautiful flowers, *schöne Blume.* Then I'll come up and sing to you in German— I will sing you to sleep.

[*Miss Gluck slowly rises with coffee and crullers. Bodey conducts her gently to the door.*]

MISS GLUCK [*crying out*]: *Ich bin allein, allein! In der Welt, freundlos!*

160

BODEY: No, no, Sophie, that is negative thinking.

MISS GLUCK: *Ich habe niemand in der Welt!*

BODEY: Sophie, God is with you, I'm with you. Your mother, all your relations are waiting for you in Heaven!

[*Shepherding Miss Gluck into the hall, Bodey repeats this assurance in German.*]

HELENA: Sometimes despair is just being realistic, the only logical thing for certain persons to *feel*. [*She addresses herself with a certain seriousness, now.*] Loss. Despair. I've faced them and actually they have—fortified and protected, not overcome me at all . . .

BODEY [*in the hall with Miss Gluck*]: Okay? *Verstehst du,* Sophie?

HELENA [*still ruminating privately*]: The weak. The strong. Only important division between living creatures. [*She nods birdlike affirmation.*]

[*Miss Gluck remains visible in the hall, afraid to return upstairs.*]

MISS GLUCK: *Allein, allein.*

[*There is a change in the light. Helena moves a small chair downstage and delivers the following to herself.*]

HELENA: *Allein, allein* means alone, alone. [*A frightened look appears in her eyes.*] Last week I dined alone, alone three nights in a row. There's nothing lonelier than a woman dining alone, and although I loathe preparing food for myself, I cannot bear the humiliation of occupying a restaurant table for one. Dining *au solitaire!* But I would rather starve than reduce my social

161

standards by accepting dinner invitations from that middle-aged gaggle of preposterously vulgar old maids that wants to suck me into their group despite my total ,abhorrence of all they stand for. Loneliness in the company of five intellectually destitute spinsters is simply loneliness multiplied by five . . .

[*There is a crash in the hallway.*]

DOROTHEA [*from the bedroom*]: Is it the phone?

HELENA: Another visit so soon? Miss Bodenheifer, your bereaved friend from upstairs is favoring you with another visit.

MISS GLUCK [*wildly*]: *Mein Zimmer is gespukt, gespukt!*

HELENA: "Spooked, spooked"?

BODEY: Sophie, your apartment isn't haunted.

HELENA: Perhaps if you went up with her, it would de-spook the apartment.

BODEY: Aw, no, I got to stay down and keep a sharp eye on *you.*

HELENA: Which means that she will remain here?

BODEY: Long as she pleases to. What's it to you? She got nothin' contagious. You can't catch heartbreak if you have got no heart.

HELENA: May I suggest that you put her in the back yard in the sun. I think that woman's complexion could stand a touch of color.

BODEY: I am puttin' her nowhere she don't want to be. How

162

about you settin' in the back yard? Some natural color would do your face good for a change.

[*Sensing the hostile "vibes," Miss Gluck moans, swaying a little.*]

HELENA: Miss Bodenheifer, I will not dignify your insults with response or attention!

[*Miss Gluck moans louder.*]

Aren't you able to see that this Miss Gluck is mental? Distressing to hear and to look at! . . . Be that as it may, I shall wait.

BODEY: Sitting? Tight as a tombstone? Huh?

HELENA: I can assure you that for me to remain in this place is at least as unpleasant to me as to you. [*She cries out to Dorothea who is still in the bedroom.*] Dorothea? Dorothea? Can you hear me?

DOROTHEA [*clinging to something in the bedroom*]: See you— Blewett—t'morrow . . .

HELENA: No, no, at once, Dorothea, the situation out here is dreadful beyond endurance.

[*Abruptly, Miss Gluck cries out, clutching her abdomen.*]

BODEY: Sophie, what is it, Sophie?

MISS GLUCK: *Heisser Kaffee gibt mir immer Krampf und Durchfall.*

[*This episode in the play must be handled carefully to avoid excessive scatology but keep the humor.*]

163

BODEY: You got the runs? *Zum Badezimmer?* Sophie's got to go to the bathroom, Dotty.

DOROTHEA: Hasn't she got one upstairs?

BODEY: After hot coffee, it gives her diarrhea!

DOROTHEA: Must she have it down here?

MISS GLUCK [*in German*]: *KANN NICHT WARTEN!*

BODEY: She can't wait, here, bathroom, Sophie! *Badezimmer!*

[*Miss Gluck rushes through the bedroom into the bathroom.*]

DOROTHEA: What a scene for Helena to report at Blewett. Miss Gluck, turn on both water faucets full force.

BODEY: Sophie, *beide Wasser rennen.*

DOROTHEA: Bodey, while I am here don't serve her hot coffee again since it results in these—crises!

BODEY: Dotty, you know that Sophie's got this problem.

DOROTHEA: Then send her coffee upstairs.

BODEY: Dotty, you know she needs companionship, Dotty.

DOROTHEA: That I cannot provide her with just now!

[*Bodey returns to the living room.*]

HELENA: How did Dorothea react to Miss Gluck's sudden indisposition?

BODEY: Dotty's a girl that understands human afflictions.

[*There is a crash in the bathroom.*]

DOROTHEA: Phone, Ralph's call—has he—did he?

BODEY: Phone, Dotty? No, no phone.

HELENA: I wouldn't expect—

BODEY [*to Helena*]: Watch it!

HELENA: Watch what, Miss Bodenheifer? What is it you want me to watch?

BODEY: That mouth of yours, the tongue in it, with such a tongue in a mouth you could dig your grave with like a shovel!

HELENA [*her laughter tinkling like ice in a glass*]: —The syntax of that sentence was rather confusing. You know, I suspect that English is not your native language but one that you've not quite adequately adopted.

BODEY: I was born on South Grand, a block from Tower Grove Park in this city of St. Louis!

HELENA: Ah, the German section. Your parents were German speaking?

BODEY: I learned plenty English at school, had eight grades of school and a year of business college.

HELENA: I see, I see, forgive me. [*She turns to a window, possibly in the "fourth wall."*] Is a visitor permitted to look out the window?

BODEY: A visitor like you's permitted to jump out it.

HELENA [*laughing indulgently*]: With so many restrictions placed on one's speech and actions—

[*Bodey turns up her hearing aid so high that it screeches shrilly.*]

DOROTHEA: Is it the phone?

HELENA: Please. Is it controllable, that electric hearing device?

BODEY: What did you say?

[*The screeching continues.*]

HELENA: Ow . . . ow . . .

[*Bodey finally manages to turn down the hearing aid.*]

DOROTHEA: Oh please bring a mop, Bodey. Water's streaming under—the bathroom door. Miss Gluck's flooded the bathroom.

BODEY: What? Bring?

HELENA: *Mop, mop!*

[*Helena moves toward the bedroom door but Bodey shoves her back.*]

BODEY: Stay! Put! Stay put!

[*Bodey grabs a mop from the closet and then rushes into the bedroom.*]

DOROTHEA: See? Water? Flooding?

166

BODEY: You told her to turn on both faucets. SOPHIE! *Halte das Wasser ab*, Sophie! [*Bodey opens the bathroom door and thrusts in the mop.*] Here, *das Wust, das Wust*, Sophie!

DOROTHEA [*to herself*]: This is incredible to me, I simply do not believe it! [*She then speaks to Bodey who has started back toward the living room.*] May I detain you a moment? The truth has finally struck me. Ralph's calls have been intercepted. He has been repeatedly calling me on that phone, and you have been just as repeatedly lying to me that he hasn't.

BODEY: LYING TO—?

DOROTHEA: YES, LYING! [*She stumbles to the door of the bedroom.*] Helena, will *you* please watch that phone for me now?

HELENA [*crossing to the bedroom door*]: I'm afraid, Dorothea, that a watched phone never rings!

[*Bodey emerges from the bedroom. She and Helena return to the living room while Dorothea retreats to the bed, shutting the door behind her.*]

What a view through this window, totally devoid of—why, no, a living creature, a pigeon! Capable of flight but perched for a moment in this absolute desolation . . .

INTERVAL

SCENE TWO

The scene is the same as before. The spotlight focuses on the lefthand, "bedroom" portion of the stage where Dorothea, seated at her vanity table and mellowed by her mebaral and sherry "cocktail," soliloquizes.

DOROTHEA [*taking a large swallow of sherry*]: Best years of my youth thrown away, wasted on poor Hathaway James. [*She removes his picture from the vanity table and with closed eyes thrusts it out of sight.*] Shouldn't say wasted but so unwisely devoted. Not even sure it was love. Unconsummated love, is it really love? More likely just a reverence for his talent—precocious achievements . . . musical prodigy. Scholarship to Juilliard, performed a concerto with the Nashville Symphony at fifteen. [*She sips more sherry.*] But those dreadful embarrassing evenings on Aunt Belle's front porch in Memphis! He'd say: "Turn out the light, it's attracting insects." I'd switch it out. He'd grab me so tight it would take my breath away, and invariably I'd feel plunging, plunging against me that—that—frantic part of him . . . then he'd release me at once and collapse on the porch swing, breathing hoarsely. With the corner gas lamp shining through the wisteria vines, it was impossible not to notice the wet stain spreading on his light flannel trousers. . . . Miss Gluck, MOP IN!!

[*Miss Gluck, who has timidly opened the bathroom door and begun to emerge, with the mop, into the bedroom, hastily retreats from sight.*]

Such afflictions—visited on the gifted. . . . Finally worked up the courage to discuss the—Hathaway's—problem with the family doctor, delicately but clearly as I could. "Honey, this Hathaway fellow's afflicted with something clinically known as—chronic case of—premature ejaculation—must have a large laundry bill. . . ." "Is it curable, Doctor?" —"Maybe with great patience, honey, but remember you're only young once, don't gamble on it, relinquish him to his interest in music, let him go."

[*Miss Gluck's mop protrudes from the bathroom again.*]

MISS GLUCK, I SAID MOP IN. REMAIN IN BATH-ROOM WITH WET MOP TILL MOP UP COMPLETED. MERCIFUL HEAVENS.

[*Helena and Bodey are now seen in the living room.*]

HELENA: Is Dorothea attempting a conversation with Miss Gluck in there?

BODEY: No, no just to herself—you gave her the sherry on top of mebaral tablets.

HELENA: She talks to herself? That isn't a practice that I would encourage her in.

BODEY: She don't need no encouragement in it, and as for you, I got an idea you'd encourage nobody in nothing.

DOROTHEA [*in the bedroom*]: After Hathaway James, there was nothing left for me but—CIVICS.

HELENA [*who has moved to the bedroom door the better to hear Dorothea's "confessions"*]: This is not to B. B.!

BODEY: Stop listening at the door. Go back to your pigeon watching.

HELENA: How long is this apt to continue?

170

DOROTHEA: Oh, God, thank you that Ralph Ellis has no such affliction—is healthily aggressive.

HELENA: I have a luncheon engagement in La Due at two!

BODEY: Well, go keep it! On time!

HELENA: My business with Dorothea must take precedence over anything else! [*Helena pauses to watch with amused suspicion as Bodey "attacks" the Sunday* Post-Dispatch *which she has picked up from the chair.*] What is that you're doing, Miss Bodenheifer?

BODEY: Tearing a certain item out of the paper.

HELENA: A ludicrous thing to do since the news will be all over Blewett High School tomorrow.

BODEY: Never mind tomorrow. There's ways and ways to break a piece of news like that to a girl with a heart like Dotty. You wouldn't know about that, no, you'd do it right now—malicious! —You got eyes like a bird and I don't mean a songbird.

HELENA: Oh, is that *so?*

BODEY: Yeh, yeh, that's so, I know!

[*Pause. Bodey, who has torn out about half of the top page of one section, puts the rest of the paper on the sofa, and takes the section from which the piece has been torn with her as she crosses to the kitchenette, crumpling and throwing the torn piece into the wastebasket on her way.*]

HELENA: Miss Bodenheifer.

BODEY [*from the kitchenette*]: Hafer!

HELENA: I have no wish to offend you, but surely you're able to see that for Dorothea to stay in these circumstances must be extremely embarrassing to her at least.

BODEY: Aw, you think Dotty's embarrassed here, do you?

[*Bodey has begun to line a shoebox with the section of news-paper she took with her. During the following exchange with Helena, Bodey packs the fried chicken and other picnic fare in the shoebox.*]

HELENA: She has hinted it's almost intolerable to her. The visitations of this Gluck person who has rushed to the bath-room, this nightmare of clashing colors, the purple carpet, orange drapes at the windows looking out at that view of brick and concrete and asphalt, lamp shades with violent yellow daisies on them, and wallpaper with roses exploding like bombshells, why it would give her a breakdown! It's giving me claustrophobia briefly as I have been here. Why, this is not a place for a civilized person to possibly exist in!

BODEY: What's so civilized about you, Miss Brooks-it? Stylish, yes, civilized, no, unless a hawk or a buzzard is a civilized creature. Now you see, you got a tongue in your mouth, but I got one in mine, too.

HELENA: You are being hysterical and offensive!

BODEY: You ain't heard nothing compared to what you'll hear if you continue to try to offer all this concern you feel about Dotty to Dotty in this apartment.

HELENA: Dorothea Gallaway and I keep nothing from each other and naturally I intend, as soon as she has recovered, to

172

prepare her for what she can hardly avoid facing sooner or later and I—

BODEY [*cutting in*]: I don't want heartbreak for Dotty. For Dotty I want a—life.

HELENA: A life of—?

BODEY: A life, a *life*—

HELENA: You mean as opposed to a death?

BODEY: Don't get smart with me. I got your number the moment you come in that door like a well-dressed snake.

HELENA: So far you have compared me to a snake and a bird. Please decide which—since the archaeopteryx, the only known combination of bird and snake, is long extinct!

BODEY: Yes, well, you talk with a kind of a hiss. Awright, you just hiss away but not in this room which you think ain't a civilized room. Okay, it's too cheerful for you but for me and Dotty it's fine. And this afternoon, at the picnic at Creve Coeur Lake, I will tell Dotty, gentle, in my own way, if it's necessary to tell her, that this unprincipled man has just been using her. But Buddy, my brother Buddy, if in some ways he don't suit her like he is now, I will see he quits beer, I will see he cuts out his cigars, I will see he continues to take off five pounds a week. And by Dotty and Buddy there will be children—children! —I will never have none, myself, no! But Dotty and Buddy will have beautiful kiddies. Me? Nieces—nephews. . . . —Now you! I've wrapped up the picnic. It's nice and cool at Creve Coeur Lake and the ride on the open-air streetcar is lickety-split through green country and there's flowers you can pull off the bushes you pass. It's a fine excursion. Dotty will forget not gettin' that phone call. We'll stay out till it's close to dark and

173

the fireflies—fly. I will slip away and Buddy will be alone with her on the lake shore. He will smoke no smelly cigar. He will just respectfully hold her hand and say—"I love you, Dotty. Please be mine," not meanin' a girl in a car parked up on Art Hill but—for the long run of life.

HELENA: —Can Dorothea be really attached to your brother? Is it a mutual attraction?

BODEY: Dotty will settle for Buddy. She's got a few reservations about him so far, but at Creve Coeur she'll suddenly recognize the—wonderful side of his nature.

HELENA: Miss Bodenheifer, Dorothea is not intending to remain in this tasteless apartment. Hasn't she informed you that she is planning to share a lovely apartment with me? The upstairs of a duplex on Westmoreland Place?

BODEY: Stylish? Civilized, huh? And too expensive for you to swing it alone, so you want to rope Dotty in, rope her into a place that far from Blewett? Share expenses? You prob'ly mean pay most.

HELENA: To move from such an unsuitable environment must naturally involve some expense.

[*Miss Gluck falls out of the bathroom onto Dorothea's bed.*]

DOROTHEA: MISS GLUCK! CAREFUL! Bodey, Bodey, Sophie Gluck's collapsed on my bed in a cloud of steam!

HELENA: Has Miss Gluck broken a steam pipe?

[*Bodey rushes from the kitchenette into the bedroom.*]

BODEY [*to Helena*]: You stay out.

174

[*Dorothea emerges from the bedroom. She closes the door and leans against it briefly, closing her eyes as if dizzy or faint.*]

HELENA: At last.

DOROTHEA: I'm so mortified.

HELENA: Are you feeling better?

DOROTHEA: Sundays are always different—

HELENA: This one exceptionally so.

DOROTHEA: I don't know why but—I don't quite understand why I am so—agitated. Something happened last week, just a few evenings ago that—

HELENA: Yes? What?

DOROTHEA: Nothing that I'm—something I can't discuss with you. I was and still am expecting a very important phone call—

HELENA: May I ask you from whom?

DOROTHEA: No, please.

HELENA: Then may I hazard a guess that the expected call not received was from a young gentleman who cuts a quite spectacular figure in the country club set but somehow became involved in the educational system?

DOROTHEA: If you don't mind, Helena, I'd much prefer not to discuss anything of a—private nature right now.

HELENA: Yes, I understand, dear. And since you've located that chair, why don't you seat yourself in it?

175

DOROTHEA: Oh, yes, excuse me. [*She sits down, weakly, her hand lifted to her throat.*] The happenings here today are still a bit confused in my head. I was doing my exercises before you dropped by.

HELENA: And for quite a while after.

DOROTHEA: I was about to—no, I'd taken my shower. I was about to get dressed.

HELENA: But the Gluck intervened. Such discipline! Well! I've had the privilege of an extended meeting with Miss Bodenheifer—[*She lowers her voice.*] She seemed completely surprised when I mentioned that you were moving to Westmoreland Place.

DOROTHEA: Oh, you told her. —I'm glad. —I'm such a coward, I couldn't.

HELENA: Well, I broke the news to her.

DOROTHEA: I—just hadn't the heart to.

[*Miss Gluck advances from the bedroom with a dripping wet mop and a dazed look.*]

HELENA [*to Dorothea*]: Can't you see she's already found a replacement?

DOROTHEA: Oh, no, there's a limit even to Bodey's endurance! Miss Gluck, would you please return that wet mop to the kitchen and wring it out. *Küche*—mop—Sophie.

HELENA: Appears to be catatonic.

DOROTHEA [*as she goes into the bedroom to get Bodey*]: Excuse me.

[*Bodey enters from the bedroom and takes Miss Gluck, with mop, into the kitchenette.*]

BODEY [*singing nervously in the kitchenette*]: "I'm just breezing along with the breeze, pleasing to live, and living to please!"

[*Dorothea returns to the living room.*]

DOROTHEA: How did Bodey take the news I was moving?

HELENA: "That far from *Blewett!*" she said as if it were transcontinental.

DOROTHEA: Well, it is a bit far, compared to this location.

HELENA: Surely you wouldn't compare it to *this* location.

DOROTHEA: Oh, no, Westmoreland Place is a—fashionable address, incomparable in that respect, but it is quite a distance. Of course, just a block from Delmar Boulevard and the Olive Street car-line, that would let me off at—what point closest to Blewett?

HELENA: Dorothea, forget transportation, that problem. We're going by automobile.

DOROTHEA: By—what automobile do you—?

HELENA: I have a lovely surprise for you, dear.

DOROTHEA: Someone is going to drive us?

HELENA: Yes, I will be the chauffeur and you the passenger, dear. You see, my wealthy cousin Dee-Dee, who lives in La Due, has replaced her foreign-made car, an Hispano-Suiza, no

177

less, practically brand-new, with a Pierce Arrow limousine and has offered to sell us the Hispano for just a song! Immediately, as soon as she made me this offer, I applied for a driver's license.

[*A moment of shocked silence is interrupted by a short squawk from Bodey's hearing aid.*]

BODEY [*advancing quickly from the kitchenette*]: Limazine? What limazine? With a show-fer?

HELENA: Miss Bodenheifer, how does this concern you?

BODEY: Who's gonna foot the bill for it, that's how!

HELENA: My cousin Dee-Dee in La Due will accept payment on time.

BODEY: Whose time and how much?

HELENA: *Negligible! A rich cousin!* —Oh, my Lord, I've always heard that Germans—

BODEY: Lay off Germans!

HELENA: Have this excessive concern with money matters.

BODEY: *Whose* money?

HELENA: Practicality can be a stupefying—

MISS GLUCK: Bodey?

HELENA: —virtue, if it *is* one.

MISS GLUCK: *Ich kann nicht*—go up.

HELENA: Go up just one step to the kitchen! Please, Dorothea, can't we—have a private discussion, briefly?

MISS GLUCK: *Das Schlafzimmer* is *gespukt!*

HELENA: Because you see, Dorothea, as I told you, I do have to make a payment on the Westmoreland Place apartment early tomorrow, and so must collect your half of it today.

DOROTHEA: —My half would amount to—?

HELENA: Seventy.

DOROTHEA: Ohhh! —Would the real estate people accept a—postdated check?

HELENA: Reluctantly—very.

DOROTHEA: You see, I had unusually heavy expenses this week—clothes, lingerie, a suitcase . . .

HELENA: Sounds as if you'd been purchasing a trousseau. —Miss Bodenhafer says that her brother, "Buddy," is seriously interested in you. How selfish of you to keep it such a secret!—even from me!

DOROTHEA: Oh, my heavens, has Miss Bodenhafer—how fantastic!

HELENA: Yes, she is a bit, to put it politely.

DOROTHEA: I meant has she given you the preposterous impression that I am interested in her brother? Oh, my Lord, what a fantàstic visit you've had! Believe me, the circumstances aren't always so—chaotic. Well! *Il n'y a rien à faire.* When I tell you that she calls her brother Buddy and that he is her *twin!* [*She throws up her arms.*]

HELENA: Identical?

DOROTHEA: Except for gender, alike as two peas in a pod. You're not so gullible, Helena, that you could really imagine for a moment that I'd—you know me better than that!

HELENA: Sometimes when a girl is on the rebound from a disappointing infatuation, she will leap without looking into the most improbable sort of—liaison—

DOROTHEA: Maybe some girls, but certainly not I. And what makes you think that I'm the victim of a "disappointing infatuation," Helena?

HELENA: Sometimes a thing will seem like the end of the world, and yet the world continues.

DOROTHEA: I personally feel that my world is just beginning. . . . Excuse me for a moment. I'll get my checkbook. . . .

[*Dorothea goes into the bedroom. Miss Gluck wanders back into the living room from the kitchenette, wringing her hands and sobbing.*]

HELENA: MISS BODENHEIFER!

BODEY: Don't bother to tell me good-bye.

HELENA: I am not yet leaving.

BODEY: And it ain't necessary to shake the walls when you call me, I got my hearing aid on.

HELENA: Would you be so kind as to confine Miss Gluck to that charming little kitchen while I'm completing my business with Dorothea?

[*Bodey crosses toward Miss Gluck.*]

BODEY: Sophie, come in here with me. You like a deviled egg don't you? And a nice fried drumstick when your— digestion is better? Just stay in here with me.

[*Bodey leads Miss Gluck back to the kitchenette, then turns to Helena.*]

I can catch every word that you say to Dotty in there, and you better be careful the conversation don't take the wrong turn!

MISS GLUCK [*half in German*]: *Ich kann nicht* liven opstairs no more, *nimmer, nimmer—kann nicht*—can't go!

BODEY: You know what, Sophie? You better change apart- ments. There's a brand-new vacancy. See—right over there, the fifth floor. It's bright and cheerful—I used to go up there sometimes—it's a sublet, furnished, everything in cheerful colors. I'll speak to Mr. Schlogger, no, no, to *Mrs.* Schlogger, she makes better terms. Him, bein' paralyzed, he's got to accept 'em, y'know.

MISS GLUCK: I think— [*She sobs.*] —Missus Schlogger don't like me.

BODEY: That's—*impossible*, Sophie. I think she just had a little misunderstanding with your—[*She stops herself.*]

MISS GLUCK: *Meine Mutter, ja*—

BODEY: Sophie, speak of the Schloggers, she's wheeling that old *Halunke* out on their fire escape.

[*The Schloggers are heard from offstage.*]

181

MR. SCHLOGGER'S VOICE: I didn't say *out* in the sun.

MRS. SCHLOGGER'S VOICE: You said out, so you're out.

BODEY [*shouting out the window*]: Oh, my *Gott*, Missus Schlogger, a stranger that didn't know you would think you meant to push him offa the landin'. Haul him back in, you better. Watch his cane, he's about to hit you with it. Amazin' the strength he's still got in his good arm.

MRS. SCHLOGGER'S VOICE: Now you want back in?

[*Helena rises to watch this episode on the fire escape.*]

MR. SCHLOGGER'S VOICE: Not in the kitchen with you.

HELENA [*to herself but rather loudly*]. Schloggers, so those are Schloggers.

BODEY [*to Miss Gluck*]: She's got him back in. I'm gonna speak to her right now. —HEY MISSUS SCHLOGGER, YOU KNOW MISS GLUCK? AW, SURE YOU REMEMBER SOPHIE UPSTAIRS IN 4-F? SHE LOST HER MOTHER LAST SUNDAY. Sophie, come here, stick your head out, Sophie. NOW YOU REMEMBER HER, DON'T YOU?

MRS. SCHLOGGER'S VOICE: *Ja, ja.*

BODEY: *JA, JA,* SURE YOU REMEMBER! MRS. SCHLOGGER, POOR SOPHIE CAN'T LIVE ALONE IN 4-F WHERE SHE LOST HER MOTHER. SHE NEEDS A NEW APARTMENT THAT'S BRIGHT AND CHEERFUL TO GET HER OUT OF DEPRESSION. HOW ABOUT THE VACANCY ON THE FIFTH FLOOR FOR

182

SOPHIE. WE GOT TO LOOK OUT FOR EACH OTHER
IN TIMES OF SORROW. *VERSTEHEN SIE?*

MRS. SCHLOGGER'S VOICE: I don't know.

BODEY: GIVE SOPHIE THAT VACANCY UP THERE.
THEN TERMS I'LL DISCUSS WITH YOU. [*She draws
Miss Gluck back from the window.*] Sophie, I think that done
it, and that apartment on five is bright and cheerful like here.
And you're not gonna be lonely. We got three chairs at this
table, and we can work out an arrangement so you can eat
here with us, more economical that way. It's no good cooking
for one, cookin' and eatin' alone is—lonely after—

[*Helena resumes her seat as Bodey and Miss Gluck return
to the kitchenette.*]

HELENA [*with obscure meaning*]: Yes— [*She draws a long
breath and calls out.*] Dorothea, can't you locate your checkbook in there?

[*Dorothea returns from the bedroom wearing a girlish
summer print dress and looking quite pretty.*]

DOROTHEA: I was just slipping into a dress. Now, then, here
it is, my checkbook.

HELENA: Good. Where did you buy that new dress?

DOROTHEA: Why, at Scruggs-Vandervoort.

HELENA: Let me remove the price tag. [*As she removes the
tag, she looks at it and assumes an amused and slightly superior
air.*] Oh, my dear. I must teach you where to find the best
values in clothes. In La Due there is a little French boutique,
not expensive but excellent taste. I think a woman looks best

183

when she dresses without the illusion she's still a girl in her teens. Don't you?

DOROTHEA [*stung*]: —My half will be—how much did you say?

HELENA: To be exact, $82.50.

DOROTHEA: My goodness, that will take a good bite out of my savings. Helena, I thought you mentioned a lower amount. Didn't you say it would be seventy?

HELENA: Yes, I'd forgotten—utilities, dear. Now, we don't want to move into a place with the phone turned off, the lights off. Utilities must be *on*, wouldn't you say?

DOROTHEA: —Yes. —Of course, I don't think I'll be dependent on my savings much longer, and a duplex on Westmoreland Place— [*She writes out a check.*] —is a—quite a—worthwhile —investment . . .

HELENA: I should think it would strike you as one after confinement with Miss Bodenhafer in this nightmare of colors.

DOROTHEA: Oh. —Yes. —Excuse me . . . [*She extends the check slightly.*]

HELENA: —Are you holding it out for the ink to dry on it?

DOROTHEA: —Sorry. —Here. [*She crosses to Helena and hands the check to her.*]

[*Helena puts on her glasses to examine the check carefully. She then folds it, puts it into her purse, and snaps the purse shut.*]

HELENA: Well, that's that. I hate financial dealings but they do have to be dealt with. Don't they?

DOROTHEA: Yes, they seem to . . .

HELENA: Require it. —Oh, contract.

DOROTHEA: Contract? For the apartment?

HELENA: Oh, no, a book on contract bridge, the bidding system and so forth. You do play bridge a little? I asked you once before and you said you did sometimes.

DOROTHEA: Here?

HELENA: Naturally not here. But on Westmoreland Place I hope you'll join in the twice-weekly games. You remember Joan Goode?

DOROTHEA: Yes, vaguely. Why?

HELENA: We were partners in duplicate bridge, which we usually played, worked out our own set of bidding conventions. But now Joan's gone to Wellesley for her Master's degree in, of all things, the pre-Ptolemaic dynasties of Egypt.

DOROTHEA: Did she do that? I didn't know what she did.

HELENA: You were only very casually—

DOROTHEA: Acquainted.

HELENA: My cousin Dee-Dee from La Due takes part whenever her social calendar permits her to. She often sends over dainty little sandwiches, watercress, tomato, sherbets from Zeller's in the summer. And a nicely uniformed maid to serve.

185

Well, now we're converting from auction to contract, which is more complicated but stimulates the mind. —Dorothea, you have an abstracted look. Are you troubled over something?

DOROTHEA: Are these parties mixed?

HELENA: "Mixed" in what manner?

DOROTHEA: I mean would I invite Ralph?

HELENA: I have a feeling that Mr. T. Ralph Ellis might not be able to spare the time this summer. And anyway, professional women do need social occasions without the—male intrusion . . .

DOROTHEA [*with spirit*]: I've never thought of the presence of men as being an intrusion.

HELENA: Dorothea, that's just a lingering symptom of your Southern belle complex.

DOROTHEA: In order to be completely honest with you, Helena, I think I ought to tell you—I probably won't be able to share expenses with you in Westmoreland Place for very long, Helena!

HELENA: Oh, is that so? Is that why you've given me the postdated check which you could cancel tomorrow?

DOROTHEA: You know I wouldn't do that, but—

HELENA: Yes, but—you could and possibly you would. . . . Look before you, there stands the specter that confronts you . . .

DOROTHEA: Miss??

HELENA: Gluck, the perennial, the irremediable, Miss Gluck! You probably think me superficial to value as much as I do, cousin Dee-Dee of La Due, contract bridge, possession of an elegant foreign car. Dorothea, only such things can protect us from a future of descent into the Gluck abyss of surrender to the bottom level of squalor. Look at it and tell me honestly that you can afford not to provide yourself with the Westmoreland Place apartment . . . its elevation, its style, its kind of *éclat*.

[*Miss Gluck, who has come out of the kitchenette and moved downstage during Helena's speech, throws a glass of water in Helena's face.*]

DOROTHEA: Bodey, RESTRAIN HER, RESTRAIN MISS GLUCK, SHE'S TURNED VIOLENT.

BODEY: Sophie, no, no. I didn't say you done wrong. I think you done right. I don't think you did enough.

HELENA: Violence does exist in the vegetable kingdom, you see! It doesn't terrify me since I shall soon be safely out of its range. . . . Just let me draw two good deep breaths and I'll be myself again. [*She does so.*] That did it. . . . I'm back in my skin. Oh, Dorothea, we must, must advance in appearances. You don't seem to know how vastly important it is, the move to Westmoreland Place, particularly now at this time when you must escape from reminders of, specters of, that alternative there! Surrender without conditions . . .

DOROTHEA: Sorry. I am a little abstracted. Helena, you sound as if you haven't even suspected that Ralph and I have been dating . . .

HELENA: Seriously?

187

DOROTHEA: Well, now that I've mentioned it to you, yes, quite. You see, I don't intend to devote the rest of my life to teaching civics at Blewett. I dream, I've always dreamed, of a marriage someday, and I think you should know that it might become a reality this summer.

HELENA: With whom?

DOROTHEA: Why, naturally with the person whom I love. And obviously loves me.

HELENA: T? RALPH? ELLIS?

[*Bodey, still in the kitchenette, nervously sings "Me and My Shadow."*]

DOROTHEA: I thought I'd made that clear, thought I'd made everything clear.

HELENA: Oh, Dorothea, my dear. I hope and pray that you haven't allowed him to take advantage of your—generous nature.

DOROTHEA: Miss Bodenhafer has the same apprehension.

HELENA: That is the one and only respect in which your friend, Miss Bodenhafer, and I have something in common.

DOROTHEA: Poor Miss Bodenhafer is terribly naïve for a girl approaching forty.

HELENA: Miss Bodenhafer is not approaching forty. She has encountered forty and continued past it, undaunted.

DOROTHEA: I don't believe she's the sort of girl who would conceal her age.

HELENA [*laughing like a cawing crow*]: Dorothea, no girl could tell me she's under forty and still be singing a song of that vintage. Why, she knows every word of it, including— what do they call it? The introductory verse? Why is she cracking hard-boiled eggs in there?

DOROTHEA: She's making deviled eggs for a picnic lunch.

HELENA: Oh. In Forest Park.

DOROTHEA: No, at Creve Coeur.

HELENA: Oh, at Creve Coeur, that amusement park on a lake, of which Miss Bodenheifer gave such a lyrical account. Would you like a Lucky?

DOROTHEA: No. Thank you. My father smoked Chesterfields. Do you know Creve Coeur?

HELENA: Heard of it. Only. You go out, just the two of you?

DOROTHEA: No, her brother, Buddy, usually goes with us on these excursions. They say they've been going out there since they were children, Bodey and Buddy. They still ride the Ferris wheel, you know, and there's a sort of loop-the-loop that takes you down to the lake shore. Seats much too narrow sometimes. You see, it's become embarrassing to me lately, the brother you know . . .

HELENA: Who doesn't interest you?

DOROTHEA: Heavens, no, it's—pathetic. I don't want to hurt Bodey's feelings, but the infatuation is hardly a mutual thing and it never could be, of course, since I am—well, involved with—

189

HELENA: The dashing, the irresistible new principal at Blewett.

[*Bodey sings.*]

DOROTHEA: —I'd rather not talk about that—prematurely, you know. Ralph feels it's not quite proper for a principal to be involved with a teacher. He's—a very, very scrupulous young man.

HELENA: Oh? Is that the impression he gives you? I'm rather surprised he's given you that impression.

DOROTHEA: I don't see why. Is it just because he's young and attractive with breeding, background? Frequently mentioned in the social columns? Therefore beyond involvement with a person of my ignominious position.

HELENA: Personally, I'd avoid him like a—snakebite!

[*Bodey, in the kitchenette, sings "I'm Just Breezing along with the Breeze" again.*]

Another one of her oldies! The prospect of this picnic at Creve Coeur seems to make her absolutely euphoric.

DOROTHEA: I'm afraid that they're the high points in her life. Sad . . . Helena, I'm very puzzled by your attitude toward Ralph Ellis. Why on earth would a girl want to avoid a charming young man like Ralph?

HELENA: Perhaps you'll understand a little later.

[*Dorothea glances at her watch and the silent phone.*]

DOROTHEA [*raising her voice*]: Bodey, please not quite so loud in there! Miss Brookmire and I are holding a conversation in here, you know. [*She turns back to Helena and continues the conversation with an abrupt vehemence.*] —Helena, that woman wants to absorb my life like a blotter, and I'm not an ink splash! I'm sorry you had to meet her. I'm awfully—embarrassed, believe me.

HELENA: I don't regret it at all. I found her most amusing. Even the Gluck!

DOROTHEA [*resuming with the same intensity*]: Bodey wants me to follow the same, same old routine that she follows day in and day out and I—feel sympathy for the loneliness of the girl, but we have nothing, nothing, but *nothing* at all, in common. [*She interrupts herself.*] Shall we have some coffee?

HELENA: Yes, please. I do love iced coffee, but perhaps the ice is depleted.

BODEY [*from the kitchenette*]: She knows darn well she used the last piece.

HELENA: Is it still warm?

[*Dorothea has risen and gone into the kitchenette where she pours two cups of coffee.*]

DOROTHEA: It never cools off in this electric percolator, runs out, but never cools off. Do you take cream?

HELENA: No, thank you.

DOROTHEA [*bringing the coffee into the living room*]: Bodey does make very good coffee. I think she was born and raised in a kitchen and will probably die in a kitchen if ever she does break her routine that way.

[*Bodey crosses to the kitchen table with Dorothea's purse*

191

and hat which she has collected from the living room while Helena and Dorothea sip their coffee.]

BODEY: Dotty, remember, Buddy is waiting for us at the Creve Coeur station, we mustn't let him think we've stood him up.

DOROTHEA [*sighing*]: Excuse me, Helena, there really has been a terrible problem with communication today. [*She crosses to Bodey and adjusts her hearing aid for her.*] Can you hear me clearly, now at last?

BODEY: You got something to tell me?

DOROTHEA: Something I've told you already, frequently, loudly, and clearly, but which you simply will not admit because of your hostility toward Ralph Ellis. I'm waiting here to receive an important call from him, and I am not going anywhere till it's come through.

BODEY: Dotty. It's past noon and he still hasn't called.

DOROTHEA: On Saturday evenings he's out late at social affairs and consequently sleeps late on Sundays.

BODEY: This late?

HELENA: Miss Bodenhafer doesn't know how the privileged classes live.

BODEY: No, I guess not, we're ignorant of the history of art, but Buddy and me, we've got a life going on, you understand, we got a life . . .

DOROTHEA: Bodey, you know I'm sorry to disappoint your plans for the Creve Coeur picnic, but you must realize by now

192

—after our conversation before Miss Brookmire dropped in— that I can't allow this well-meant design of yours to get me involved with your brother to go any further. So that even if I were *not* expecting this important phone call, I would not go to Creve Coeur with you and your brother this afternoon—or ever! It wouldn't be fair to your brother to, to—lead him on that way . . .

BODEY: Well, I did fry up three chickens and I boiled a dozen eggs, but, well, that's—

HELENA: Life for you, Miss Bodenhafer. We've got to face it.

BODEY: But I really was hoping—expecting—

[*Tears appear in Bodey's large, childlike eyes.*]

HELENA: Dorothea, I believe she's beginning to weep over this. Say something comforting to her.

DOROTHEA: Bodey? Bodey? This afternoon you must break the news to your brother that—much as I appreciate his attentions—I am seriously involved with someone else, and I think you can do this without hurting his feelings. Let him have some beer first and a—cigar. . . . And about this superabundance of chicken and deviled eggs, Bodey, why don't you call some girl who works in your office and get her to go to Creve Coeur and enjoy the picnic with you this afternoon?

BODEY: Buddy and I, we—don't have fun with—strangers . . .

DOROTHEA: Now, how can you call them strangers when you've been working in the same office with these girls at International Shoe for—how many years? Almost twenty? Strangers? Still?

BODEY: —Not all of 'em have been there long as me . . . [*She blows her nose.*]

DOROTHEA: Oh, some of them must have, surely, unless the death rate in the office is higher than—a cat's back.

[*Dorothea smiles half-apologetically at Helena. Helena stifles a malicious chuckle.*]

BODEY: —You see, Dotty, Buddy and me feel so at home with you now.

DOROTHEA: Bodey, we knew that I was here just for a while because it's so close to Blewett. Please don't make me feel *guilty*. I have no reason to, do I?

BODEY: —No, no, Dotty—but don't worry about it. Buddy and me, we are both—big eaters, and if there's somethin' left over, there's always cute little children around Creve Coeur that we could share with, Dotty, so—

DOROTHEA: Yes, there must be. Do that. Let's not prolong this discussion. I see it's painful to you.

BODEY: —Do you? No. It's—you I'm thinking of, Dotty. —Now if for some reason you should change your mind, here is the schedule of the open-air streetcars to Creve Coeur.

HELENA: Yellowing with antiquity. Is it legible still?

BODEY: We'll still be hoping that you might decide to join us, you know that, Dotty.

DOROTHEA: Yes, of course—I know that. Now why don't you finish packing and start out to the station?

194

BODEY: —Yes. —But remember how welcome you would be if—shoes. [*She starts into the bedroom to put on her shoes.*] I still have my slippers on.

DOROTHEA [*to Helena after Bodey has gone into the bedroom*]: So! You've got the postdated check. I will move to Westmoreland Place with you July first, although I'll have to stretch quite a bit to make ends meet in such an expensive apartment.

HELENA: Think of the advantages. A fashionable address, two bedrooms, a baby grand in the front room and—

DOROTHEA: Yes, I know. It would be a very good place to entertain Ralph.

HELENA: I trust that entertaining Ralph is not your only motive in making this move to Westmoreland Place.

DOROTHEA: Not the only, but the principal one.

HELENA [*leaning forward slowly, eyes widening*]: Oh, my dear Dorothea! I have the very odd feeling that I saw the name Ralph Ellis in the newspaper. In the society section.

DOROTHEA: In the society section?

HELENA: I think so, yes. I'm sure so.

[*Rising tensely, Dorothea locates the Sunday paper which Bodey had left on the sofa, in some disarray, after removing the "certain item"—the society page. She hurriedly looks through the various sections trying to find the society news.*]

DOROTHEA: Bodey? —BOOO-DEYY!

195

BODEY: What, Dotty?

DOROTHEA: Where is the society page of the *Post-Dispatch?*

BODEY: —Oh . . .

DOROTHEA: What does "oh" mean? It's disappeared from the paper and I'd like to know where.

BODEY: Dotty, I—

DOROTHEA: What's wrong with you? Why are you upset? I just want to know if you've seen the society page of the Sunday paper?

BODEY: —Why, I—used it to wrap fried chicken up with, honey.

DOROTHEA [*to Helena*]: The only part of the paper in which I have any interest. She takes it and wraps fried chicken in it before I get up in the morning! You see what I mean? Do you understand now? [*She turns back to Bodey.*] Please remove the fried chicken from the society page and *let me have it!*

BODEY: —Honey, the chicken makes the paper so greasy that—

DOROTHEA: *I will unwrap it myself!* [*She charges into the kitchenette, unwraps the chicken, and folds out the section of pages.*] —A section has been torn out of it? Why? What for?

BODEY: Is it? I—

DOROTHEA: Nobody possibly could have done it but you. What did you do with the torn out piece of the paper?

196

BODEY: —I— [*She shakes her head helplessly.*]

DOROTHEA: Here it is! —Crumpled and tossed in the waste-basket!—What for, I wonder? [*She snatches up the crumpled paper from the wastebasket and straightens it, using both palms to press it hard against the kitchen table so as to flatten it. She holds up the torn-out section of the paper so the audience can see a large photograph of a young woman, good looking in a plain fashion, wearing a hard smile of triumph, then she reads aloud in a hoarse, stricken voice.*] Mr. and Mrs. James Finley announce the engagement of their daughter, Miss Constance Finley, to Mr.—T. Ralph Ellis, principal of—

[*Pause. There is much stage business. Dorothea is stunned for some moments but then comes to violent life and action. She picks up the picnic shoebox, thrusts it fiercely into Bodey's hands, opens the door for her but rushes back to pick up Bodey's small black straw hat trimmed with paper daises, then opens the door for Bodey again with a violent gesture meaning, "Go quick!" Bodey goes. In the hall we hear various articles falling from Bodey's hold and a small, panting gasp. Then there is silence. Helena gets up with a mechanical air of sympathy.*]

HELENA: That woman is sly all right but not as sly as she's stupid. She might have guessed you'd want the society page and notice Mr. Ellis's engagement had been torn out. Anyhow, the news would have reached you at the school tomorrow. Of course I can't understand how you could be taken in by what-ever little attentions you may have received from Ralph Ellis.

DOROTHEA: —"Little—attentions?" I assure you they were not—"little attentions," they were—

HELENA: Little attentions which you magnified in your imagi-nation. Well, now, let us dismiss the matter, which has dis-

197

missed itself! Dorothea, about the postdated check, I'm not sure the real estate agents would be satisfied with that. Now surely, Dorothea, surely you have relatives who could help you with a down payment in cash?

DOROTHEA: —Helena, I'm not interested in Westmoreland Place. —Now.

HELENA: What!

DOROTHEA: I've—abandoned that idea. I've decided not to move.

HELENA [*aghast*]: —Do you realize what a shockingly irresponsible thing you are doing? Don't you realize that you are placing me in a very unfair position? You led me to believe I could count on your sharing the expense of the place, and now, at the last moment, when I have no time to get hold of someone else, you suddenly—pull out. It's really irresponsible of you. It's a really very irresponsible thing to do.

DOROTHEA: —I'm afraid we wouldn't have really gotten along together. I'm not uncomfortable here. It's only two blocks from the school and—I won't be needing a place I can't afford to entertain—anyone now. —I think I would like to be alone.

HELENA: All I can say is, the only thing I can say is—

DOROTHEA: Don't say it, just, just—leave me alone, now, Helena.

HELENA: Well, that I shall do. You may be right, we wouldn't have gotten along. Perhaps Miss Bodenheifer and her twin brother are much more on your social and cultural level than I'd hoped. And of course there's always the charm of Miss Gluck from upstairs.

DOROTHEA: The prospect of that is not as dismaying to me, Helena, as the little card parties and teas you'd had in mind for us on Westmoreland Place . . .

HELENA: *Chacun à son goût.*

DOROTHEA: Yes, yes.

HELENA [*at the door*]: There is rarely a graceful way to say good-bye. [*She exits.*]

[*Pause. Dorothea shuts her eyes very tight and raises a clenched hand in the air, nodding her head several times as if affirming an unhappy suspicion regarding the way of the world. This gesture suffices to discharge her sense of defeat. Now she springs up determinedly and goes to the phone.*

[*While waiting for a connection, she notices Miss Gluck seated disconsolately in a corner of the kitchenette.*]

DOROTHEA: Now Miss Gluck, now Sophie, we must pull ourselves together and go on. Go on, we must just go on, that's all that life seems to offer and—demand. [*She turns her attention to the phone.*] Hello, operator, can you get me information, please? —Hello? Information? Can you get me the number of the little station at the end of the Delmar car-line where you catch the, the—open streetcar that goes out to Creve Coeur Lake? —Thank you.

MISS GLUCK [*speaking English wih difficulty and a heavy German accent*]: Please don't leave me alone. I can't go up!

DOROTHEA [*her attention still occupied with the phone*]: Creve Coeur car-line station? Look. On the platform in a few minutes will be a plumpish little woman with a big artificial flower over one ear and a stoutish man with her, probably with a cigar. I have to get an important message to them. Tell them that Dotty called and has decided to go to Creve Coeur with them after all so will they please wait. You'll have to shout to the woman because she's—*deaf* . . .

[*For some reason the word "deaf" chokes her and she begins to sob as she hangs up the phone. Miss Gluck rises, sobbing louder.*]

No, no, Sophie, come here. [*Impulsively she draws Miss Gluck into her arms.*] I know, Sophie, I know, crying is a release, but it—inflames the eyes.

[*She takes Miss Gluck to the armchair and seats her there. Then she goes to the kitchenette, gets a cup of coffee and a cruller, and brings them to Sophie.*]

Make yourself comfortable, Sophie.

[*She goes to the bedroom, gets a pair of gloves, then returns and crosses to the kitchen table to collect her hat and pocketbook. She goes to the door, opens it, and says . . .*]

We'll be back before dark.

THE LIGHTS DIM OUT

CLOTHES FOR A SUMMER HOTEL

Copyright © 1980, 1981, by Tennessee Williams
Copyright © 1983 by the Estate of Tennessee Williams

AUTHOR'S NOTE: This is a ghost play.

Of course in a sense all plays are ghost plays, since players are not actually whom they play.

Our reason for taking extraordinary license with time and place is that in an asylum and on its grounds liberties of this kind are quite prevalent: and also these liberties allow us to explore in more depth what we believe is truth of character.

And so we ask you to indulge us with the licenses we take for a purpose which we consider quite earnest.

This edition of *Clothes for a Summer Hotel* is a further revision, by the author, of the acting text published by Dramatists Play Service in 1981, which was itself a revision of the script of the Broadway production. The play now includes the following characters (in order of appearance):

F. SCOTT FITZGERALD
SISTER ONE
SISTER TWO
GERALD MURPHY
ZELDA FITZGERALD
INTERN
BECKY
SARA MURPHY
DR. ZELLER
BOO-BOO
HER NURSE
EDOUARD, played by the same actor as the INTERN
MRS. PATRICK CAMPBELL
ERNEST HEMINGWAY
HADLEY HEMINGWAY
A BLACK MALE SINGER
SEVERAL DANCERS
ASSORTED PARTY GUESTS

Clothes for a Summer Hotel was presented by Elliot Martin, in association with Donald Cecil and Columbia Pictures, at the Cort Theatre, in New York City, on March 26, 1980. It was directed by Jose Quintero; the scenic production was designed by Oliver Smith; costumes were by Theoni V. Aldredge; lighting was by Marilyn Rennagel; the original music was by Michael Valenti; and the dance consultant was Anna Sokolow. The cast, in order of appearance, was as follows:

GERMAN SISTER #1	MADELEINE LE ROUX
GERMAN SISTER #2	JOSEPHINE NICHOLS
GHOST	MARILYN ROCKAFELLOW
GHOST	TANNY McDONALD
GHOST	GARRISON PHILLIPS
GHOST	SCOTT PALMER
GHOST	WEYMAN THOMPSON
GHOST	AUDREE RAE
F. SCOTT FITZGERALD	KENNETH HAIGH
GERALD MURPHY	MICHAEL CONNOLLY
BECKY	MARY DOYLE
ZELDA FITZGERALD	GERALDINE PAGE
JOURNALIST	ROBERT BAYS
PHOTOGRAPHER	SCOTT PALMER
NURSE #1	MADELEINE LE ROUX
INTERN	DAVID CANARY
SARA MURPHY	MARILYN ROCKAFELLOW
MADAME EGOROVA	AUDREE RAE
EDOUARD	DAVID CANARY
MRS. PATRICK CAMPBELL	JOSEPHINE NICHOLS
DOCTOR ZELLER	MICHAEL GRANGER
HEMINGWAY	ROBERT BLACK
HADLEY HEMINGWAY	TANNY McDONALD
SINGER	WEYMAN THOMPSON
DANCER	MADELEINE LE ROUX
DOCTOR BAUM	MICHAEL GRANGER
NURSE #2	TANNY McDONALD

THE SET: The stage is raked downward somewhat from the "mock-up" facade of Zelda's final asylum (Highland Hospital on a windy hilltop near Asheville, North Carolina) which is entered through a pair of Gothic-looking black iron gates, rather unrealistically tall. At curtain-rise there are three other set-pieces, a dark green bench downstage and, just behind it and slightly stage right of it, a bush of flickering red leaves that suggest flames; further downstage is a large rock which should seem a natural out-cropping on the asylum lawn, but which will later serve as a cliff above the sea in the scene between Zelda and Edouard.

Only the door of the asylum building is realistically designed for entrances and exits: the entire building must be in "sudden perspective" so that the third (top) floor of it—the one floor with barred windows, in which Zelda was confined with other patients taking insulin shock and in which she and the other shock patients were burned to "indistinguishable ash" in the autumn of 1947, years after Scott's death on the West Coast— is seen.

This must be regarded as a ghost play because of the chronological licenses which are taken, comparable to those that were taken in *Camino Real*, the purpose being to penetrate into character more deeply and to encompass dreamlike passages of time in a scene.

The windy hill was called Sunset, and the setting sun at the end of the play should be fierily reflected in the barred third floor windows.

The extent to which the characters should betray an awareness of their apparitional state will be determined more precisely in the course of a production.

ACT ONE

<hr>

SCENE ONE

<hr>

At curtain-rise F. Scott Fitzgerald is standing before the mock-up building. He appears as he did when he died in his mid-forties, a man with blurred edges, a tentative manner, but with a surviving dignity and capacity for deep feeling.

<hr>

SISTER ONE: If you are tired of waiting—

SCOTT [*cutting in*]: Yes, I am tired but I will continue to wait as long as she keeps me waiting.

[*There is a pause, the sound of wind.*]

SISTER TWO: There was a discussion among the staff lately about whether to paint the gates red to make them appear more cheerful.

SISTER ONE: To the patients and visitors. Do you think they should be painted red?

SCOTT: No.

SISTER ONE: Why?

SCOTT: I think it would make no perceptible difference.

SISTER ONE: The building is red.

SCOTT: *Is* it?

205

SISTER ONE: What?

SCOTT: Red.

SISTER ONE: Oh, yes, it is red, a dark red.

SCOTT: In some areas it appears to be black as if scorched by fire.

SISTER ONE: What did he say?

SISTER TWO: I didn't catch what he said—the wind blew his voice away.

SISTER ONE: And so that is your opinion?

SCOTT: What?

SISTER ONE: The gates should not be painted red to look cheerful?

SCOTT: Frankly speaking—

SISTER ONE: Yes?

SCOTT: If the objective is to create a cheerful impression, I would begin by removing the two of you from beside the gates.

SISTER ONE: Oh, no, we must guard them until they are locked for the evening.

SCOTT: Then why don't you wear red robes with dashes of white and blue. Sprinkle a few stars on them! Jesus!

[*Sister One crosses herself.*]

SISTER TWO: What did he say?

SISTER ONE: He spoke the name of our Lord.

[*Sister Two crosses herself. Gerald Murphy appears behind Scott.*]

MURPHY: It does no good antagonizing them, Scott.

SCOTT: Murph!

MURPHY: It will all be over in— [*He looks at his wristwatch.*] —one hour and forty-five minutes.

SCOTT: —It? [*Murphy nods. Scott staggers. Murphy catches his arm.*] Not drunk. Exhausted. You said "it"? —What is "it"?

VOICE BOOMING ON SPEAKERS: *La question est défendue.*

SCOTT: Is Sara with you, Murph?

MURPHY: Yes, she's gone back to the inn, you know, the Pine Grove Inn.

SCOTT: Yes. I know. —Dreary place for—

MURPHY: For a bit of rest. Pretty tired from the trip. Surprisingly long, considering . . .

SCOTT [*dazed, nodding in a bewildered way*]: Yes, I—

MURPHY: —She—she caught a glimpse of Zelda—practicing ballet.

SCOTT: Where?

MURPHY: Therapy room.

SCOTT: —Oh. Yes. —Excuse me, I'm—

MURPHY: You must have found it a long trip, too.

SCOTT: Long and—tiring. I'm only here for the afternoon and the night. [*Murphy nods.*] So. Sara saw Zelda, did she?

MURPHY: Saw her practicing—

SCOTT: Ballet . . .

MURPHY: Scott? Sara was so distressed, I'd better tell you this to prepare you when you see her. Scott, Sara—burst into tears. Scott? You ought to try to come out here more often, more for your own sake than hers. She has her fantasy world which we'll take part in later—

SISTER ONE: Thin ice.

SISTER TWO: Very thin ice.

[*The two men exchange wary glances. Scott clears his throat; Murphy kicks at some fallen autumn leaves.*]

MURPHY: I was going to say—oh, yes—working on the West Coast—right? [*Scott nods uncertainly.*] You see her rarely, now. So. The change you'll notice in her is going to be a shock. She's taking insulin; it's put a good deal of weight on her, and, well, regardless of what the doctors—

SCOTT: —I know—doctors . . .

MURPHY: They tell you what it's—

SCOTT: To their advantage, what's—expedient to tell you . . .

MURPHY: Of course that's understandable. You naturally realize that her reality is very different from ours even in these—circumstances.

SCOTT: She's still afflicted with that dancing craze, even now when any kind of a career, especially dancing, is—sadly—impractical.

MURPHY: Scott, we feel she was driven to it because—

SCOTT: I had to discourage her attempt to compete with my success as a writer: precocious, I face that now, have to bleed for it now. Have you seen Zelda's writing?

MURPHY: —Yes. That was her talent. I hear you made her promise not to publish *Save Me the Waltz* till your *Tender Is the Night* had come out.

SCOTT: Without apology, yes, I did. Didn't I have to pay for her treatment, for Scotty's Vassar and—I did. So much of Zelda's material was mine and she put it into her novel—a beautiful but cloudy, indistinct mirror of—

MURPHY: Yours! [*He turns away.*] I suppose all professional writers are self-protective first—and maybe last . . . [*He crosses offstage.*]

SCOTT: Where are you going, Murph? [*The reply is indistinct.*] They slip away from me now, dissolve about me . . . —Something strange here—unreal . . . disturbing!

ZELDA'S VOICE IN THERAPY: *Un, deux, pliez, un, deux, pliez,* etc.

[*Scott draws his coat collar about him, shivering.*]

SISTER ONE: The wind is cold on the hilltop; you could wait inside till she finishes her dancing.

SCOTT [*shouting*]: ZELDA! IT'S ME, SCOTT!

[*There is a slight pause.*]

ZELDA'S VOICE: —*Him? Impossible! —A dream* . . .

[*Another pause, then Zelda appears at the asylum doorway in a tutu and other ballet accoutrements, all a bit gray and bedraggled.*]

ZELDA: *For me, a visitor? Where?*

[*Murphy reappears, arrested by Zelda's outcry.*]

SCOTT: My God. Is that—? —Murph! Is that—?

MURPHY: Zelda.

SISTER ONE: Miss Zelda, get into your coat.

SISTER TWO: It's cold out.

ZELDA: I am not going out. Why would I go out?

SISTER TWO: Your visitor is waiting.

ZELDA: What visitor?

SISTER ONE: Your husband.

ZELDA: Impossible.

SISTER ONE: Look, he is by the bench.

ZELDA: No, no, no! An imposter! —No resemblance to Scott. [*She spins angrily about and rushes back into the asylum.*]

SCOTT: —That apparition was—! [*Scott covers his eyes.*]

MURPHY: Apparently she didn't recognize you either, Scott. You were a remarkably handsome young man, but—time has a habit of passing.

SCOTT: For me remorselessly—yes. . . . Murph, you mustn't leave me, I can't get through it alone!

MURPHY: Afraid you'd better.

SCOTT: I'd crack.

MURPHY: What's one more crack among all the others? I wouldn't think another would be very distinguishable from the rest.

SCOTT: —All right. God! —That was a beastly remark . . .

MURPHY: We are all obliged to make one now and then . . . [*He has retreated into the foliage, then calls back in a somewhat spectral voice.*] You and Zelda will be at our dance tonight at the villa? [*This line is almost drowned in the wind.*]

SCOTT: Dance? Where?

[*Zelda, wearing a coat, reappears at the asylum entrance with an intern.*]

ZELDA: How shall I play it?

INTERN: Delicately, delicately.

ZELDA: Delicacy is not the style of a hawk. [*She draws the coat tightly about her throat: her eyes are wide with shock.*]

SCOTT [*calling from downstage*]: Zelda, is that you?

ZELDA: Do I answer that pathetic mockery of my once attractive husband?

[*The intern nods, gripping her arm.*]

SCOTT: Come down where I can hear you! —I've waited hours!

ZELDA [*calling out*]: Hours, only hours. [*She turns to the intern.*] It's an impossible meeting, one that he would regret.

INTERN: Zelda, you must play it.

ZELDA: As if it existed?

INTERN: After a while, it will seem to exist.

ZELDA: I'll try to keep that in mind but the mind of a lunatic is not—retentive of present things. [*She advances slightly.*] You'll come to my assistance when I need you?

INTERN: Yes. Now go on out.

ZELDA: Why should this be demanded of me now after all the other demands? —I thought that obligations stopped with death!

INTERN: Zelda, you must go on.

ZELDA: I'm afraid.

INTERN: You've never known your courage.

ZELDA: I should be relieved of it now.

INTERN: Don't hold back! Don't let the dream dissolve. I'll follow a little behind you. You should receive him alone. *À bientôt.*

SCOTT [*calling*]: *Zelda?*

[*The intern exits into the asylum closing the doors behind him. Zelda begins a slow descent and moves downstage. Despite her increase of weight and the shapeless coat, her approach has the majesty of those purified by madness and by fire. Her eyes open very wide. Scott is barely able to hold his ground before their blaze. Zelda has to shout above the wind.*]

ZELDA: Is that really you, Scott? Are you my lawful husband, the celebrated F. Scott Fitzgerald, author of my life? Sorry to say you're hard to recognize now. Why didn't you warn me of this—startling reunion, Scott?

SCOTT: I had to come at once when the doctors advised me of your remarkable improvement.

ZELDA: —Not exactly an accurate report. —Aren't you somewhat unseasonably dressed for a chilly autumn afternoon?

SCOTT: When I got the doctors' report, well, I forgot the difference in weather between the West Coast and here, just hopped right onto the first plane—bought a spare shirt at a shop at the airport.

ZELDA: I see, I see, that's why you're dressed as if about to check in at a summer hotel.

SCOTT: It's all right, Zelda.

ZELDA: Is it all right, Scott?

SCOTT: Since I have to fly back tomorrow. —Don't be so standoffish, let me kiss you.

[*He goes to Zelda and tentatively embraces and kisses her in a detached manner.*]

ZELDA: —Well.

SCOTT: I would describe that as a somewhat perfunctory response.

ZELDA: And I'd describe it as a meaninglessly conventional— gesture to have embraced at all—after all . . . [*He draws back wounded: she smiles, a touch of ferocity in her look.*] —Sorry, Goofo. It's been so long since we've exchanged more than letters. . . . And you fly back tomorrow? We have only this late afternoon in which to renew our—acquaintance.

SCOTT [*uncomfortably*]: Work on the Coast, film-work, is very exacting, Zelda. Inhumanly exacting. People pretend to feel but don't feel at all.

ZELDA: Don't they call it the world of make-believe? Isn't it a sort of a madhouse, too? You occupy one there, and I occupy one here.

SCOTT: I'm working on such a tight schedule. Never mind. Here's the big news I bring you. I'm completing a novel, a new one at last, and it will be one that will rank with my very best, controlled as *Gatsby* but emotionally charged as *Tender Is the*—

[*Pause.*]

ZELDA: —Good . . . will I be in it?

SCOTT: Not—recognizably . . .

ZELDA: Good. —So what is the program for us now? Shall we make a run for it and fall into a ditch to satisfy our carnal longings, Scott?

SCOTT: That was never the really important thing between us, beautiful, yes, but less important than—

ZELDA [*striking out*]: *What was important to you was to absorb and devour!*

SCOTT: I didn't expect to find you in this—agitated mood. Zelda, I brought you a little gift. A new wedding band to replace the one you lost.

ZELDA: I didn't lose it, Scott, I threw it away.

SCOTT: Why would you, how could you have—?

ZELDA: Scott, we're no longer really married and I despise pretenses.

SCOTT: I don't look at it that way.

ZELDA: Because you still pay for my confinement? Exorbitant, for torture.

SCOTT: You always want to return here; you're not forced to, Zelda.

ZELDA: I only come back here when I know I'm too much for Mother and the conventions of Montgomery, Alabama. I am pointed out on the street as a lunatic now.

SCOTT: Whatever the reason, Zelda, you do return by choice,

215

so don't call it confinement. And even if you don't want a new marriage ring, call it a ring of, of—a covenant with the past that's always still present, dearest.

ZELDA: I don't want it; I will not take it!

SCOTT [*with a baffled sigh*]: Of course we do have nonmaterial bonds, memories such as— "Do you remember before keys turned in locks—when life was a close-up, not an occasional letter— how I hated swimming naked off the rocks—but you liked nothing better?"

ZELDA: No, no, Scott, don't try to break my heart with early romantic effusions. No, Goofo, it's much too late!

SCOTT: I wasn't warned to expect this cold, violent attitude in you!

ZELDA: Never in all those years of coexistence in time did you make the discovery that I have the eyes of a hawk which is a bird of nature as predatory as a husband who appropriates your life as material for his writing. Poor Scott. Before you offered marriage to the Montgomery belle, you should have studied a bit of ornithology at Princeton.

SCOTT: I don't believe a course in ornithology was on the curriculum at Princeton in my day!

ZELDA [*distracted, looking vaguely about*]: What a pity! You could have been saved completely for your art—and I for mine . . .

SCOTT: Didn't hear that, the wind blows your voice away unless you shout. Is it always so windy here?

[*The wind blows.*]

216

ZELDA: Sunset Hill on which this cage is erected is the highest to catch the most wind to whip the flame-like skirts as red as the sisters' skirts are black. Isn't that why you selected this place for my confinement?

[*Scott moves toward her, extending his arms and gesturing toward the bench.*]

Are you studying ballet, too?

SCOTT [*attempting to laugh*]: Me, studying ballet?

ZELDA: You made a gesture out of classic ballet, extending your arms toward me, then extending the right arm toward that bench which I will not go near—again.

SCOTT: Now, now, Zelda, stop play acting, come here!

ZELDA: I won't approach that bench because of the bush next to it. Besides I'm only taking a little recess from O.T.

BECKY [*offstage voice*]: The head of the Harlow, the platinum of it, the bleach! —My personal salon was only a block from Goldwyn's . . .

[*Zelda starts drifting back to the doorway of the asylum. Scott grabs her.*]

SCOTT: *Zelda, don't withdraw!*—What are you— Tell me, Zelda, what are you working on mostly in Occupational Therapy now, dear?

ZELDA: The career that I undertook because you forbade me to write!

SCOTT: Writing calls for discipline! Continual!

ZELDA: And drink, continual, too? No, I respect your priority in the career of writing although it preceded and eclipsed my own. I made that sacrifice to you and so elected ballet. Isadora Duncan said, "I want to teach the whole world to dance!" —I'm more selfish, just want to teach myself.

SCOTT: The strenuous exercises will keep your figure trimmer.

ZELDA: Than writing and drinking?

SCOTT: Oh, I've quit that.

ZELDA: Quit writing?

SCOTT: Quit drinking.

ZELDA: QUIT? DRINKING?

SCOTT: Completely.

ZELDA: Cross your heart and hope to die?

SCOTT: I cross my heart but I don't hope to die until my new book is finished. [*Scott has maneuvered Zelda toward the bench. He sits and gets her to sit.*] Zelda, I've had—several little heart disturbances lately . . .

ZELDA: You mean the romance? Or romances?

SCOTT: I mean—cardiac—incidents. At a movie premiere last week, as the film ended, it all started—fading out . . .

ZELDA: Films always end with the fade-out.

SCOTT: I staggered so. I thought the audience would think I was drunk.

ZELDA [*sarcastically*]: Were they as foolish as that?

SCOTT: Luckily I had a friend with me who helped me out.

ZELDA: Oh, yes, I know about her.

SCOTT: You—she—you'd like her.

ZELDA: Certainly, if you do. Well—Scott? Let me say this quickly before I become disturbed and am hauled back in for restraint. You were not to blame. You needed a better influence, someone much more stable as a companion on the—roller-coaster ride which collapsed at the peak. You needed—*her*? Out there, utterly vulgar but—functioning well on that level.

SCOTT: Who are you, what are you—referring to, Zelda?

ZELDA: Who or what, which is it? Some are whats, some are whos. Which is she? —Never mind. You are in luck which-ever. . . . But can we turn this bench at an angle that doesn't force me to look at the flaming bush here?

SCOTT: It's such a lovely bush.

ZELDA: If you're attracted by fire. Are you attracted by fire?

SCOTT: The leaves are—radiant, yes, they're radiant as little torches. I feel as if they'd warm my hands if I—

ZELDA: I feel as if they'd burn me to unrecognizable ash. You see, the demented often have the gift of Cassandra, the gift of—

SCOTT: The gift of—?

ZELDA: Premonition! I WILL DIE IN FLAMES!

219

SCOTT: Please, Zelda, don't shout, don't draw attention. The doctors will think my visits disturb you—I won't be allowed to come back.

ZELDA: Visits? Did you say visits? That is plural. I wouldn't say that your presence here today qualifies as a very plural event.

[*She starts toward the gates. Scott rises to follow.*]

SCOTT: You're going inside?

ZELDA: I have my own little Victrola. Mama sent it to me for Christmas. I'm preparing for Diaghilev; he's offered me an audition. I'm going to do a Bach fugue with almost impossible *tempi* I was told. *Hah!*

SCOTT: Zelda, I didn't come all the way out here to listen to a Bach fugue, and watching you dance is a pleasure I've—exhausted . . .

ZELDA: Sorry. But I'm working against time! [*She continues imperiously.*] Sister, Sister, I want my little Victrola; my husband wants to see the dance I'm preparing for my audition for Diaghilev this—

SISTER ONE: You'll have to bring it out.

SISTER TWO: Or bring your visitor in.

SISTER ONE: We have to stay at the gates.

ZELDA: Oh, God damn you, bitches, all right, I'll fetch it out myself! Scott, wait! The idiot teacher, fuck her, said the *tempi* were impossible for me! I'll show her!

SCOTT: You'll come back out?

[*Zelda's voice is lost in the wind as she rushes to the entrance of the asylum. Scott speaks to the sisters.*]

She never spoke that way, never, never vulgarly before.

SISTER ONE: In an asylum they talk, they scream like that.

SISTER TWO: They pick it up from each other.

SCOTT: She didn't ever.

SISTER ONE: The excitement of your visit she did not expect. If I were you—

BECKY [*offstage voice, shouting*]: My personal salon! Transferred heads of stars!

SISTER TWO: Look who's coming back out! Shall I stop her?

[*Sister One shrugs. Becky appears in the doorway and moves to the middle of the platform.*]

Now what is it, Becky?

BECKY: I'm not talking to you so shut up. [*She sees Scott and calls to him.*] Mister? You, Mister?

[*Scott retreats downstage near the rock below the bench. Becky moves around the bench and then toward Scott.*]

You're from Hollywood, aren't you? Yes? Somebody said so! I am, too! My salon was a block from Goldwyn. Dressed hair for gentlemen, too. The Navarro! Was called to Falcon's Lair for the great Valentino, the Sheik!

SCOTT: Not now, not necessary, no time, just—visiting my—

221

[*Zelda reappears from the asylum, lugging a portable wind-up Victrola.*]

Zelda, please! Can't somebody restrain this—

ZELDA: Fight them off, you've got to fight them off! Hit her, give her a—

SCOTT: A demented woman, I—

ZELDA: Can't? Ungentlemanly? Well, look. I can, I can! [*She delivers a blow to Becky who kicks back at her.*] In, in, get this lunatic in!

[*Becky is captured by the sisters and herded into the mock-up asylum.*]

SCOTT: Distressing—distressing that you are exposed to—have to associate with—

ZELDA: Please wind up my Victrola. Dr. Bleumer, is that the name, have I got the name right? —He thought they would draw me out. "Mrs. Fitzgerald, converse with the other ladies." —There was a fake countess, there was a pretender to the throne of— [*She laughs harshly.*] —something! —"Dr. Bleumer," I said, "I have no social ambitions whatsoever." —Oh, God, Scott, can't you even wind a Victrola?

[*Gerald and Sara Murphy appear from the wings.*]

I'm working against time, only a week to prepare for my audition for—DIAGHILEV! Ballet Russe de—

MURPHY: Don't let her see you crying!

ZELDA [*rushing to the Murphys*]: Sara! Gerald!

SARA [*embracing her*]: Darling! We just dropped by to—

MURPHY: We happened to be in—

ZELDA [*hallucinating*]: Paris? On your way to St. Rapheal? Where is Mme. Egorova? Secretly tipples a bit but such a wonderful, wonderful instructor of classic ballet. [*She calls out.*] *MADAME? MADAME? MES AMIS LES MURPHYS SONT ICI POUR—* Gerald, Scott's in a daze! Would you please wind up my Victrola? Mme. Egorova feels I've embarked upon a dance career rather late in life, but she says that with such application and such longing, such dedication, I can make up for delay. You know that old poem? "She that comes late to the dance/more wildly must dance than the rest/though the strings of the violins/are a thousand knives at her breast."

SARA [*sotto voce*]: Start the Victrola for her, we'll act it out.

SCOTT: No, no, don't encourage—hallucinations, I wasn't advised—correctly . . .

[*But a Bach partita is now playing and Zelda is dancing. Gerald Murphy holds Sara's hand tightly as Sara holds a handkerchief to her nostrils. Zelda stumbles to the ground.*]

SARA: Oh, Zelda!

ZELDA: I'm all right. It was the *pizzicato*, most difficult part of—but I'm—determined: must master it for Diaghilev next week.

MURPHY: The poor child, she received no offer except from the *Moulin Rouge* . . .

SARA: Shhh! Shout "*Brava!*"

MURPHY: *Brava! Bravissima!*

SCOTT: You think it kind to encourage hallucination? Excuse me, I don't agree! The doctors who called me out here, cross-country despite heart condition, have ignored my requests for consultation about her. [*He rushes to the door of the mock-up asylum.*] Doctor! Doctor! Bleumer!

SARA [*to Murphy*]: I'm afraid!

MURPHY: It won't go?

SARA: Scott will break it down. Couldn't you prepare him?

MURPHY: Tell him that—?

SARA: Something, anything.

MURPHY: Couldn't! Which of them suffered more?

SARA: Wasn't there a woman with him on the Coast?

MURPHY: Yes, but—we know the compromises Scott had to make and finally—almost the indignity of Chekhov's body returned to Russia in a freight car labeled—"Oysters". . . . If anybody's discovered dignity in death—

[*The intern, who will also appear as Edouard, appears at the asylum door in response to Scott's shouts.*]

Oh, it may be reported as having "occurred quietly" in sleep, and so forth, but—the only reliable witness is the deceased, and reports by the deceased aren't—publicly reported.

SCOTT [*to the intern, advancing to the gates*]: Who are you? Surely you're not Dr. Bleumer, why, you look like—

224

MURPHY: If he should recognize him as—

SARA: Edouard?

MURPHY: It will all explode.

SCOTT: Well, whoever! Did you see her out there?

INTERN: Zelda?

[*Zelda, in a frozen position, stares at the intern, fist pressed to her mouth.*]

SCOTT: Please refer to my wife as Mrs. Fitzgerald, not— Zelda . . .

INTERN: We call patients by the first name to create an intimacy with them to make them feel they're at home.

SCOTT: Her home's not here. And not in a—long-ago ballet studio in Paris.

INTERN: Isn't it where she prefers it? If offering her some comfort is the object?

SCOTT: You're not Dr. Bleumer? Nor Zeller?

INTERN: No, no, just an intern, but all of us here are acquainted with Zelda's case, the tragedy she's borne with such—gallantry, *monsieur.*

SCOTT: I see. I hope that I see. —BUT I was falsely informed that she had nearly recovered, flew out from the Coast to make sure—and discover what? More demented than ever, and now violent, too. Look, you. I want to tell you something! —I've sold, am selling my talent, bartering my life and my daughter's future

225

in the obviously vain hope that—here at Highland you could—
[*He covers his face for a moment.*] —return her to—

INTERN: What?

SCOTT: *REASON, REASON, GOD DAMN IT!* What the
hell else did you offer?

[*Zelda has started advancing slowly to Scott and the intern.*]

INTERN: A refuge.

ZELDA: I AM NOT A SALAMANDER! —Just tell him that.

[*Murphy has led Sara off.*]

INTERN: Salamander, she said?

SCOTT: The salamander does not exist, never did; it is a mythological creature that can live in fire and suffer no hurt or—
[*Scott utters a gasp, almost a sob.*] —injury from—the element
of fire.

ZELDA: I am not a salamander. Do you hear? You've mistaken
my spirit for my body! Because my spirit exists in fire does not
mean that my body will not be consumed if caught in fire behind
barred gates and windows on this windy hill.

[*Zelda, trembling, faces the two men: she looks from one to
the other with wild, imploring eyes.*]

INTERN: Salamander, sal-a-mander. Hmm. We've heard her
refer to a salamander before but no one seems to know what she
is talking about.

SCOTT: By no one you mean yourself and the patients? You

surely don't mean the doctors! Why, doctors are men of education, I thought! Such a degree of illiteracy doesn't exist among—men of science.

INTERN: By none of us of course I spoke for the staff at Highland.

SCOTT: You've heard my wife repeatedly refer to a salamander and yet you stand there and tell me that not a goddam one of you bothered to look it up!

[*The doctor appears behind the intern.*]

DR. ZELLER: Is there some trouble? Can I be of assistance?

SCOTT: You are—

DR. ZELLER: Dr. Zeller. You are Zelda's husband?

SCOTT [*furiously*]: I am sometimes known, in fact I am usually known—perhaps because I haven't been in the right places—as F. SCOTT FITZGERALD!

DR. ZELLER: Ahh? You are the husband?

SCOTT: You receive my monthly checks and still you don't know who I am?

[*The intern is supporting Zelda.*]

Tell that impertinent young—

DR. ZELLER: Since I am in consultation, staff meeting, tell quickly the trouble, *bitte*!

VOICE [*offstage, calling*]: Dr. Zeller?

DR. ZELLER: *Ja*—yes, *ein Moment!* You see . . . and so?

INTERN: He has disturbed his wife. She started to collapse.

DR. ZELLER: Give her—reassurance. She deserves comfort.

INTERN [*to Zelda*]: *Mieux, maintenant? Ma chère?*

ZELDA: I don't want to hurt him, I never wanted to hurt him. But tell him I am—not—a salamander.

DR. ZELLER: *Ach, der Salamander!* You see, being German, the word is not the same to me, I do not know what it is.

SCOTT: German, French—someone here must be English-speaking. Is no one English-speaking? To look up the word "salamander"?

DR. ZELLER: I will ask Dr. Baum who is more English-speaking to, to—what?

SCOTT: LOOK UP THE WORD! OTHERWISE HOW CAN YOU UNDERSTAND WHAT SHE MEANS BY IT?

DR. ZELLER [*to the intern*]: *Betrunken?*

SCOTT: Since it is obvious that she's obsessed with fire for some reason and keeps crying out "I am not a salamander," one of you might bother to look it up! —It's—mythological—meaning . . .

INTERN: In what?

SCOTT: A DICTIONARY, goddam it . . .

DR. ZELLER: *Ja, BETRUNKEN.* —Offer him a cold shower. I must go in. [*He enters the asylum.*]

228

INTERN: Of course. *Soyez un peu plus calme pour la visite, Monsieur*—Fitzgerald. —Would it help to have a cold shower as Dr. Zeller—suggests?

SCOTT: Thinks me drunk!

ZELDA: A frequent—misapprehension. Seems like—old times, Scott.

SCOTT: *UNBEARABLE!*

ZELDA: Yes, that's life for us, Goofo. —Did I say life? I tried to understand, I did, I did so hard.

INTERN: *Pauvre homme.* I was always concerned. Wondered what effect the indiscretion—

SCOTT: To be ridiculed, called drunk when Sheilah won't permit me to touch liquor.

ZELDA: Then the West Coast companion is better for you, Goofo.

SCOTT: Salvaging what's left of— [*He fumbles in his pocket.*] —Left my nitro? —No, wouldn't dare. —Little bottle of tablets for—man with heart condition, induced by false report to fly across country and witness this—

INTERN: Here it is. In this pocket. Now come in for—

SCOTT: NOT DRUNK! —DON'T NEED SHOWER! FREEZING COLD ON THIS WIND TOP!

INTERN: Just rest—Mr. Fitzgerald.

SCOTT: Yes, I—work mostly in bed . . .

229

[*Zelda utters a barely audible laugh. The intern/Edouard has seated Zelda on the bench. Then he places an arm about Scott and leads him toward the entrance of the mock-up asylum.*]

Don't touch me—can move—unassisted. But tell them all, the whole money-grubbing, lying staff of the—I will not—where's Zelda?

[*The voices are quieter: there is faint, elegaic music.*]

INTERN: Recovering from the disturbance of your unexpected visit.

SCOTT: Oh, but I won't leave without discovering who's responsible for my wife's deteriorating condition, *MUST! LEARN!*

INTERN: And if you learn it is *you*?

SCOTT: You're taken in, all of you, by her crazed accusations?

[*They enter the asylum. Zelda rises from the bench and crosses to the proscenium. Her eyes make it apparent she is about to attempt to make a meaningful statement. Author's note: In this scene Zelda must somehow suggest the desperate longing of the "insane" to communicate something of their private world to those from whom they're secluded. The words are mostly blown away by the wind: but the eyes—imploring though proud—the gestures—trembling though rigid with the urgency of their huge need—must win the audience to her inescapably from this point through the play: the present words given her are tentative: they may or may not suffice in themselves: the presentation—performance—must.*]

ZELDA: There's something I— [*The wind sound comes up and drowns her voice, then subsides.*] —But the winds, the winds, this

230

continual—lamentation of winds as if— [*The wind sound rises again and subsides.*] —they were trying to give one single tongue to all our agonies here. . . . Oh, but I write home cheerful letters to reassure Mother, lonely, family scattered to—winds. . . . Speak of pleasant strolls through the hills, not mentioning the escort of female dragons keeping us in line, bearing straps to restrain us if we—attempt to break ranks—ha, ha. . . . No need to distress her with actualities now. At our last parting in Montgomery, I said to her as I left, "Don't worry, Mother. I'm not afraid to die." —Not knowing how it would happen.

[*The upper stories light with flame and she cries out, crouching, hand to her eyes. There is the ghostly echo of women burning at a locked gate. The intern/Edouard, the doctor, the two sisters, all rush toward her. Zelda waves them away.*]

Sorry, nothing happened, it was a trick of light . . .

DR. ZELLER: May we continue without disturbance of this kind.

ZELDA: For what purpose? I don't understand the purpose.

DR. ZELLER [*to intern*]: Explain!

ZELDA: Yes, do! —Explain the inexplicable to me, please.

[*All except the intern/Edouard withdraw.*]

INTERN: Shadows of lives, tricks of light, sometimes illuminate things.

ZELDA: Not to us. To audiences of a performance of things past. Wasn't there once a little *auberge*, the *Reve Bleu*—where I cried out so wildly in your embrace that you were shocked and abandoned me to this long retreat into—

231

[*An idiotically cheerful white-starched nurse wheels a patient, Boo-Boo, up to Zelda.*]

this . . .

NURSE: Boo-Boo saw her roommate and wanted to say hello.

[*The spectral Boo-Boo is past all "wanting."*]

ZELDA: Hello, Boo-Boo—bye-bye—Boo-Boo.

[*Bells ring inside the asylum as the nurse wheels Boo-Boo that way.*]

Five o'clock—feeding time at the zoo . . .

[*As if sadly sensing a failure to receive them properly into her haunted world, Zelda offers the audience a polite social smile and a slight bow as—*]

THE LIGHT DIMS OUT

SCENE TWO

The table is pre-set with a bulletin board with a chart and several clippings attached with thumb tacks, sharpened pencils, and a book or two.

The music for this change ends and Scott, wearing a white knit sweater, enters from the rear of the stage. He was the most methodical of writers, charting out the course of a work in progress with the most astute care.

Zelda is dimly visible at the edge of the lighted area (behind Scott) looking as she did in about 1926. She advances into the scene more clearly when she speaks.

SCOTT [*setting a gin bottle on the table*]: There! Christ—when a writer starts drinking at work—who was it said he's only got ten years to go? Oh, yes—Galbraith, who never really got started.

[*He pours himself half a tumbler of gin and regards it moodily. Then he touches his slender waist.*]

—Hasn't put fat on me yet—but there's time. Hemingway's still in good shape and drinks more than me. —Or does he? —There's time . . . [*He settles down to work at the table.*] No more decor, surface of the work, too damn easy for me. Chapter Five is where it must begin to bite hard and deep.

[*Zelda approaches the table.*]

ZELDA: Dear Scott, dear Goofo—"bite hard and deep"—are you writing about a shark, a tiger—a hawk—or a human composite of all three?

SCOTT: —How long have you been standing back there, Zelda?

ZELDA: Just crept in against orders, to admire you at work.

233

[*He shuts his eyes tight for a moment.*]

SCOTT: I don't work to be admired at it.

ZELDA: I know, for the work to be admired. But, Goofo, you look so pretty working, at least till— [*She points at the bottle.*]

SCOTT [*still facing front*]: Pretty did you say?

ZELDA: Admirable, and pretty. At first, you know, I had reservations about marriage to a young man prettier than me.

SCOTT: Than you?

ZELDA: I'm not pretty, only mistaken for it. [*Her eyes are dark, tender, disturbed.*] But, Goofo, you really *are*.

SCOTT [*with an edge*]: Don't keep on with that, Zelda, that's insulting.

ZELDA [*approaching him, touching his throat*]: I don't understand why you should find it so objectionable.

SCOTT: The adjective "pretty" is for girls, or pretty boys of— ambiguous gender . . .

ZELDA: Girls, boys, whatever's pretty is pretty. Never mind ambiguity of—

SCOTT: In a man?

ZELDA: What? In a man?

SCOTT: Being called pretty implies—

ZELDA: Implies? What? —Implication?

scott: A disparagement of—

zelda: What?

scott: You know as well as I know that what it disparages is— the virility of— [*He takes another drink.*]

zelda: Oh, but that's so established in your case. And even if it wasn't—know what I think?

scott: Never.

zelda: I think that to write well about women, there's got to be that, a part of that, in the writer, oh, not too much, not so much that he flits about like a—

scott: Fairy?

zelda: You're too hard on them, Scott. I don't know why. Do they keep chasing you because you're so pretty they think you must be a secret one of them?

scott: Zelda, quit this, it's downright mockery.

zelda: Don't take it seriously, it's just envy, Scott—I'm not pretty at all.

scott: Zelda, you know that you're an internationally celebrated beauty.

zelda: Oh? Am I?

scott: The latest issue of *Cosmopolitan* magazine has a shipboard photograph of us with Scotty, and the caption says—

zelda: Headed for an iceberg?

scott: Says: "Brilliant young F. Scott Fitzgerald and his *beautiful* wife, Zelda, sail for France. *Bon voyage!*"

zelda: A slightly sinister—caption. Scott? Desperate can go with beauty, with an illusion of it.

scott: —Desperate? —Are you desperate, Zelda?

[*Pause: music comes in at a low level. Zelda runs her hands tenderly through Scott's blond hair and along his face.*]

zelda [*looking darkly over his head*]: Have no right to be, but—

scott: But you are? —Are you?

zelda: —You fall asleep first, before me.

scott: Do I?

zelda: Yes. I hold you. I caress your smooth body, sleeping; then feel mine. —Mine's harder, not so delicate to the touch.

scott: What are you telling me, Zelda? I'm not satisfactory to you? As a—

zelda: Sometimes I wish that the fires were equal.

scott: Too much of mine goes to work, but—

zelda: —Work. —Loveliest of all four-letter words. . . . Circumstances such as—disparities—might some day—come between us. A little, or seem to—but this golden band on my finger's the truth. . . . [*She establishes the ring, removing it from her finger and slipping it on his.*] The lasting truth, even—whatever—time brings little divisions and you are better than me at the cover-up,

236

Scott. [*She opens a copy of the* Princeton Triangle Club.] —Why didn't you ever show me this?

SCOTT: —*That?*

ZELDA: Is this really a picture of you?

[*A blowup of the picture appears on the drop behind the desk.*]

SCOTT: —Zelda, you know very well that every year the Princeton Triangle Club put on a show. Somebody had to appear as the ingénue in it. —That year, I was chosen to play it. Yes, that's me. What of it?

ZELDA: —Exquisite . . . a perfect illusion. I'd never achieve it so well.

SCOTT: Who showed that to you? For what purpose?

ZELDA: A lady fan of your fiction—came up to me with it on the beach today. —A gushy type, probably meant no harm but was so loud, "Why, Mrs. Fitzgerald, Mrs. Scott Fitzgerald, can't believe it, but they swear it's your husband! Surely not, but the name is—" —Sara said, "Please! You're interrupting—"

SCOTT: Zelda, you are interrupting my work! Mustn't *do* that, thought it was agreed you wouldn't!

ZELDA: What about my work?

SCOTT: Your—?

ZELDA: You're not going out tonight? —To the casino and the masquerade?

SCOTT: Obviously not—since working!

237

ZELDA: Scott? Goofo? You need a night off to refresh you. You're driving yourself too hard.

SCOTT: That may be, but the purpose is—necessary. To live and live well. In keeping with our—

ZELDA: What?

SCOTT: Reputation!

ZELDA: Regardless of price? Scott, you're wearing yourself thin for something that I already suspect isn't worth it, at the price. We're on the *Cote d'Azur* with golden people. Generous to us. But the effort to match their bets at the casino, to run in their tracks is—too demanding of my nerves and your—liver . . .

SCOTT: What about my liver?

ZELDA: Dr. D'Amboise had a private talk with me.

SCOTT: About my—

ZELDA: Liver. He didn't want to alarm you but there is already some damage to it, and going on like this—the damage will be progressive. —*Oh! Widow's moon!*

SCOTT: What's a widow's moon?

ZELDA: Nearly full. When it's full the cherries will be ripe and when the cherries are ripe the nightingales stop singing. —Bearing the cherries home to their hungry little nestlings.

SCOTT: You seem to have picked up a lot of local lore. But, Zelda, regardless of my liver and the charms of the widow's moon, I do have to get on with my work. Did you hear me? I must GET ON WITH MY WORK!

ZELDA: What about mine, my work? —What sort of face are you making? Turn around, let me see!

[*Scott whirls about to face her. This short scene must catch the paradox of the love-hate relationship which existed between them at this point in their marriage.*]

Oh, that *is* quite a face! A face to strike terror to the heart of any person not equally savage. Well, there is equality in us there: savagery equal, both sides.

SCOTT: Zelda, we are *one* side, indivisible. You know that, by God, you'd better know that since I've staked my life on it, that you'd know it and accept it and—respect it!

[*His shaking hand seizes the glass; he drains it and then hurls it away.*]

ZELDA: Naughty, naughty young writer, drinking while working. So. One side, indivisible, created in liberty and justice with freedom for all? Ha, ha, paraphrase of the oath of allegiance to the classroom flag. So. Sit down. I only want a minute of your time.

SCOTT: I am not going to sit down again. I am standing to face you and hear you.

ZELDA: Hear me, good, a change. But answer me, this time, that would be a change, too. I want an answer to my first question, "What about *my* work?"

SCOTT: You are the wife of a highly respected and successful writer who works night and day to maintain you in—

ZELDA [*overlapping*]: An impossible situation? Oh, yes, you do that; I don't dispute your intense absorption in work. Yours!

I still say, "What about *mine,* meaning my *work?*"—Answer? None? —You threw the glass away, drink out of the bottle.

SCOTT [*throwing the bottle away*]: Your work is the work that all young Southern ladies dream of performing some day. Living well with a devoted husband and a beautiful child.

ZELDA: Are you certain, Scott, that I fit the classification of dreamy young Southern lady? Damn it, Scott. Sorry, wrong size, it pinches! —Can't wear that shoe, too confining.

SCOTT: I see. It's too confining. But it's all that we have in stock!

ZELDA: —Excuse my interruption. I'll not prolong it; I'll not do it again; I'll—find my own way somehow. Used to have some aptitude for dancing: could take that up again, or—I could betray you by taking a lover. . . . Could I? —I could give it a try . . .

[*Zelda exits into the asylum and is masked by the sisters who hold their positions till she returns. Scott exits at the rear of the stage. Two men enter from the same point and remove the table and chairs. Two dancers enter from either side of the stage for a* pas de deux *as the light changes into long, late afternoon shadows on a beach. Zelda reappears in a large, white straw hat and beach robe and sits on the rock, downstage. Edouard appears wearing the intern's jacket. The sisters mask him as he takes off the jacket and reappears in a swimsuit of the period. The dancers exit to the rear as Edouard moves down to Zelda on the rocks. He dries his head with a towel.*]

ZELDA: What a beautiful dive you made off the rocks. We call it a swan dive.

EDOUARD: I went very deep, so deep I nearly touched bottom.

ZELDA: You are reckless, you have a reckless nature and so have I!

EDOUARD: I know when to be careful: but do you?

ZELDA: I don't care to be careful! Anyway, we are alone!

EDOUARD: There could be hidden observers.

[*Zelda laughs and clasps his shining head between her hands and kisses him intensely.*]

Zelda, Zelda, your hands, please: the *plage* is public! You are—

ZELDA: Unnatural?

EDOUARD: Impulsive—dangerously—this is not the way of the French; we know passion but we also know caution. With public caution, our passions can be indulged in private. There must be the fictitious names on the register of the—

ZELDA: *Chambre de convenance!* You see, I've picked up the idiom for it in case, just in case—

EDOUARD: I know you've never used such a room before.

ZELDA: No, but how would you know?

EDOUARD: By intuition, Frenchmen have intuition.

ZELDA: And as for the fictitious name, mine I'd like to be Daisy.

EDOUARD: Why Daisy?

241

ZELDA: I was quite infatuated with the mysterious, dashing young Gatsby, and Daisy was his love: a wanton creature, not encumbered with morals, scruples, gifted with—how did Scott put it?—the enormous carelessness of the very rich.

EDOUARD: This is a matter to be approached seriously, Zelda.

ZELDA: Later, yes, not yet. If I approached the matter seriously now, at this moment, with you all wet and gleaming from your swan dive off the rocks, I think I'd cry—diamond tears.

EDOUARD: If serious precautions aren't taken about this—much as I want it to happen and to be altogether happy—we've got to recognize the gravity of the possibilities— In French I could say it easily; the words come right in French; our language was made for making arrangements of this kind—not so close. Can you look casual, Zelda, and listen? I think I know the little hotel. Fictitious names, yes, but not Daisy and not Gatsby, on the register. I'll use the names of my maternal grandparents!

ZELDA: Who were named?

EDOUARD: Better that you don't know them, you'd blab them out at some—hysterical moment.

ZELDA: It's probably not Southern-lady-like to have secrets which are held sacred but—I shall have one, a secret kept securely. I've turned away from you; I've picked up a shell, coiled, iridescent—an innocent occupation for possible observers while we complete our plans for the illicit occasion in private. Behind a locked door, a securely locked door?

EDOUARD: A door that's locked and bolted.

ZELDA: With a window facing the sea, open, to admit the sea-wind and the wave sounds, but with curtains that blow inward as if wanting to participate in our caresses! —Here's another, shell, not coiled, but—the window not so high that we'd break bones if we had to escape that way, the door being stormed by—

EDOUARD: You're trembling, Zelda. Are you cold?

ZELDA: *Au contraire.*

EDOUARD: Frightened?

ZELDA: God, no! Are *you*?

EDOUARD: A bit shocked by the—imprudence.

ZELDA: But not repelled? Not wanting to call it off?

EDOUARD: *Non, non au contraire.* —Shells, birds, creatures of sea and sky . . .

ZELDA: You'll have your security measures, *cher*, locked, bolted door, but behind closed curtains there must be light in the room, you must be all visible to me, indelibly—*im-mem-orially!*—in my heart's eye, if this adventure blows out the eye of the mind. So? When? Tomorrow? *Demain?*

EDOUARD: At noon, tomorrow, here, *sur la plage*. We'll swim a ways up to the pier. I'll have a taxi waiting to take us to a little *auberge*—the *Reve Bleu*.

ZELDA: Promise? Sacred as secret?

EDOUARD: *D'accord, d'accord, entendu!*

ZELDA: *Merci mille fois!*

EDOUARD: A beautiful girl does not thank a man for enjoying

intimacy with her. —We're being observed by a woman with binoculars on the *plage.*

ZELDA [*loudly, almost shouting*]: How many shells have we collected.

EDOUARD: Only these two.

ZELDA: Two will be sufficient for our purpose at the *Auberge Reve Bleu.*

EDOUARD: How strange and lovely you are . . .

[*The dancers reappear and as soon as they have reached center-stage, Edouard exits into the asylum. Zelda remains seated on the floor while the* pas de deux *continues upstage of her.*]

ZELDA [*to herself*]: And so the appointment is made! The hawk and the hawk will meet in light near the sun!

[*Zelda stretches out onto the floor in her spotlight while the love* pas de deux *finishes as the curtain comes down.*]

END OF ACT I

ACT TWO

SCENE ONE

|||||||||||||||||||||||||||||||||||||||||||||||||||||||||||||||||||||||||||||||||||||||||||||||||||||||||

The scene opens with the sound of wind sweeping the hilltop: as if a dark cloud had blown over it, the asylum lawn is dimmed out.

The little hotel room is set up downstage of the flaming bush. There is a double bed with an arched headboard and two chairs, one on either side of the bed.

On the chair to the left of the bed are Edouard's jacket, shirt, and pants—also his wallet with a photograph, an ash tray, and a pack of cigarettes and matches.

On the chair to the right of the bed are Zelda's dress, a bottle of opened champagne, and two glasses. Her shoes are near the chair.

The light is brought up, cool, as if the light of a full moon shone through the shutters.

Edouard and Zelda (in her younger guise) are visible, nude except for whatever conventions of stage propriety may be in order.

|||||||||||||||||||||||||||||||||||||||||||||||||||||||||||||||||||||||||||||||||||||||||||||||||||||||||

ZELDA: The little hotel has such an appropriate name.

EDOUARD: *Reve Bleu. C'est àpropos. Vraiment.* How do you feel, Zelda?

ZELDA: Innocent, quite innocent. A lunatic is innocent until proven sane.

EDOUARD: *C'est lui, je crois.*

ZELDA: Meaning who?

245

EDOUARD: I believe it is your husband.

ZELDA: Oh. My very late husband. Is he pacing the garden?

EDOUARD: *Non. Il est assis.*

ZELDA: When you forget me, you speak in French. Where is he seated?

EDOUARD: *Sur la*—excuse me, on the bench.

ZELDA: How like him, how terribly like him, patiently seated outside while his wife and heroine of his fiction betrays him upstairs.

EDOUARD: I made sure that no one would be admitted. I heard loud voices downstairs—while you were crying out so wildly during your—

ZELDA: Creating a drunken disturbance was he? Sometimes I think his whole life has been a drunken disturbance, except—

EDOUARD: I believe he suspects. I think he knows. And the American husband takes a slight infidelity on the part of his wife very seriously, it appears, from the look on his face.

ZELDA: Slight, did you say? A slight infidelity, was it? Scott and I always made love in silence. Tonight was the one time that I cried out wildly. But, oh, how quiet you were: strong, enormously, and assured, completely, but not—not impassioned. Of course, your adventures of this kind are many and probably varied—mine, this once. . . . And I think never again . . .

EDOUARD: I think he knows but he cannot be certain until we leave the hotel, if he continues to wait that long on the bench.

246

ZELDA: He must fly back to the Coast where he has a new love of his own.

EDOUARD: Shhh.

ZELDA: The champagne is still cool as the counterfeit moon, and I am cold without you. Return. Come back to the bed. We haven't slept together, only made love. These are words. Words are the love acts of writers. Don't turn. I love your back. It's sculptured by Praxiteles and even in the moon wash, it's copper gleaming. Except for the groin which is dark with imagination . . .

EDOUARD: You found me unusually quiet?

ZELDA: No, no, he is quiet, too. Even his work is never loud with passion. It is controlled—desperately. Very beautifully, often . . . sometimes classic . . .

EDOUARD: I had to be controlled, and I had to be quiet. He may have recognized your cries.

ZELDA: How could he, having never heard them before? I am out of bed; I am on my feet, approaching you. . . . No, don't turn. I want to flatten my body against your back.

EDOUARD: *Pas si fort, la voix.*

ZELDA: But if he knows, he knows. Throw the shutters open and cry out, "I have taken your wife!"

EDOUARD: Just be quiet, and he will have no proof.

ZELDA [*shouting through the shutters*]: The flyer has taken me from you! You do not respond, Edouard.

EDOUARD: Response is for the living. And passion, too.

ZELDA: I felt even your memory with passion.

EDOUARD: I am an aviator, you know, and for those of my calling which is flight in the sky—that is true passion and it will always take me away.

ZELDA: I know. For better or worse. I know that I must resume the part created for me. Mrs. F. Scott Fitzgerald. Without that part, would I have ever been known, except as a woman who cried out wildly in the arms of a man married to the sky? Did I love Scott? Belonging to, is it love? *Ça depend.* If he makes of me a monument with his carefully arranged words, is that my life, my recompense for madness? There is none. Have you nothing to leave me when you've flown? In terror of this beautiful indiscretion between us?

EDOUARD: I have this photograph.

[*She takes it. There is a pause.*]

ZELDA: All photographs are a poor likeness and so are paintings; they don't have the warmth of the living flesh so loved, nor even the warmth of the memory of it. You want to go. Leaving a poor photograph of you. Photographs contain no likeness of heads gold as Christmas coins, or bronze hands cupping the breast, cupping the groin and the thighs, as if to engrave remembrance after madness and death.

EDOUARD: I think it may be possible to dissolve, to leave unnoticed. Strange things are occurring tonight. There's a magic about it. I see it in the sky, I hear it in the wind. [*A birdcall is heard.*] *Un rossignol.* [*He lifts his face to the sky.*] *Oui, je reviens!*

248

ZELDA: I know what you said, you said that you were returning; you said it to the sky and the bird, not to me.

[*Dance music of the twenties fades in.*]

EDOUARD: Music—the party's started.

ZELDA: Here? At the hotel *Reve Bleu?*

EDOUARD: At the Murphy's dance. We're expected. *Non—non!* —Child of Alabama . . . we must arrive on time to avoid suspicion.

ZELDA [*dressing rapidly*]: Into my party dress, and you—

EDOUARD: Into my dress uniform. What a lovely dress for the party.

ZELDA: A whisper of cerise chiffon. And under? Nothing! Remember? We danced at the edge of the light and we danced as if lovemaking. . . . You know I expected our affair to continue, no matter what it might cost.

EDOUARD: Could I have saved you, Zelda? We must arrive separately so I'll leave first.

ZELDA: *Attends, un moment de plus!* —Why they've removed our room! Our little hotel!

EDOUARD: A dream dissolves that way.

ZELDA: But it wasn't a dream. It happened.

EDOUARD: Once, yes. But now? —Don't claw my shoulders! I'd have to explain it in the barracks tonight.

[*They exit to the rear. There is a medley of indistinct voices, animated and gay, voices of people gathering for a party. The asylum lawn is lighted again, strewn with lanterns, and party guests in evening dress are seen dancing. Edouard enters from the rear of the stage and makes his way through the dancing couples. He moves downstage near the rocks. Zelda enters seconds later from the rear and wanders between the rocks and the downstage end of the bench, making her way through the party guests, following Edouard.*]

ZELDA [*to Edouard*]: Why—hello! —It's so long since I've seen you that I thought you were gone for good, but you've dropped by for the Murphy's party?

EDOUARD: No, not really for that. I have only dropped by to thank you for an unearthly adventure and to wish you—no regrets. How lovely you are in that *robe-de-soir* with the—ruby necklace . . .

ZELDA: I have no rubies. Wives of writers, even eminent writers, well-paid by the *Saturday Evening Post*—are not decked out with many precious stones; no, these were loaned me by Sara Murphy for this—bizarre occasion. Some people were so kind, and afterwards it's the kindness you remember, the rest is trivia, dissolved, dropped away . . .

EDOUARD: How lovely you are in that—

ZELDA: You said that before.

EDOUARD: Have you no photograph for *me*?

ZELDA: You want it back? The one of you that you gave me?

EDOUARD: I meant one of you, dear savage.

250

ZELDA: I would have to inscribe it and I'm afraid the inscription would be embarrassingly candid for a gentleman-flyer so attached to convention.

EDOUARD: I would not expose it to anyone but myself in private at night.

ZELDA: Privacy? In a barracks? —I am going to return your photograph to you. I am careless with things. I would be likely to leave it on my bedside table, that's how careless I am with Caesar's things. Here. Take it back, I don't need it. Don't want it. Photographs are a *petit souvenir* but not a good likeness at all. They can't penetrate the flesh, they have no heart, no fury, no explosion of molten—I was about to say fire, oh, God, about to say to you fire, that element you crashed in! Didn't you, later on, love?

[*Edouard gently disengages himself from Zelda's hands.*]

EDOUARD: —No, I—

ZELDA: I was certain that eventually you and that plane, in which you performed aerial acrobatics over the red-tiled roof of the Villa Marie, would crash in fire.

EDOUARD: I must disappoint you. Nothing like that happened to me at all.

ZELDA: Then what did happen to you? After you left me that summer?

EDOUARD: Well, gradually, as such things occur to most living creatures, Zelda, I—*grew old* . . .

ZELDA: No, not to you, that is not permitted! *C'est défendu! C'est impossible pour toi!*

251

EDOUARD: You're too romantic. I did grow old—weighted down with honors. *Grand-croix de la Légion d'honneur, Croix de guerre*, and finally—*Grand-croix au Mérite de l'ordre de Malte* . . .

ZELDA: So many impressive honors! I never knew. My congratulations if not too long delayed?

EDOUARD: I'm afraid that that sort of thing—public esteem, orders of merit—are what we must live for.

ZELDA: The only respected alternative to descent in flame.

EDOUARD: Little Alabama, your head's still full of "huge, cloudy symbols of high romance." They—dissolve, too. —Hold onto your benefits, Zelda.

ZELDA: Such as what? I'm glad I was spared the sight of your gentle decline into age. . . . I'm sure you managed it with as much grace as could be hoped for. Now say something gallant to *me*.

EDOUARD: You were—you are—radiant with beauty.

ZELDA: Tonight at that trick of a hotel called *Reve Bleu*, I thought I was holding your body against me inseparably close, so tight that I felt the blades of your bones carved to mine. You were bronze gold; you smelled of the sand and the sun (on a bed cooled by a Mediterranean moon). Yes, I felt you underneath starched linen. I think I frightened you a little. Is it bad of a woman, I mean a well-bred Southern lady, not a professional *putain*, to be sensual?

EDOUARD: No, but—

ZELDA: I think Scott feels it is; he thinks a woman's love should

252

be delicate as a fairy-tale romance. I don't think he's ever looked deeply enough into my eyes. If he did I wouldn't serve so well as the heroine of his fiction. But you're an aviator; you dare the sky. But I think even you are a little frightened of—

EDOUARD: Of such intensity, yes. A Frenchman has a male conceit that makes him prefer to be dominant in love. Zelda, I must go back to quarters at Fréjus, now.

ZELDA: Away to grow old and weighted down with honors, *Croix de*—everything but—*Calvary's Christ?*

EDOUARD: We must hold our benefits, Zelda, make much of them, a life.

ZELDA: Of what? For me? A flame burning nothing? Not even casting a shadow? A match for a cigarette does better than that. Look. Edouard? I'll ask Scott for my freedom if you'll have me!

EDOUARD: Careful, careful, hold on to what's secure.

ZELDA: I'd be quite willing to perform the act of love with you at the height of a cloudless noon, on top of the *Arc de triomphe*, enormously magnified for all of Paris, all the *world* to see.

EDOUARD: That sketch of a room with shutters served us better.

ZELDA [*with a touch of bitterness, now*]: How dearly you do value discretion! *Is it worth it?* You're looking around, you're looking this way and that way! [*She is approaching a kind of fury at his concern for what she regards as inconsequential values.*] *Is there a woman with binoculars in the bushes?* Is the *secret* called *truth* being overheard by someone or everyone that's hostile to it? My benefits, are they *discretions*, are they deceptions?

253

EDOUARD: Zelda, please, we mustn't create a *scandale*.

ZELDA: I think you mean, "*Don't live!*" —Well—I didn't want to when you'd gone. And I think you ought to know this because someday you may wear it on your dress uniform with your other decorations. After you'd gone back to the sky, I did this in honor of my love for you—I swallowed all the contents of a bottle of narcotics!

EDOUARD: Zelda! Hush!

ZELDA: And Sara Murphy walked me up and down the bedroom to keep me from falling asleep for always, alll-wayyys!

[*The passion of her cry makes Edouard clap a hand to her mouth. She twists violently for a moment; then her fury passed, she leans against his shoulder.*]

EDOUARD: *Pourquoi?* Why did you?

ZELDA: The only message I ever thought I had was four pirouettes and a *fouetté*, and—it turned out to be about as cryptic as a Chinese laundry ticket . . . but the will to cry out remains. The orchestra's playing a tango. Please, please—take me to the dance floor?

[*Zelda leads Edouard toward the music; they exit to the rear as Scott enters from the asylum doors—as he appeared much younger—and rushes onto the lawn. He gasps, covers his face, and sways.*]

MURPHY: Has he seen them together, Zelda and the flyer?

SCOTT: My God, Gilbert Seldes just called out to me from his balcony next to ours.

254

MURPHY: Called out what?

SCOTT [*in a choked voice*]: That Joseph Conrad just died.

MURPHY [*insufficiently moved or surprised*]: Really?

SCOTT [*mocking his unemotional tone*]: "Really?"

MRS. PATRICK CAMPBELL: My dear young man, to a party one brings the latest fashions and gossip, not obituaries.

SCOTT [*turning to her furiously*]: What you bring to a party is a fading reputation and a double chin.

MURPHY: Eventually we all bring that to parties, if we're still invited to parties. And being offensive to ladies doesn't increase your popularity at them. You've insulted a friend of ours: apologize to her, Scott.

MRS. PATRICK CAMPBELL: No, no, no, I haven't been insulted in much too long!

SCOTT: You amaze me, all of you amaze me! I bring you word that Joseph Conrad's just died and you go right on—what are you doing? Setting up a Maypole? If I had known that this was a children's party, I'd have brought Scotty. Set up a Maypole in honor of Conrad's death.

SARA: I must have missed something. What is it?

SCOTT: Gilbert Seldes—

SARA: Oh, Gilbert Seldes! Did we forget to ask him?

SCOTT: Sara, I said that Gilbert Seldes has just shouted to me

255

from the balcony next to ours that Conrad has just died. We've lost our only writer with a great tragic sense.

MRS. PATRICK CAMPBELL: Oh, that's why I found him so difficult to read!

SCOTT: May I—may I have a drink?

SARA: Was that your reply?

SCOTT: No, that's my need at the moment.

MURPHY: Scott, will you please hold it down tonight?

SCOTT: Hold down what? —The shock of being informed of Joseph Conrad's death?

SARA: Yes, of course, but please don't talk about death at a dance and please don't smash Venetian goblets or Baccarat crystal.

SCOTT: Okay, *touché*. —Is Zelda here?

[*Tango music begins.*]

SARA: Yes, and I asked her, "Where's Scott?" —She said, "Oh, working—working."

[*Zelda and Edouard appear dancing the tango. They move centerstage and then exit opposite.*]

—She's lost when you're lost in work, and it's difficult for her, you know.

SCOTT: I know. She's jealous of it. Well, she has her French aviator and swimming and nude sunbathing on the rocks, probably not alone.

SARA: It's just an innocent little flirtation, Scott.

SCOTT: There they are dancing together. Does it look innocent to you?

SARA: The tango isn't supposed to look like a Quaker square dance! That elegant new nigra we enticed from the Moulin Rouge is going to sing.

SCOTT: It's disgraceful. It's got to be stopped! Something's got to be done. Something's—Doctor—

[*Scott seems abruptly confused. The light changes. The party guests exit left and right and Dr. Zeller enters from the doors of the asylum. He approaches Scott.*]

Dr., uh—Bleumer . . .

DR. ZELLER: I am Dr. Zeller.

SCOTT: May I talk to Dr. Bleumer with whom I talked by phone from the Coast this morning?

DR. ZELLER: Mr. Fitzgerald, I think you must be confused.

SCOTT: I regard that as an impertinent remark. When I say that I talked to Dr. Bleumer this morning—

DR. ZELLER: It's not an unnatural confusion.

SCOTT: Dr. Bleumer assured me that Zelda's condition was much improved, that she was enjoying such a long and encouraging state of remission that it might soon be possible to release her.

257

DR. ZELLER: I've heard of Dr. Bleumer but—I'm sorry, he's never been on our staff. I say that it's a natural confusion because we have your wife's complete history, of course, and she's been a patient of sanitariums in Switzerland where Dr. Bleumer practiced.

SCOTT: God damn it, whoever talked to me, called me here from the Coast, did assure me I'd find her transformed, so I caught the first plane out without stopping for suitable clothes. And look down there! Do you recognize that overblown middle-aged woman down there?

DR. ZELLER: Mr. Fitzgerald, I would not have recognized you from the photograph on the dust jacket of *The Great Gatsby*.

SCOTT: Taken sixteen years ago, *Gatsby* was published sixteen years ago, before that pathetic creature—turned me to this middle-aged—robbed me of my—

DR. ZELLER: Youth, were you going to say youth?

SCOTT: —I don't say—obvious things. If you know my work you should know—I never write or say—obvious—things . . .
[*Dr. Zeller, having observed Scott's shaken condition, places a supportive arm about Scott's shoulder.*]

Take your arm off me! I don't like being touched by men!

DR. ZELLER: Mr. Fitzgerald, you were about to fall.

[*The word "fall" is repeated as if an echo was fading into the wind.*]

SCOTT: Yes—sometimes—nearly. —Zelda is with a young man down there, behaving with no regard for the public appearance of it.

DR. ZELLER: Oh, yes. —One of our young interns is with her.

SCOTT: She calls him by the name of a young French aviator with whom she had an affair in the south of France. She calls him, "Edouard—Edouard!"

DR. ZELLER: Yes, well—Mr. Fitzgerald, we've found it a privilege to treat your wife Zelda for her own sake, not just because she's your wife. It's lucky we've had this meeting. I like to read important writing, and I feel that your wife's novel *Save Me the Waltz*—I'm sure you won't mind my saying that there are passages in it that have a lyrical imagery that moves me, sometimes, more than your own.

SCOTT: My publishers and I edited that book! —Tried to make it coherent.

DR. ZELLER: I'm not deprecating your work; I wouldn't think of deprecating your work, but I stand by my belief that—

SCOTT: That none of my—desperately—well-ordered—understood writing is equal to the—

DR. ZELLER: More desperately—somehow controlled—in spite of the—

SCOTT: Madness . . .

DR. ZELLER: All right. —Mr. Fitzgerald, I think you suspect as well as I know that Zelda has sometimes struck a sort of fire in her work that—I'm sorry to say this to you, but I never quite found anything in yours, even yours, that was—equal to it . . .

[*Scott sways and uses the bench for support.*]

Sisters! —Take Mr. Fitzgerald inside; he should have a little sedation—a little something to calm him.

scott: No, no, angina again. I'll take a nitro tablet and just rest a bit.

[*The lights change. The scene returns to the party and music begins. The Hemingways are arriving. They enter from up-stage left and move centerstage behind the pavilion ribbons.*]

sara: Hadley! Hem!

murphy: What do you think, Ernest?

hemingway: About what, Gerry?

murphy: Zelda's infatuation with the handsome young French aviator? Innocent or not?

hemingway: Zelda's a crazy, Scott's a rummy, so speculation is useless and interest is wasted.

murphy: She's wandering among us as if completely alone.

hemingway: The solitude of the lunatic is never broken by no matter what number.

sara [*calling out*]: Zelda!

zelda [*calls softly*]: Edouard?

hemingway: Surrounded by thousands, she'd still be completely alone.

sara: Do you think that Scott's alcoholism is driving Zelda mad, or is Zelda's madness driving Scott to alcoholism?

HEMINGWAY: Scott has talent: delicate sensibilities for a male writer—

MURPHY: You do allow him a certain talent, Ernest?

HADLEY: Scott's pushing Ernest's work harder than he pushes his own.

[*Zelda has come through the ribbons of the pavilion and moves behind/between Murphy and Hemingway.*]

ZELDA: —Why? [*Zelda steps back and continues to move to the right before turning to the group.*] I said, "Why?" Didn't anyone hear me? Is it the attraction of Ernest's invulnerable, virile nature? Isn't that the implication, that Scott is magnetized, infatuated with Ernest's somewhat too carefully cultivated aura of the prizefight and the bullring and the man-to-man attitude acquired from Gertrude Stein?

HEMINGWAY: I'm acquainted with the other side of the coin. The excessive praise on the one side and the—envious other. I will go on: strong—oh, will accept convenient introductions but don't need them. My work will be hard and disciplined till it stops. Then—quit by choice—and rich . . . but—

HADLEY: Will I still be your girl?

HEMINGWAY: Be good.

HADLEY: You mean devoutly devoted to you, even when discarded for the next?

[*The elegant black entertainer has started singing a haunting song of the period, offstage left. He hums as he enters upstage of the pavilion and sings as he moves to the opening of the pavilion.*]

261

Who's that *exotic* young man singing my favorite song?

MURPHY: The latest sensation of the Moulin Rouge.

SARA: We flew him down for our party.

[*Zelda has seated herself on the rock, downstage. Sara watches her and then joins her on the rock. The singer sings throughout the following dialogue.*]

Zelda, are you looking for someone?

ZELDA: I was with Edouard. Where is he? Where's he gone?

SARA: Why, he just said good night, had to get back to—his barracks.

ZELDA: Edouard's left me *alone* here?

SARA: Zelda, you're not alone here.

ZELDA: I'm afraid so, Sara—I have no gift for friendship.

SARA: I meant Scott.

ZELDA: What about Scott?

SARA: He's arrived at the party.

ZELDA: Do you think Scott's arrival means that I'm not alone?

[*The song ends.*]

SARA: He's had a shock—someone's death.

[*The singer exits stage right.*]

I'm not sure who it was. [*She lowers her voice.*] Please be careful, Zelda!

ZELDA: Are you warning me not to make a remark on the tip of my tongue? —A remark that would violate the rules of the game? Well. I'm not sure that I could ever be intimidated by rules into sticking quite faithfully to them, especially when abandoned by—the young man with whom I've committed my first infidelity to Scott, a young man to whom I'd offered myself as mistress in preference to continuing my shadow of an existence as Mrs.— Eminent Author . . .

[*Scott abruptly confronts Zelda, shaking her.*]

SCOTT: Hush, hush! Privately. I knew! Here we're in public!

ZELDA: The young man declined. "Hold on to your benefits," he warned me, and then I think my heart died and I—went—mad.

[*Overlap.*]

[*Scott claps his hand over Zelda's mouth. She bites him.*]

SCOTT: Christ, you bit my hand. She bit my— Most men would have struck you down for what you've announced at this—

HEMINGWAY: Scott had better have a rabies shot.

[*Hemingway laughs loudly, coarsely drunk.*]

SARA: Ernest, don't! We must all try to smooth this over or the party will be spoiled, and it's such a lovely party, probably the last party this season.

[*The dance music begins again. The singer and an extremely thin woman with a lovely face, in a twenties evening gown, enter from upstage left and dance their way to downstage right.*]

MURPHY: Sara, darling, your wonderful black singer is dancing now.

MRS. PATRICK CAMPBELL: And what is that?

SARA: Did you say what or who?

MRS. PATRICK CAMPBELL: Whichever suits the case.

SARA: The singer or the dancer?

MRS. PATRICK CAMPBELL: They both appear to be dancing and in a highly provocative fashion.

SARA: He is the latest craze of Paris. Appears at the Moulin Rouge.

MRS. PATRICK CAMPBELL: And she? Of the scarcely tangible physique?

[*The dancers have made their exit.*]

SARA: Anorexia nervosa.

MRS. PATRICK CAMPBELL: Ah, you know everybody. —Would he do an apache dance with me? I've always wanted to do an apache dance, not a violent one, but—*adagio* . . .

SARA: He's very accommodating, but if I ask him, will you tell me if this is a true or apocryphal story about an adventure of yours in Hollywood?

MRS. PATRICK CAMPBELL: Very few stories about me are too outrageous to be true, or even outrageous enough. Which one is this?

SARA: That your poodle relieved his bowels in a cab and when you arrived at your destination, the cabdriver discovered what had occurred and made a scene about it in vulgar language. And you said, "It wasn't my dog—it was me."

MRS. PATRICK CAMPBELL: Even if it weren't true would I disown such an hilarious anecdote as that? And now, the apache dance?

[*There is a reprise of the song.*]

SARA: Soon as he's finished.

[*The singer begins to hum offstage.*]

MRS. PATRICK CAMPBELL: What a rare and lovely party this is: are all of us—you know what?

SARA: I'll have to check the guest list.

MRS. PATRICK CAMPBELL: Surely nothing comparable to it before. Why, there's Scott, again.

SARA: Whenever he approaches Ernest I alert the waiters to prepare for a disturbance.

MRS. PATRICK CAMPBELL: —Yes . . .

SARA: What?

MRS. PATRICK CAMPBELL: I just said, "Yes"—I've said wittier things but none so appropriate to an occasion of unlimited license.

265

Death is that: and after many outraged cries of "no," well, it's finally, "yes" and "yes" and "yes" . . .

[*The singer has entered from the right and now begins to sing "Sophisticated Lady" softly as he moves to the opening of the pavilion. Scott crosses to Hemingway.*]

SCOTT: What's that milk-choc'late fairy know about sophisticated ladies?

HEMINGWAY: Why don't you ask him, Scott, go right on up and ask him.

SCOTT: Think I'm scared to?

HEMINGWAY: You're not drunk enough yet.

SCOTT: Watch this! [*Scott approaches the singer.*] HEY! MILK-CHOC'LATE, WANTA ASK YOU SOMETHING! Which gender do you prefer?

[*The singer springs at Scott and flattens him with one blow; then he exits stage right. Sara goes to Murphy.*]

SARA: How did it happen?

MURPHY: Hemingway put him up to it.

SARA: We must never have them together at a party. [*She raises her voice.*] A buffet's being served in the pavilion, if anybody's interested in supper.

MRS. PATRICK CAMPBELL: Do I smell bouillabaisse?

[*The party drifts into the pavilion.*]

HEMINGWAY: Old bitches never die, just smell bouillabaisse.

[*Scott rises. Hemingway crosses to a waiter who is holding a tray of drinks.*]

The ladies and gentlemen seem to have left us alone together. For what? A *mano-mano?*

[*Scott looks bewildered.*]

Oh, but you're not acquainted with the idioms of the bullring.

SCOTT: I'm afraid they're mostly meaningless to me, Hem.

HEMINGWAY [*handing him a drink*]: *À chacun sa merde!* Careful don't spill.

SCOTT: A damaged ticker makes you shaky sometimes, even after a—nitro . . .

HEMINGWAY: I suppose it makes it difficult for you to sleep—always wondering if you'll ever wake up. But you were always a light sleeper. I remember that trip to Lyon to pick up your topless Renault from a repair shop—you had a sleepless night when the rain stopped us on the way back.

SCOTT: A bitch of a cold.

HEMINGWAY: You had a cold—oh, yes . . . [*He is restless, paces.*] Scott, I've always had a feeling that it's a mistake for writers to know each other. The competitive element in the normal male nature is especially prominent in the nature of writers.

SCOTT: With so much in common? As you and I?

267

HEMINGWAY: A profession—only.

SCOTT: Not sensibilities?

HEMINGWAY: Yours and mine are totally different, Scott.

SCOTT: And yet—it's said of us both that we always write of the same woman, you of Lady Brett Ashley in various guises and me of—

HEMINGWAY: Zelda and Zelda and more Zelda. As if you'd like to appropriate her identity and her—

SCOTT: And her?

HEMINGWAY: Sorry, Scott, but I almost said—gender. That wouldn't have been fair. It's often been observed that duality of gender can serve some writers well.

[*He approaches Scott. For a moment we see their true depth of pure feeling for each other. Hemingway is frightened of it, however.*]

—Yes, some—to create equally good male and—

SCOTT: You are fortunate in having such an inexhaustibly interesting and complex nature, Hem, that regardless of how often you portray yourself in a book—

HEMINGWAY: Don't be a bitch. Where's the resemblance between Colonel Cantwell of *Across the River and into the Trees* and, say, the wounded American deserter from the Italian army in *Farewell to Arms*?

SCOTT: I don't recall the Colonel but I've no doubt he's one of your many and always fascinating self-portraits.

HEMINGWAY: Fuck it! —You know as well as I know that every goddam character an honest writer creates is part of himself. Don't you? —Well, *don't* you?

SCOTT: We do have multiple selves as well as what you call dual genders. —Hem? Let's admit we're—

HEMINGWAY: What?

SCOTT: Friends, Hem—true and very deep friends. You brought up the trip to Lyon for the topless Renault, which was topless because Zelda hated tops on cars.

HEMINGWAY: In all weather?

SCOTT: Hem, you never understood Zelda, not as much as me.

HEMINGWAY: Not as much as *you* understood Zelda?

SCOTT: I didn't understand Zelda either, no, I know that, now, but I loved her.

HEMINGWAY: And hated her, enemy, lover, same same, as the Chinaman says.

SCOTT: You just hated her and blamed her for my drinking and there was a double reason for that, you know. You wanted to believe that I had only one great book in me, *Gatsby*, that Zelda and drinking would preclude the possibility of anything to equal *Gatsby*—after . . .

HEMINGWAY: Which you attribute to professional envy, Scott?

SCOTT: More to the fact that I saved *The Sun Also Rises* from starting with the entire past history of Lady Brett Ashley, a thing that would have—

269

HEMINGWAY: If my own critical faculty hadn't been capable of— there was Maxwell Perkins—

SCOTT: To whom I'd introduced you. But, Hem, admit this much. You could *not* admit, then that anybody gave you professional help.

HEMINGWAY: Don't admit the truth of anyone's—cherished— illusions. Oh, hell, believe whatever's a comfort to you, believe it, but don't ask me to confirm the imagined truth of it, I don't offer that kind of comfort.

SCOTT: Ernest, you've always been able to be kind as well as cruel. Why, that night when I was so sick in Lyon—

HEMINGWAY: Not Lyon, *after* Lyon, at Chalon-sur—

SCOTT: Wherever's—no matter. I was catching pneumonia. You cared for me with the tenderness of—

HEMINGWAY [*cutting in quickly*]: The night? —Scott? You had the skin of a girl, mouth of a girl, the soft eyes of a girl, you— you solicited attention. I gave it, yes, I found you touchingly vulnerable.

SCOTT: These attributes, if I did have them in—

HEMINGWAY: You did have them.

SCOTT: And they were—repellent to you?

HEMINGWAY: They were disturbing to me.

SCOTT: Why?

HEMINGWAY: I'd rather not examine the reason too closely. Wouldn't you? Rather not?

SCOTT: In privacy, under such special circumstances, why not, I don't see why not?

HEMINGWAY: You were so innocent, so guileless, Scott. Did you ever grow up? I don't mean older, but up. —Well? Can't you say?

SCOTT: I'm trying to recall a certain short story of yours. The title doesn't come back to me right now but the story does. An Italian officer has been removed from any contact with women for weeks or months in some snowbound Alpine encampment during the war, the First. He has a young orderly waiting on him, a boy with the sort of androgynous appeal that you said I had in wherever after Lyon. —At last he asks the boy if he's engaged. The boy says he is married. He says it blushing, avoiding the officer's eyes, and goes out quickly. The officer wonders—significantly—if the boy was lying about it.

HEMINGWAY: I've also written a story called "Sea Change" about a couple, young man and older young man, on a ship sailing to Europe and—at first the younger man is shocked, or pretends to be shocked, by the older one's—attentions at night. However the sea change occurs and by the end of the voyage, the protesting one is more than reconciled to his patron's attentions. Look, Scott, it's my profession to observe and interpret all kinds of human relations. That's what serious writers hire out to do. Maybe it's rough, this commitment, but we honor it with truth as we observe and interpret it. And some day, I'll certainly write about a man not me, or at all related to me. He'll be completely you, Scott. In it, aspects, embarrassing aspects of you, will be suggested clearly to the knowledgeable reader. You see, I can betray even my oldest close friend, the one most helpful in the beginning. That may have been at least partly the reason for which I executed myself not long after, first by attempting to walk into the propeller of a plane—that having failed, by blasting my exhausted brains out with an elephant gun. Yes, I may have pronounced on myself this violent death sentence to

271

expiate the betrayals I've strewn behind me in my solitary, all but totally solitary—

[*Pause. Hemingway turns from Scott and faces the audience with cold, hard pride.*]

There I stop it, this game. Would never appeal for sympathy with such a confession containing the word "solitary" which I never was. —*Was I?* [*Obviously he is not convinced of the matter.*] *WAS I?*

[*Scott faces him.*]

SCOTT: Ernest, you may regret that you asked for an answer to that. Do you want an answer to that?

HEMINGWAY: If you've got one to give me.

SCOTT: I suspect that you were lonelier than I and possibly you were even as lonely as Zelda.

[*They stare at each other.*]

HEMINGWAY: *Fuck it! Hadley, Hadley, call me, the game's gone soft, can't play it any longer!* [*Offstage, a woman's voice sings "Ma bionda."*]—That's Miss Mary whom you never knew, a good, loving friend, and a hunting, fishing companion—at the end. We sang that song together the night before I chose to blast my brains out for no reason but the good and sufficient reason that my work was finished, strong, hard work, all done—no reason for me to continue. . . . What do you make of that, Scott?

[*He hoarsely joins in Miss Mary's song as he crosses off, roughly brushing aside the delicate silk ribbons of the pavilion drop. Pause.*]

SCOTT: Zelda? —Zelda?

FADE OUT

SCENE TWO

We are back in the time and place of the play's beginnings. Shadows are long on the front lawn of Highland Hospital as sunset approaches. Scott is seated as at the end of the preceding scene, on the bench near the flaming bush.

Nuns flank the entrance. They slowly lift their arms so that their batwing sleeves mask Zelda's costume change. Scott rises unsteadily and looks incredulously about him at the spectral scene. Low clouds scudding over are projected on the "cyc." Shreds of vapor drift across the proscenium. There is a fragile and elegiac music of the sort that Prokofiev or Stravinsky might have composed. It fades out as the sisters slowly lower their masking sleeves from the entrance, disclosing Zelda as she appeared in the first scene of the play.

ZELDA [*to Sister One*]: Is he still waiting out there to say good-bye, as late and cold as this, in such unseasonable clothes?

[*Edouard appears behind her in the white jacket of the intern.*]

INTERN: Be kind. He's a gentleman and an artist.

ZELDA: Fatal combination.

INTERN: Now, yes: he died for attempting to exist as both. And so be kind to him, Zelda.

SCOTT [*calling*]: Zelda?

ZELDA: Of course I will be kind as possible to him.

INTERN: Offer him a sort of last sacrament. You know what I mean. "Drink this in remembrance of me whose blood was shed for thee to give thee—"

ZELDA: The Everlasting ticket that doesn't exist. The lies of Christ were such beautiful lies, especially on the night before crucifixion on The Place of the Skull.

273

INTERN: His disciples said that he rose again from the dead.

ZELDA: And ascended to the lawn of Highland Hospital.

SCOTT: Zelda?

ZELDA [*to the intern*]: I'll see you again before this occasion is over?

INTERN: Yes.

[*Zelda advances slowly toward Scott.*]

ZELDA: —I'm approaching him now, no son of God but a gentleman shadow of him. It's incredible how, against appalling odds, dear Scott achieved a Christly parallel through his honoring of long commitments, even now to me, a savage ghost in a bedraggled tutu, yes, it's a true and incredible thing.

SCOTT [*softly, as he falls back onto the bench*]: Incredible? —Yes.

[*She pauses briefly before him; then touches his shoulder and crosses to downstage center.*]

ZELDA [*her back to the feared bush*]: The incredible things are the only true things, Scott. Why do you have to go mad to make a discovery as simple as that? Who is fooling whom with this pretense that to exist is a credible thing? The mad are not so gullible. We're not taken in by such a transparent falsity, oh, no, what we know that you don't know— [*She is now facing the audience.*] Or don't dare admit that you know is that to exist is the original and greatest of incredible things. Between the first wail of an infant and the last gasp of the dying—it's all an arranged pattern of—submission to what's been prescribed for us unless we escape into madness or into acts of creation. . . . The latter option was denied me, Scott, by someone not a thousand miles from here. [*She faces Scott.*] Look at what was left me!

scott: I thought you'd gone in to dinner.

zelda: I won't be forced to dine at five o'clock, especially with a visitor still on the grounds. I have not forgotten all manners, after all . . .

[*She goes to the bench.*]

scott: Then sit down a while.

zelda: Help me turn the bench away from that flaming bush.

[*He rises and they turn the bench at a sharper angle. She then sits beside him, holding his hand, caressing his faded hair.*]

—As I grew older, Goofo, the losses accumulated in my heart, the disenchantments steadily increased. That's usual, yes? Simply the process of aging. —Adjustments had to be made to faiths that had faded as candles into daybreak. In their place, what? Sharp light cast on things that appalled me, that blew my mind out, Goofo. Then. —The wisdom, the sorrowful wisdom of acceptance. Wouldn't accept it. Romantics won't, you know. Liquor, madness, more or less the same thing. We're abandoned or we're put away, and if put away, why, then, fantasy runs riot, hallucinations bring back times lost. Loves you'd frightened away return in dreams. —A remission occurs. You fall out of a cloud to what's called real—a rock! Cold, barren. To be endured only briefly. —Goofo? The last time I was home with Mother in Montgomery I used to ride the trolley car to the end of the line and back again, going nowhere, just going. Someone asked me one time, "Why do you do that?" and I said, "Just for something to do." —Yes, I went back to the world of vision which was my only true home. I said to Mother, the last time I told her good-bye, "Don't worry about me. I'm not afraid to die." —Why were *you* afraid to? The sentence is imposed—there's no appeal, no reprieve!—Don't be so gutless about it.

scott: Zelda, haven't you something more comforting to offer me on this cold, windy hilltop than—worn-out recriminations?

[*She rises and picks up her coat.*]

ZELDA: I offer you my horse blanket, Scott. And in return for its comfort, I have to make a request, a last one, of you. —If there should be nine mounds of indistinguishable ash at the barred door up there, persuade them somehow to scatter all to the wind to be blown out to sea: that's the purification, *give me that!* God damn you, enemy, love, *give—me—that!*

[*He frees himself from her fierce hands and rises, breathing heavily.*]

Oh, dear you're agitated. Is it the prospect of writing a film for the Crawford? She's not Eleanora Duse nor even Bernhardt but she has her own territory that she'll fight hard to hold and she'll hold it a while. —I only mentioned her, Goofo, to show a bit of polite interest in things at the Garden of Allah, and look, you're all worked up—not good for a failing heart. Didn't you say you'd had frightening attacks of—?

SCOTT: You must have—misunderstood me.

ZELDA: Oh. Good. I'm relieved.

SCOTT: This *is* a windy hilltop.

ZELDA: Serious conversation's wasted, it's blown away. So let's return to the cheerful little idiocies that we began with.

SCOTT: They were blown away, too.

ZELDA: You're shivering, you're still breathing too rapidly over the Crawford assignment.

[*She attempts to draw the shapeless coat about him; he hurls it away again. The action dizzies him; he clutches hold of the bench.*]

Why, Scott! You're as dizzy as I was when I attempted the *pizzicato*! Let's—stretch out on the grass like we used to after picnics—*au bord de l'Oise* . . .

[*He shakes his head helplessly.*]

Breathe quietly, rest. [*She takes hold of his wrist.*] —Where's your pulse? I can't feel your pulse.

SCOTT: Never mind . . .

ZELDA: Somebody has to point out to you these little physical symptoms, not to alarm you but—

SCOTT [*exploding involuntarily*]: You've pointed out to me nothing I haven't observed myself. —The mistake of our ever having met! —The monumental error of the effort to channel our lives together in an institution called marriage. Tragic for us both. Result—slag heap of a—dream . . .

ZELDA: Poor Scott.

SCOTT: Meaning "poor son of a bitch."

ZELDA: What a way to speak of your irreproachably proper mother!

SCOTT: CUT!

ZELDA: What?

SCOTT: That's what a film director shouts when a scene is finished . . .

ZELDA: Finished, is it? The visitor's bell has rung and we can withdraw to our separate worlds now?

277

[*She throws back her head and shouts "CUT!" He attempts to rise from the bench, gasps, and falls back onto it. The intern advances rapidly to Zelda and takes hold of her hand.*]

INTERN: What is it, Zelda? Why'd you shout like that?

ZELDA: This gentleman on the bench was once my husband and I was once his wife, sort of a storybook marriage, legendary. Yes, well, legends fade. It seems he's finally faced that. He just now admitted that despite its ideal, relentlessly public appearance, it had been, I quote him, a monumental error, and that it had been a mistake for us ever to have met. Something's been accomplished: a recognition—painful, but good therapy's often painful.

SCOTT: Let go of her hand. She isn't yours.

ZELDA: Oh, yes, I was his once. You didn't hear the confession, or did you doubt the truth of it?

SCOTT [*trembling*]: I said let go of her hand. Remember you're just employed here.

INTERN: Employed to care for patients.

ZELDA: Scott used to be quicker at games.

SCOTT: LET GO OF HER HAND, I SAID! God damn it, let her hand go, or I'll have you discharged.

ZELDA: —Neither of us is cruel but we're hurting each other unbearably. Can't you stop it?

INTERN: Visiting hours are nearly over. [*He rises and starts away.*]

SCOTT: Hold on a moment more! Maybe *you* can explain to

her the advantage she's had in being psychotic, since it seems you've acquired, by means I won't inquire into—

ZELDA: Advise him to remain—

INTERN: Let him speak it out.

ZELDA: Within the safe, sunny woodlands called Holly, not to venture into—

SCOTT: Oh, I've known darker places, I've been places where it's always—

ZELDA: Three o'clock in the morning? Dark night of the soul again?

SCOTT: Followed you but went further—without escort or guide or protector . . .

ZELDA: Oh, not caught and led into and locked! For incineration?

INTERN: Zelda!

[*Overlap.*]

[*Scott clenches his fists impotently.*]

SCOTT: The name of this woman—

ZELDA: Once known as a lady.

SCOTT: Is still Mrs. F. Scott Fitzgerald.

ZELDA: As distinguished from Lily Sheil? —As acceptable insult, leaves me quite unabashed.

INTERN: Mr. Fitzgerald, it's permissible to leave before visiting hours are over, and the—

279

ZELDA: Iron gates are closed . . .

INTERN: Zelda? [*He extends his hand to her.*]

ZELDA: How sweet of Scott to have flown such a long way to see me. A delightful surprise to find myself still remembered by an old beau that I thought must have filed me away long ago among his—fantasies discarded . . .

SISTERS [*at the gate*]: Visiting hours are over. The gates are about to be closed.

SCOTT: Allow me a moment or two with my wife alone.

INTERN: A moment only. Your visit has disturbed her, Mr. Fitzgerald. [*He enters the asylum.*]

ZELDA [*following intern*]: Such a fiery sunset . . .

[*Scott stumbles toward her.*]

What are you following me for?

SCOTT: Taking you to the gates.

ZELDA: The gates are iron, they won't admit you or ever release me again. [*She enters; the gates close.*] I'm not your book! Anymore! *I can't be your book anymore! Write yourself a new book!*

SCOTT [*reaching desperately through the bars*]: The ring, please take it, the covenant with the past— [*She disappears.*] —still always present, Zelda!

[*A wind seems to sweep him back as the stage dims slowly. Mist drifts in. Scott turns downstage; his haunted eyes ask a silent question which he must know cannot be answered.*]

THE END

THE RED DEVIL BATTERY SIGN

||||||||||||||||||||||||||||||||||||||||||||||||||||||||||||||||||||||||||||||||||||||||||||||||||||||||||||||||||||||||||||||||||||||||||||||||||||||||||||||||||||||||||

TO KEITH BAXTER

The City's fiery parcels all undone
— Hart Crane, "To Brooklyn Bridge"

||||||||||||||||||||||||||||||||||||||||||||||||||||||||||||||||||||||||||||||||||||||||||||||||||||||||||||||||||||||||||||||||||||||||||||||||||||

The Red Devil Battery Sign was presented by Gene Persson for Ruby Productions Limited at the Round House, London, on June 8, 1977, and at the Phoenix Theatre, London, on July 7, 1977. It was directed by Keith Baxter and David Leland; it was designed by Bob Ringwood and Kate Owen; lighting and projections were by David Hersey; and original music was by Mario Ramos. The cast, in order of appearance, was as follows:

WOLF	KEN SHORTER
GRIFFIN	MICHAEL ENSIGN
CHARLIE	GARRY MCDERMOTT
FIRST DRUNK	GLENN WILLIAMS
SECOND DRUNK	DON STAITON
HOTEL GUEST	SIMON WALSH
HOOKER	DEBORAH BENZIMRA
WOMAN DOWNTOWN	ESTELLE KOHLER
MARIACHIS	MARIO RAMOS, ALEJANDRO VASQUEZ, ALFONSO SALAZAR,
CREWCUT	PETER LUKAS
KING	KEITH BAXTER
PERLA	MARIA BRITNEVA
McCABE	PIERCE BROSNAN
LA NIÑA	NITZA SAUL
JUDGE COLLISTER	ROBERT HENDERSON
FIRST CONVENTIONEER	SIMON WALSH
SECOND CONVENTIONEER	GLENN WILLIAMS
DRUMMER	RAAD RAWI
PHARMACIST	ROBERT HENDERSON
WASTELAND BOYS	TONY GARNER, TONY LONDON, KELVIN OMARD, ELVIS PAYNE, MARIO RENZULLO, DON STAITON, SIMON WALSH

This edition of *The Red Devil Battery Sign* is based on a 1979 revision, by the author, of the text used for the London production. The play now includes the following characters (in order of appearance):

GRIFFIN
HOOKER
DRUNK
WOMAN DOWNTOWN
CHARLIE
KING
THREE MARIACHIS
JULIO (the oldest Mariachi)
CREWCUT
PERLA
LA NIÑA
McCABE
FIRST CONVENTIONEER
SECOND CONVENTIONEER
DRUMMER
OLD MAN (the Pharmacist)
CAB DRIVER (offstage)
WOLF
BOY
OTHER WASTELAND BOYS

ACT ONE

‖‖‖

SCENE ONE

‖‖‖

The cocktail lounge of the Yellow Rose Hotel in downtown Dallas. At curtain-rise, only the bar is hotly lighted. A small group of Mariachis play softly. A Drunk is talking to Charlie, the barman. At a slight distance, the hotel manager, Mr. Griffin, is looking on with disapproval. A restless Hooker crosses to a bar stool adjoining the Drunk's.

‖‖‖

GRIFFIN: I'm sorry, Miss, but unescorted ladies aren't allowed at the bar.

HOOKER [*in a broad Texas drawl*]: What makes you think I'm unescawted, huh? [*She nudges the Drunk, who pivots to inspect her, and speaks to him.*] He calls me not escawted. [*She digs an elbow lower into the Drunk's paunch.*]

DRUNK: This young lady's escawted, personally by me.

[*The Woman Downtown enters the upstage perimeter of the lighted area. She is tall, with a pale, exquisitely molded face: an immediately striking elegance of presence. She has a light coat (loose-woven cloth of gold) thrown over her dress. She stands by a rear table and surveys the lounge as if she suspected some menacing element in it.*]

GRIFFIN [*to Drunk*]: Are you registered *here*?

DRUNK: Here's my room-key, here.

[*The Drunk digs into a pants' pocket and empties an avalanche of coins and crumpled bills on the floor.*]

285

HOOKER: Aw!

[*She stoops immediately to collect the bills, returning some to the Drunk and slipping others into her bag. The Woman Downtown laughs wryly, softly. She removes the light coat and reveals a stunning iridescent Oriental sheath with a delicate dragon design on it.*]

DRUNK: And here's my bus'ness card. See what firm I'm with? To check out this hotel as possible headquarters for our next month convention?

GRIFFIN [*abruptly, very impressed*]: —Thank you, sir. Charlie, offer this young couple drinks on the house, excuse me. [*He crosses to the Woman Downtown. A blond Crewcut enters.*] Well! Good evening, Ma'am.

WOMAN DOWNTOWN [*icily*]: Good evening, Mr.—

GRIFFIN: Griffin. —I was surprised to see you down here.

WOMAN DOWNTOWN: Why? What surprised you about it?

GRIFFIN: When you were checked in here by Judge Collister.

WOMAN DOWNTOWN: When I checked in was when?

GRIFFIN: I'd have to check the books to give you the exact night—

WOMAN DOWNTOWN: The approximate night, a week ago, two weeks, since the last ice age?

GRIFFIN: What I do remember clearly right now is that Judge Collister said that you were to have complete anonymity here and complete rest and seclusion.

WOMAN DOWNTOWN: Oh, rest and seclusion I've had a massive dose of. Only morning visits from a doctor who *said* he'd been told to visit me by the *Judge*.

GRIFFIN [*repeatedly, nervously*]: Yes. Fine. I see. Hmmm.

WOMAN DOWNTOWN [*overlapping*]: —At first the injections were agreeably sedative, then not so agreeably, then not agreeably at all since I found myself falling to the floor when I got out of bed. [*She gets progressively louder.*] Then I stopped letting him in, locked and bolted the door against him when he knocked.

GRIFFIN: You're being overheard by strangers at the bar. You don't want attention in the public rooms. You see, I regard your anonymity here more highly than you, Ma'am. With such a distinguished person we—

WOMAN DOWNTOWN: You give yourself away.

GRIFFIN: I haven't spoken your name.

WOMAN DOWNTOWN: You refer to me as "a distinguished person."

GRIFFIN: There's something so apparent about you.

WOMAN DOWNTOWN [*cutting through contemptuously*]: I came in here covered from *head* to *foot* by the Judge's car-blanket and *said* and *did* nothing . . . stayed speechless in a wheelchair while the Judge said that I must have anonymity here and paid you exceptionally well for providing it for me. But since you've penetrated that anonymity—I am ready to check out, my luggage is packed. I want to get word to my guardian, Judge Collister, to come here for me at once. I've made continual efforts to reach the Judge by phone. For some reason I'm not able to make outside calls from my suite; the calls are not completed. I've complained to the operator; still they're not *completed*.

GRIFFIN: You are raising your voice, Ma'am. I don't think you realize that your face is recognizable—

WOMAN DOWNTOWN [*putting on dark glasses*]: There he is, the blond Crewcut. *He* certainly *recognizes* me! Whenever I enter the corridor, he starts to follow a couple of paces behind me, and I retreat to my rest and seclusion.

GRIFFIN: That young man is our house detective, Ma'am.

WOMAN DOWNTOWN: Oh, your house dick. What is he trailing me for, of what does he *suspect* me? Call him over, tell him I'd like to *know*.

GRIFFIN: He has to stay by the door. Undesirables try to enter, you know. My wife had a sister who spent a few months at Paradise Meadows Nursing Home. She had some treatments there called electric shock.

WOMAN DOWNTOWN: Shock, yes, electric.

GRIFFIN: The treatments were highly effective in the case I mentioned—

WOMAN DOWNTOWN: Brainwashed. . . . Well, I am not. My foster father the Judge maneuvered my escape from Paradise Meadows after five days of their marvelous treatment.

GRIFFIN: Now, as to the Judge, you would naturally be unable to call him at his residence or office. —Would you allow me to order you a drink? Brandy? Charlie, the lady would like some brandy.

WOMAN DOWNTOWN: No she would *not*. A glass of champagne *laced* with a little brandy; I need to keep a clear head in this atmosphere of intrigue here. —What about Judge Collister?

GRIFFIN: Just have your drink first, before we—hmmm . . .

[*Charlie serves the drink; she drains it immediately.*]

WOMAN DOWNTOWN: I said laced with, not loaded. Now what have you to tell me?

GRIFFIN: That grand old man has been on the critical list at the New Medical Center since later on the night he delivered you here, Ma'am.

WOMAN DOWNTOWN: Christ, on the—critical—which night? —He brought me here—and you haven't informed me? I want a car, a rental limousine. [*She has caught hold of his jacket.*]

GRIFFIN: If you'll let go of my jacket, I will call the limousine service. [*He glances away, picks up the bar phone, glancing back at her, nodding, smiling—a grimace.*] Car for the lady at the bar.

WOMAN DOWNTOWN: Perhaps you'd like the button I tore off your jacket.

[*Griffin leaves. The subdued talk among the men at the bar is brought up.*]

DRUNK: Any goddam kid won't register for draft is a traitor to—

CHARLIE: Yestuhday, f'rinstance, Nation'l Guard tried to round up those kids that live in the Hollow, west a city, register 'em. I tell yuh they couldn't get near 'em, blown up two squad cars with bottles of nitro!

DRUNK: Savages in city. Oughta go in there with flame throwers, burn 'em outa their dug-outs like we done gooks in 'Nam.

WOMAN DOWNTOWN: Hear! Hear! It's a patriotic duty for you middle-aged gentlemen over draft age! DO IT! You're not too old to discharge a missile, are you, at— Sorry, did I speak? I'm not supposed to speak!

DRUNK: You spoke distinctly, baby. I'd like t' discharge a missile into . . . [*He completes the lewd remark behind his hand.*]

WOMAN DOWNTOWN [*laughing mockingly*]: That *would* be a little beyond your capacity just now, and if lightning does not strike once, it cannot strike twice.

CHARLIE [*in response to a whisper*]: Bananas.

DRUNK: Aw? Could use a chiquita banana and I don't mean *mañana*. [*He stumbles toward the Woman Downtown.*]

WOMAN DOWNTOWN: Your vision must be blurred. Your wife has retired to the ladies' loo.

DRUNK: That hooker?

WOMAN DOWNTOWN: What a shocking term to use for your *wife.*

DRUNK: Me? Married to a hooker?

WOMAN DOWNTOWN: Some gentlemen do marry above their station.

DRUNK: Nah me, Babe. Here, take this key while I finish my drink. Go up to my room and I promise I won't disappoint yuh!

WOMAN DOWNTOWN: —*Hands off!* —I don't want that, I never did want that, all that I ever wanted was—

[*Her face and voice soften. She makes a vague gesture in space. King Del Rey appears. Originally called Rey, this Texan born on the border and with some Spanish-Indian blood in him, later called himself by the English word for "Rey." He has a natural kingliness—an air of authority—about him, with just a hint of that bravado that masks an anxiety that the authority may slip from him. This hint appears only at moments. Now as he stands at stage left, having just entered the revolving door of the "club" lounge, he exaggerates the bravado, the air of command, to something almost macho.*]

MARIACHIS: *¡Hola, King! ¡Hola, amigo!*

[*The band plays "El Rey." There have been jocular greetings in Spanish from the musicians, which King has returned.*]

KING: *Es una noche caliente, ¿eh?*

[*The Woman Downtown appears diverted from her own situation by King's entrance.*]

WOMAN DOWNTOWN: —*Sí, señor, es una noche caliente.*

KING [*impressed by her beauty and style*]: The lady speaks some Spanish?

WOMAN DOWNTOWN: Oh, yes, the lady is a linguist, speaks many tongues.

DRUNK [*at the bar*]: Yeh, that lady's got a tongue in her mouth runnin' outa control.

KING [*to the Drunk*]: You are on my bar stool. Get off it before you're knocked off it.

291

[*The Drunk stares at King a moment, then shrugs and staggers from the bar.*]

DRUNK: Where's a—man's room? [*He exits.*]

WOMAN DOWNTOWN [*to King*]: Ah, now, seats at the bar, two adjoining. Will you be my escort? An unescorted lady is not allowed at the bar.

KING: *Sí. Con mucho gusto.* Sit down, please. Charlie's opened my beer. Charlie, give the lady a drink.

WOMAN DOWNTOWN: Thank you, but my "special" drink was already provided. Strong drinks aren't good in hot weather, overheat you internally. Even in a cool room, I'm conscious of heat outside. People bring it in the room with them, like—little moons of perspiration under the armpits.

KING [*embarrassed*]: I took a shower and put on clean white shirt just before I come downtown, but the shirt's already stickin' to me. I ain't crowdin' you, am I?

WOMAN DOWNTOWN: Oh, no. Am I crowding you? I find it hard to keep a completely vertical position when so tired . . . [*She is leaning against his shoulder; then she removes an atomizer from her evening bag.*] This is a cooling little imported fragrance, *Vol de Nuit,* translates to Night Flight. Everything translates to something when your head's full of tongues, you know.

CHARLIE: Sure you don't want some rest?

WOMAN DOWNTOWN: I am resting comfortably, but I must keep an eye out for that rental limousine.

CHARLIE: How is Pearla, King?

KING: Charlie, it's pronounced "Perla," like in a pear, not "Pearla" like in a pearl.

[*The four Mariachis complete a song. The oldest one calls out to King.*]

JULIO: Come up and do a solo, King.

KING: Is that a test you give me? Okay, challenge—accepted!

[*He rises to join them. The Woman Downtown clutches his arm.*]

WOMAN DOWNTOWN [*in an urgent whisper, glancing fearfully at Crewcut, who has moved by the door*]: Don't leave me, please! Stay with me!

KING: I do a song for you, special! Ha! First performance since San Antone! And without La Niña?

MARIACHI: ¿La Niña *está en* Chicago?

KING: You bet La Niña is burning up Chicago! Is at a spot called The Pump Room—

WOMAN DOWNTOWN [*rising*]: Please! Please! Later! Sing later!

KING [*not understanding her agitation*]: But I sing for you. ¡Hombres, para la señorita! [*He turns to the Woman Downtown.*] ¿Qué canción le gustaría escuchar, señorita? What song you like, lady?

WOMAN DOWNTOWN: Any, any will do!

KING: *Volver.*

[The Mariachis begin a ranchero: sensual rhythm. King sings solo, his look remaining on the Woman Downtown.]

CREWCUT: Car for the lady at the bar!

WOMAN DOWNTOWN *[with a desperate, involuntary cry]*: My car!

[She rushes dizzily toward the exit and stumbles. King rushes to help her to her feet.]

Thanks, see you don't leave!

[King remains, bewildered, by the door. Crewcut and Charlie may exchange significant glances or signs. After a few loud moments, she rushes wildly back in.]

A cab, same cab, same monster grinning at me, I swear! *I demand—*

[She collapses to her knees. Crewcut stares imperturbably ahead. Charlie lifts the bar phone. King rushes to lift the Woman Downtown.]

KING *[softly]*: What's the trouble, tell me, what's the trouble!

[She sobs, unable to speak. King turns to Charlie.]

She stay in hotel?

CHARLIE: Don't get involved—I call the doctor?

WOMAN DOWNTOWN: Noooo!

KING: Whatcha mean? "Not involved," huh?

CHARLIE: She's mental: under surveillance.

[*Griffin has entered from the lounge.*]

KING: Lady? Lady?

WOMAN DOWNTOWN [*to King*]: Please, help me upstairs, Penthouse B! —I need seclusion and rest . . .

[*King supports her gently offstage.*]

GRIFFIN [*to Crewcut*]: Follow! [*To the Mariachis.*] Music, music!

[*Crewcut follows rapidly upstage and off. The Mariachis resume.*]

THE LOUNGE IS DIMMED OUT

SCENE TWO

<hr>

The set is a sketchy evocation of the bedroom of Penthouse B, parlor entrance at left.

<hr>

WOMAN DOWNTOWN [*to King, still in the parlor*]: I suppose you think I'd gone crazy down there, isn't that what you think?

[*King appears in the doorway; he regards her with a slightly apprehensive reserve.*]

Lock that hall door, bolt it, I think they called their "doctor"! —That elevator hasn't gone down, I haven't heard the elevator door close! Did you notice the young man with close-cropped hair who came all the way up here, carefully ignoring my pretense of being unable to stand unsupported? Would you, while I get some glasses out of the little ice-chest, slip quietly into the corridor and see if he's hanging around still.

KING: Aw, him, he asked my name as we come up here.

WOMAN DOWNTOWN: Didn't give it, did you?

KING: Naw, naw, if a guy has a friendly attitude and he asked my name or he's got some reason to ask like I was witness to a car crash, I'll give my name, but—

WOMAN DOWNTOWN: Quick, please check the corridor for Crewcut who dogs my steps, every step I take outside this Penthouse B! Quickly, quietly. Don't be alarmed, I'm not demented.

[*King sets the chair behind her.*]

KING: *Estate, estate quieta—un momento.*

[*He exits. She waits tensely till he returns.*]

Tienes razón.

WOMAN DOWNTOWN: Out there, was he?

KING: Leanin' against wall, scribbling in a notebook. He snapped it shut when he seen me, give me a hard look and got in the elevator.

WOMAN DOWNTOWN: And at last I hear its descent with him in it, I trust.

KING: So why don't you sit down and catch your breath in this chair?

WOMAN DOWNTOWN [*distractedly*]: Chair?

KING: I put it right here for you.

WOMAN DOWNTOWN: Ah . . . thoughtful, but when I'm disturbed, I have to stay on my feet and keep occupied with—ice bucket, drinks?

KING: Leave that to me, you sit down before you—

WOMAN DOWNTOWN: Fall down?

KING: In that beautiful dress.

WOMAN DOWNTOWN: This iridescent sheath of goldfish color was given me by General Susang's wife. Some tyrants have exquisite tastes in fabrics. The gift has some very unpleasant associations, but you can't blame a gift for the giver's moral corruption and everything else was packed for departure if any means of escape presented itself, refuge in the country estate of my

297

guardian. [*She takes a breath.*] Jailkeeper Griffin downstairs just informed me my guardian's been hospitalized since the night he delivered me here. Shattered what's left of my nerves. God! Did you think I'd flipped out in the lounge?

KING: What I think or don't think, does it matter?

WOMAN DOWNTOWN: Yes. Very much.

KING: Why?

WOMAN DOWNTOWN: You are actually the only person I've encountered at the—Paradise—Rose?—who strikes me as being a person I could appeal to for assistance, now that—

[*She runs out of breath.*]

KING [*pressing gently down on her shoulders to seat her in the chair*]: This hotel. What was that y'called it?

WOMAN DOWNTOWN: I hope you put that word "hotel" in quotes.

KING: In?

WOMAN DOWNTOWN: Quotes—sorry. I keep forgetting your native language is Spanish. You're Mexican, aren't you?

KING: Don't let that scare you. Some people, y'know, they think all Mexicans are criminals like, like rapists, y'know, like—rapists.

WOMAN DOWNTOWN: Ridiculous—misapprehension.

KING: I was born close to the border, but I'm a Texan. —My mother tole me my father was a gringo, but his name was Spanish—Del Rey. —Oh, I brought your coat and bag up.

WOMAN DOWNTOWN: *Gracias.*

KING [*handing the bag to her*]: You better check the bag to make sure the cash is still in it.

WOMAN DOWNTOWN: There was nothing much in it *but* money.

KING: And money means nothing to you.

WOMAN DOWNTOWN: Nothing compared to some documents which I—

[*She stops, uncertain whether she can go into the subject of "documents" even with this charmingly ingenuous man. She thinks that it might be wiser to change the subject till she knows him better.*]

Didn't you say you were going to serve as bartender at the little bar? A Margarita? Or a Tequila Sunrise?

KING: For me—the limit is beer.

WOMAN DOWNTOWN: I think you mean I was loaded in the lounge.

KING: I didn't say you was. I, I—got no—opinion.

WOMAN DOWNTOWN: My drink was loaded, I wasn't.

KING: Y'say your drinks was loaded. By Charlie the barman?

WOMAN DOWNTOWN: Who else mixes drinks down there but Fatso at the bar: Charlie the barman is he? —Let me remove the luggage from the bed. I mean, would you? I'm still in a shocked condition. The news about my guardian, Judge Collister's very

299

suspiciously sudden hospitalization and on the critical list at—New Meadows—New—Medical—

KING: I got the luggage off. You rest on the bed.

WOMAN DOWNTOWN: Oh Lord, how I do long to! It wouldn't embarrass you if I—you wouldn't misinterpret it as a—provocation?

KING: No, I—don't—take advantage of—ladies . . .

[*His voice is hoarse with conflicting impulses. A Vuitton suitcase falls from his nervous fingers, spilling its contents, delicate lingerie, a leopard-skin coat, an ermine jacket, etc.*]

Perdóname, one arm, one hand, the fingers—still—don't operate right, I—

[*She has gasped and immediately snatched up some photostatic papers among the spilled articles.*]

—specially when I'm— Did, did—anything break?

WOMAN DOWNTOWN: Papers don't break—

[*They have bent together, she for the papers, he for the delicate lingerie. They straighten simultaneously, faces nearly touching. She is searching his eyes and is abruptly convinced of his total honesty. He notices he has picked up a pair of lace panties and drops them like a hot coal. She shrieks with the laughter of released tension.*]

My God, but you Latins do have an instinct for the most intimate bits of apparel!—

KING: Me? No, I'm—I didn't—notice, I—

[*His embarrassment, frustration, and their betrayal, anger him. He takes a suddenly commanding tone.*]

Set back down on the bed!—I put it in the box for you.

WOMAN DOWNTOWN [*suddenly serious, touching his face as you might a child's*]: I shouldn't have laughed. You Latin men don't understand women's laughter.

KING: You think I'm buffoon, *payaso?* A clown?

WOMAN DOWNTOWN: Oh, please no. It was a release of tension. *¿Comprende?* I realized all at once that I could trust you completely. [*There is a "moment" between them.*] —May I, just to make up?

[*She gives him a quick, light kiss. Clearly she has now decided that intimacy will secure him as a confederate.*]

KING: Why don't you just stay on the bed?

WOMAN DOWNTOWN: I'd fall asleep and who knows what I'd dream? Of my previous confinement, of that butcher's block of a bed with straps that tore my skin till I screamed—before the electric shock and the Judge saved me from them. Oh, they would have continued the shock treatments till they killed me, wouldn't have stopped short of assassination to discover who held the original copies of those documents. You see, my memory's still scrambled like—eggs ranchero . . .

KING: —*Huevos rancheros,* huh?

WOMAN DOWNTOWN: That's right, *hombre.* Exactly like *huevos rancheros,* good for breakfast, but not for—recollection . . .

KING: I like 'em for a late supper when I can't sleep, yeah, with pepper sauce, tabasco.

301

WOMAN DOWNTOWN: Oh, you like that, do you? I have McIl-henny's tabasco on my little bar here. Why don't you call room service and ask for two orders of *huevos rancheros?* Room service is the one thing that I can always get on that phone.

KING: You—serious?

[*He is now crouched by the bed, folding the delicate lingerie very neatly and tenderly into the suitcase. There is a knock at the door. She catches her breath softly.*]

WOMAN DOWNTOWN [*in a whisper*]: Must be their doctor. Did you bolt the door?

[*He nods.*]

Call through it and tell them I won't see him. Don't, don't admit that impostor!

[*King crosses rapidly out.*]

KING [*offstage*]: The lady is all right now, don't need to see you. [*There is the sound of muffled protest.*] I told you she won't see you, so get lost!

[*He returns.*]

WOMAN DOWNTOWN: Thank you—oh God, thank you.

KING: *Por nada. —Recógete en tu cama. No hay peligro conmigo—* There is no danger with me. Now I call room service.

[*She sinks, sobbing voluptuously, onto the bed. He lifts the phone, but stares at the woman as she slowly, sensuously writhes on the bed's surface. He is startled.*]

—*Oh, yes, please, room service!*

[*He speaks to the Woman Downtown, hoarsely, through dry lips.*]

Now I am calling room service—they are ringing room service. —Hey Juan, *¿qué tal? Sí ¡Rey! ¡Escucha! Queremos dos platos de huevos rancheros, Chico, para*— What is your name, Miss?

[*Pause.*]

WOMAN DOWNTOWN [*sitting up slowly to face him*]: That I can't give you. [*She smiles slowly, sadly.*] Call me the Woman Downtown—

KING [*his eyes lingering on her*]: I'll just say for Penthouse B. —*Para* Penthouse B. Ha? *Cierra la boca*—you fink. You wanta tell Perla? You wanta be dead tomorrow?

[*He starts to put down the phone.*]

WOMAN DOWNTOWN: Don't hang up!

KING: Hold on, Juan— You want something else? —To go with the *huevos rancheros?*

[*She stands thinking.*]

WOMAN DOWNTOWN: He's a good friend of yours? One you can trust, even here?

KING: *Sí, sí,* a very good friend from Piedras Negras, Texas— my hometown.

WOMAN DOWNTOWN: —Ask him to put through a call, at once, to the New Medical Center and inquire about the condition of

303

my guardian, Judge Leland Collister, who's hospitalized there—identify himself as the Judge's cook, they might give him a report.

KING: Why can't I call from here?

WOMAN DOWNTOWN: The call wouldn't be put through.

KING [*into phone*]: —Juan, *otra cosa, muy discreta, Llama el hospital—*

WOMAN DOWNTOWN: New Medical Center.

KING: *El Nuevo Centro Medical. Sí.* New Medical Center. *Y pregunta por—*

WOMAN DOWNTOWN: Judge *Le*-land *Col*-lis-ter, *su condición.*

KING: Judge Leland Collister, *su condición.* Say you work for him, cook, *cocinero, tú sabes. ¡Ahora, pronto!*

[*He cradles the phone, his eyes lingering on her. The Woman Downtown sits tensely at the foot of the bed. He tries to lighten it up.*]

He says to me, musta been up with room service, he says you're in the Penthouse with the classy—

WOMAN DOWNTOWN: —Classy what?

KING: Some a these spicks, y'know, they got a—

WOMAN DOWNTOWN: Classy *what?* Papaya? Oh, I am flattered, you know.

KING: As, some a the, y'know, they got a—*boca grosera* . . .

[*He looks away, blushing. Pause. She kicks off her high-heeled slippers and falls onto the edge of the bed. Pause. She spreads her legs slightly.*]

WOMAN DOWNTOWN: —Papaya is the name of a tropical fruit.

KING: —Hmm—yes . . .

WOMAN DOWNTOWN: And is also an idiomatic expression for a woman's—well, you know—

KING: Where do you learn such things!?

[*She rolls slowly onto her stomach and presses a button on the bedside table. The Mariachis are piped in.*]

WOMAN DOWNTOWN: Oh, let's say I was once the prisoner of a man who was hung up on that kind of language. I was forced to listen to those words over and over to—achieve his—erection. There's your Mariachis. What's the song?

KING [*hoarsely*]: —*Mujer.*

WOMAN DOWNTOWN: Just "Woman," huh?

KING: Yeah. Ain't that enough?

WOMAN DOWNTOWN: —Alone? —No. —Would you say so?

[*He rises, a hand unconsciously touching the fly of his pants.*]

KING: No. Alone is—

WOMAN DOWNTOWN: Sometimes lonely.

[*The phone rings. She springs up, catching her breath.*]

305

KING [*lifting the phone*]: *¿Juan? Sí, una noticia acerca del señor* Collister.

[*She makes an imploring gesture with her hands.*]

—Ah. —*Sí.*

[*He looks up at her.*]

—*Él está mejor.*

WOMAN DOWNTOWN: Out of danger?

KING: *¿Aparte de esto? ¿Seguro?* [*He turns to the Woman Downtown.*] They say yes.

WOMAN DOWNTOWN: When released?

KING: *¿Quándo está libre? —Muchas gracias, Chico. ¡Discreto! Ahora—los huevos rancheros, la señorita tiene hambre, ¡apúrate!*

[*He hangs up the phone.*]

En breve—soon—*cálmate.*

[*He rises again, but doesn't know what to do.*]

Listen. I will take you to the Judge. I can call a cab.

WOMAN DOWNTOWN: Don't you understand? It will always be the same cab, with the same driver, with the face of a demon. Like tonight. You must believe me. Please. *For your sake.*

KING: I could take a letter for you to him.

WOMAN DOWNTOWN: Not you. Rather your friend Juan—the one who calls me "classy papaya" . . .

[*She notes his troubled look and wants to distract him from her dilemma.*]

KING: You are gonna wrinkle that—elegant dress you got on . . .

WOMAN DOWNTOWN: I don't want to do that.

KING: Then would you—

WOMAN DOWNTOWN: —Like to remove it? Yes. My gift . . . from the General's wife . . . The skin of the Orientals is very delicate skin. She couldn't bear zippers on dresses, in fact she could wear only silk; she came of Mandarin, ancient Mandarin—lineage. She was utterly barbaric in her instincts, loved watching decapitations through binoculars from a mound of silk cushions in the cupola on the roof of the palace.

[*He has now slipped off her silk sheath and he looks down in humble awe at her delicate body in its silk lingerie.*]

I feel rather chilly. Do you?

KING: I got the, the elegant dress off you.

WOMAN DOWNTOWN: That must be why I noticed a change in the temperature of the room.

KING: —Do you enjoy a—good back-rub?

[*She laughs abruptly. There is a knock at the door.*]

WOMAN DOWNTOWN: The *huevos rancheros.*

KING: Should I tell 'em forget it?

307

WOMAN DOWNTOWN: We might be hungry—later.

KING [*reluctantly*]: —Yeah—yeah . . .

[*He crosses off. Inaudible voices come from the living room. After a few moments, King re-enters the bedroom, pushing a room service table on wheels—nervously.*]

They got tin covers over the—*huevos rancheros* and the plates are—hot . . . so no hurry . . .

WOMAN DOWNTOWN: We are all of us hurrying to the same place. So what's the hurry?

[*She stands still, smiling, trembling. He takes a faltering step toward her.*]

KING: —*¿Con permiso?*

WOMAN DOWNTOWN: —I do think you'd better!

[*He embraces her. She loses her breath and writhes involuntarily.*]

KING: *¡Por favor!* Hold still!

[*She breaks away from him. He is utterly baffled.*]

WOMAN DOWNTOWN: You—you—hu—hu—

KING: What are you trying to say?

WOMAN DOWNTOWN [*throwing her head back*]: *Human!*

KING: —Oh. —"Human." —Yes, I'm—

WOMAN DOWNTOWN [*with the same strange intensity*]: Human!

KING [*clasping her desperate head between his hands*]: You say "human" to me like something special about me. A living man is—

WOMAN DOWNTOWN: Yes! Human! To enter my life something human is special, this day, this night, this place, suddenly—you—*human! Here! What?* [*She gasps.*] I am back there, inhuman. Behind estate walls of my husband's hacienda where I play hostess to Red Devil Battery Monsters. Great tall prison walls, guarded, oh, yes, private deputies guarded with revolvers the entrance; the gates had a guard house and were slid open and shut by electric-eye power, operated by power, and all the grounds were patrolled by—sports clothes for day and dinner jackets at night. —Guards guarded, they had such short friendly names, Pat, Bill, Ray and their, oh, their smiles at the gates and in the guardhouse and along the long drive, their smiles and their laughs and their shouts, it was not at all like the atmosphere of—San Quentin, but—I was—hostess to—monsters! —The guests were not—distinguishable from the guards; the guards were not—distinguishable from the guests. The guests and the guards shouted short names to each other with the same smiles, Hey, Pat, Bill, Ray, Hiyah, Hi, Hi, Hiyah. Credentials presented at the guardhouse, then the hell of the hollering. Come *awn* in here, Hi *ah* yuh, hi, hi *hiyah*, come in here, you folks drive right on in, and a dog pack, there was also a dog pack, and the dog pack all smiled too. It was all one big hell-hollering *death grin*. "Wanta drink now or afta you been to your guest house? Anything you want dial zero for service, you heah? Wonderful to see you lookin' so well; he-lllll! Ye-lllll." Oh, they trusted me to take their attaché cases with the payola and the secrets in code, and *why not? Wasn't I perfectly NOT human, too?*!

KING: *¡Cálmate!*

[*He rushes to catch hold of her. He lifts her and bears her to the bed and places her carefully on it.*]

¡Cálmate! You are out of that prison! *Cálmate.* Now be still, we're—human—together . . .

DIM OUT. MARIACHIS PLAY.

SCENE THREE

It is a while later in the penthouse bedroom. King and the Woman Downtown are both stretched out on the bed.

KING: —Sleeping?

WOMAN DOWNTOWN: No, of course not.

KING: Tired out?

WOMAN DOWNTOWN: No.

KING: All those—cries . . .

WOMAN DOWNTOWN: I didn't hear any cries.

KING: I did. So I stopped.

WOMAN DOWNTOWN: Cries like something coming to life?

KING: I think you—exaggerate.

WOMAN DOWNTOWN: But I heard nothing at all. Just felt.

KING: What?

WOMAN DOWNTOWN: —Coming to life. [*Pause.*] —Afterwards, what do you do?

KING: What you want to do?

WOMAN DOWNTOWN: Rest. Beside you. I did a lot of talking before the—ecstatic outcries. Now you talk. Your turn.

KING: About what?

WOMAN DOWNTOWN: Your life, you—music . . .

KING: Yes . . . well. Mariachis. They gotta history to them goes back a long way. Before Maximilian—the Frenchman Napoleon sent us to be king. And in those days they played at marriages so they got them the French word *mariages* mispronounced to "mariachis." But then after Maximilian—we shot him!—and his wife Carlotta, she—

WOMAN DOWNTOWN: Went crying in the night through the palaces of Europe.

KING: Yeah. Well then they become just Mariachis that play in the streets and in cantinas. But we—we went a step better. We played in hotel lounges. Mainly I think because of La Niña.

WOMAN DOWNTOWN: Means little girl.

KING: My daughter was called La Niña. After she started work with us—you want to hear this? You're not just faking some interest?

WOMAN DOWNTOWN: I want to hear everything, please, please, I don't pretend.

[*He sits up.*]

KING [*sitting on the side of the bed*]: After La Niña started work with us, it wasn't just "King's Men," it was "King's Men with La Niña," and, honey, La Niña was so goddam terrific that after a month of singing with the vocal trio, she was singing solo *and she was dancing a flamenco better'n a gypsy fireball!*

[*The Mariachis fade in under his speech now.*]

In San Antone we played in The Ranchero Room of the big new hotel there, The Sheraton Lone Star, on the riverbank, y'know, in the heart of the city, and oh, man, they booked reservations for dinner five, six hours ahead or got no table. Outside that San Antone hotel, at the main entrance to it, La Niña's photo was blown up in color life-size; La Niña was the *Star!*

WOMAN DOWNTOWN [*stirring sensually so that her breasts are uncovered*]: I think she was just the daughter of the star. Tell me why you don't go back with King's Men and your Neen-ya. Tell me.

KING: Okay, I'll tell you straight. An accident—accident? Yeh, I guess you'd say "accident" of it. —This crazy accident happened—one week after we got a real name manager that was getting us gigs that would've made us hot as anything in the South. He said, "You start in The Hotel Reforma, the big one in Mexico City." "Man," I said, "oh, man, you got to be kidding—Reforma!!" —"Never tell me I'm kidding; it's not my profession to kid. I'm delivering the Reforma, to you, King. I'm booking you there for the summer, all of it; you can hold there all summer, and in the fall, well, on the roof of The Hotel Raleigh in Houston. Then, I think you ought to hit the Coast, at a spot like the Beverly Wilshire. Say, middle of November through the holidays."

[*He is suddenly boyish.*]

And he, my manager, he—he—criticized how I dressed; he said, "Look, dude, you're not an old dude!" —A wonderful thing to make a man believe. "Not old, and—*still*—appealing." —I thought, "Yes, older women." I said, "Yes, older women." —He said, "No, all women, because you are a big man with—"

[*Shyness makes him abruptly silent.*]

313

So I changed—outfits to suit him and—appeal to—

[*He stops, embarrassed.*]

WOMAN DOWNTOWN: Women.

KING: Yes. I did. And then—this goddam crazy thing happened. It happened that night at The Sheraton Lone Star in San Antone. We just finished a set and started to leave the bandstand, and I felt a stab in my head. I stumbled off the bandstand, fell on my face, blacked out. They broke some kinda capsule—

WOMAN DOWNTOWN: Oh, a popper . . .

KING: —Under my nose, but I—didn't get up. Well, they found this—accident—in my head.

WOMAN DOWNTOWN [*sitting up slowly*]: Found?

KING: A thing that happens to a man like that should have meaning, not be just an awful accident to *him*. Accidents don't have meaning. An yet, y'know most of the things that happen to people are accidents. You know that? Meaningless accidents? To them?

WOMAN DOWNTOWN: Yes, even birth and death, but love is not an accident.

KING: Ain't it? Are you sure?

[*She laughs richly, triumphantly.*]

Huh?

WOMAN DOWNTOWN: It seems more like . . . an Act of God to me . . .

[*She strokes his head; she abruptly catches a soft breath and leans over him.*]

KING: —I know. You just noticed the—scar.

WOMAN DOWNTOWN: And is that the accident that you were talking about? A scar from . . .

KING: Surgery, yes, a—surgical scar.

[*She rises from the bed. Her shock impels her to suddenly reach for a drink.*]

Thank you for a nice evening.

WOMAN DOWNTOWN: *What?*

KING: Have you got the time?

WOMAN DOWNTOWN: More time than a clock can hold, so don't think about it.

KING: I can't miss the last bus home. It wouldn't please my wife. And I got to please my wife because like you see, well, I am not working now. I am my wife, Perla's dependent, her—invalid dependent, and if I don't get home at night, she would hit the ceiling.

WOMAN DOWNTOWN: Good. It would knock her unconscious.

KING: Don't talk like that; she is a hard-working woman. Now I got a serious request to make of you. Don't drink no more in bed.

WOMAN DOWNTOWN: Don't deny me that comfort. I learned to do it to obliterate experience, but this night it's to hold it closer for a while.

KING: There's no future in it. No. I take that back, there *is* a future in it and it's a bitch of a future. Want to hear what a bitch of a future it is?

WOMAN DOWNTOWN: No, love, not tonight.

[*He grabs the drink from her hand.*]

KING: This much I will tell you. You drink in bed for experience and you'll wind up not a lady with some bad words in her head and some habits that don't fit a lady like, like screaming and clawing in bed. —How do I explain these marks you put on me, tell Perla I was in bed with a wild cat tonight?

WOMAN DOWNTOWN: No, with a she-wolf! —And no matter how I wind up in the future, still . . .

[*She extends her bare arms to him.*]

I would have known you, I would have lain with a king on a king-size bed.

[*Her arms extended, she grabs hold of him and draws him close again.*]

KING: —You know—

WOMAN DOWNTOWN: Yes, I know! I have known you!

KING: Love, lady, let go, I do, I do got to go, I—can't *not*—go—

WOMAN DOWNTOWN: You demand your release? Demand is granted! I relinquish you to the last bus home! And the lady that clocks you!

[*She cries this out as if she had been given a death sentence. He touches his head—shakes it.*]

KING: I think you got something in you that is wild like flamenco. You got something in you like my kid in Chicago—a heart on fire!

WOMAN DOWNTOWN: And you don't want to get burned in addition to getting those marks of the she-wolf on you? The episode is completed, not just for this night, but always? Or would it be heard in heaven if I offered a prayer that you'll be back tomorrow?

KING: I don't know about what is heard in heaven or not—but tell me, Miss Downtown Woman—what hotel are you in?

WOMAN DOWNTOWN: Answer my question first.

KING: I will be back tomorrow.

[*The Mariachis fade in, softly.*]

WOMAN DOWNTOWN: —Then the hotel I am in is the right one for the first time!

[*He stares at her from the door. Her eyes drop shut with a deep sigh of content and still he stands looking longingly back as—*]

THE ROOM DIMS OUT

SCENE FOUR

The interior and exterior of a small frame house on the outskirts of the city. The exterior is the backyard. In it are two metal chairs. The interior contains a kitchen and sitting room area. It seems as if the house has drawn in upon itself for protection from the menacing profile of the city, and here is where a visual poetry must be present: sounds of the Wasteland, a wolf-call, calls. Perhaps we see figures watching, menacing. King is lighted as he walks slowly onto the set. He sits in one of the metal yard chairs. Across the Wasteland stand, in miniature silhouette, the towers of downtown Dallas. Perla is at the kitchen table, waiting up for King. She is a small woman, about King's age but appearing a good deal older. She is probably more attractive than she now seems to King—since his illness has made him dependent upon her. A disturbance in the Wasteland, accustomed as it is, makes her gasp and set the cup down with a crash. A primitive cry, much nearer, answers the explosion. Other cries answer. Perla rises and goes to the door.

PERLA: Stay back or I call police!

[*There are more wolf calls, another distant explosion. King lights a cigarette in the yard. Perla crosses to the phone. King listens to the phone call. A ringing is heard persistently and another area of the stage is slowly lighted. La Niña is lighted, shivering in the chill of rising from love-making. McCabe is just visible.*]

LA NIÑA: *Sí, Mama, ¿qué pasa?*

[*Her voice is harsh and mocking. She is a girl of nineteen, but desperation has aged her and she is disheveled from "the bed." She continues, still harshly.*]

318

—Well, Mama, have you hung up? —I didn't hear the phone click. —Are you still on the line? What a difference in you, this silence, not shouting at me!

PERLA [*slowly and fiercely*]: There are whores at the hotel where I work as housekeeper, but I do not talk to them except to say, "Can the maid come in to make up the bed now or is the man still with you?"

[*La Niña utters a wild flamenco cry of defiance. McCabe extends a hand toward her as if to restrain her.*]

I got to whisper or your father will hear. Or else I would scream at *you, ¡Puta!*

LA NIÑA [*abruptly soft*]: —Mama. How is he?

PERLA: What time is it in Chicago? In Dallas it's half past two. Ain't it that time in Chicago? Yes! A man answered the phone at half past two at night. Blood of Jesus, this life, these lies!

[*King has risen from the chair and listens just out of the interior light. McCabe is also listening in the opposite set.*]

LA NIÑA: Call him to the phone.

PERLA: He is not home.

KING [*advancing into the lighted interior*]: I am at home!

LA NIÑA: I hear his voice! King, King!

[*Perla makes a gesture of hanging up the phone.*]

KING: Call her back.

PERLA: —Who?

KING: La Niña. I heard her shouting my name.

PERLA: —King, you have dreams.

KING: Live on them, yes. She called me. Call her back. What is the number? I will call her myself.

PERLA: You think I was talking to her? Every two weeks a new address and a new—phone number . . .

KING: You lie.

PERLA: You dream.

KING: *¡Mierda!*

PERLA: You're sweating. Fever?

[*She touches his head. He strikes her hand away.*]

KING: You're always suggesting I'm still sick in the head, you *suci mentirosa!*

[*He jerks open the Frigidaire door and searches for beer. Both the Chicago and Dallas rooms remain lighted and neither scene freezes for the other.*]

KING [*throwing things out of the box*]: Too stingy to keep a beer in the Frigidaire?

[*Perla has thrust a can of beer she has just removed from a shelf at King.*]

Hot beer? *¡Muchas gracias!*

[*He tosses it into the corner. She picks it up and pours it over*

*ice cubes. McCabe rises with a thwarted, anguished, choked
sob. The light shifts to a poster of La Niña; her hand is on
the poster and her imploring cry is heard.*]

LA NIÑA: King!

[*The poster should remain lighted through the hallucinatory
duet with her father.*]

KING [*to Perla*]: In your purse this week was a envelope
empty, empty envelope dated five days ago and from Chicago
and it was not addressed here. Why? Huh? You got secrets from
me about my daughter? A secret—correspondence between you
and her that you don't want me to know?

PERLA: When she writes home she lies. I tell her to write me
the truth, one woman to another. —Why did you look in my
purse?

KING: *Because I steal from your purse! Sí, sí,* your purse is too
tight so I take the price of two beers! Sometimes, excuse me, I
take a little more to buy in a card game! Look, you want me to
be like a beggar in front of the men at The Yellow Rose, not
able to play a game of cards between sets there, not able to buy
a beer and tip Charlie the barman?

PERLA [*shamed*]: What I have is yours . . . *Lo que tengo es
tuyo, Dios sabe.* [*She presses her face to his shoulder.*] Oh, my
God, I'm so tired.

KING: Then why don't you go to bed?

PERLA: —I smell perfume on you, a woman's perfume.

KING: Oh-ho, that. A drunk woman at the bar took out a
spray bottle and—sprayed me. [*He is deceptively quiet.*] Be
careful what you say to me.

PERLA: You don't want to go to bed with me because you got a woman downtown, I think.

KING: *Mierda.*

PERLA: I sit up for you nights, but when you come home you don't come in the house if the light is still on but you sit in the yard. Why? To look at the dump-heap, at Crestview-by-the-Dump-Heap in which we sunk our life savings? Till half an hour after I turn the light out? I say nothing, but I think, I feel, I'm a woman and I—love you.

KING: Things will work out soon. You're a brave woman. Tonight? I got up on the bandstand with the men and I—*sang!* And there was applause almost like there was before. Soon I will send for La Niña and we will hit the road again. Remember her voice and mine together. *¿Los duetos?*

[*La Niña is lighted again, spectrally, downstage. He crosses to her and they sing together—a love song. The spot goes out and he returns to the kitchen.*]

PERLA: *Sí, recuerdo.* Love songs, between father and daughter. Not natural, not right. —Let's go to bed and—fight tomorrow.

KING: You go to bed, you get up early, need sleep. I want a cold beer.

PERLA: *¡Todas, todas las noches siempre lo mismo!* Go to bed alone.

KING: Yes, I'm no good.

[*Their eyes blaze at each other. Then he turns to snatch a beer. She turns away and walks wearily off. When she is out of the light, he places the beer can back on the table. The anger goes out of his eyes. He bends his head to sniff at his shirt.*]

—Night—flight . . .

DIM OUT

ACT TWO

||||||||||||||||||||||||||||||||||||||||||||||||||||||||||||||||||||||||||||||||||||||||||||||||||||||

SCENE ONE

||||||||||||||||||||||||||||||||||||||||||||||||||||||||||||||||||||||||||||||||||||||||||||||||||||||

A dull explosion at a great distance. Sounds of the Wasteland. Cries. A clouded flare. Fade out as the Mariachi music is brought up and the lounge is lighted. The Woman Downtown enters that area slowly; she crosses to the bar. At the bar is a clutch of conventioneers in a huddle, talking rapidly in low voices, all wearing conical hats of red tin foil with the Red Devil insignia on them. It is a month later. The Woman Downtown has a light cape or stole about her shoulders, indicating a cooler season.

||||||||||||||||||||||||||||||||||||||||||||||||||||||||||||||||||||||||||||||||||||||||||||||||||||||

WOMAN DOWNTOWN: Mr. Barman, are you sure you haven't received any word from Mr. Del Rey? He's half an hour later than I expected.

CHARLIE: Maybe he's been delayed by family problems.

[*This interchange catches the attention of the conventioneers. They come out of their huddle to stare up at the Woman Downtown. Inadvertently, as she suddenly notices the insignia on their caps, she gives a little gasping cry.*]

WOMAN DOWNTOWN: —Oh, Batteries, huh?

FIRST CONVENTIONEER [*grinning lasciviously*]: You wouldn't be Mabel, would you?

SECOND CONVENTIONEER [*trying to stand*]: Is this Miss Mabel Dickens?

WOMAN DOWNTOWN: —I'm sorry to—disappoint you, but I am

324

not "Mabel." Is the Red Devil Battery Company convening here? I beg your pardon for interrupting your festivities. Battery Red Devil! What cunning caps, I mean, cute like children's at Halloween. Will all attending the battery convention allow me to offer you—Mr. Barman, champagne for the gentlemen of the Battery Convention and make sure it's imported. Battery men? —Yes, *imported!* The best! And now please call Mr. Del Rey's home; I have the number. Tell him to take a taxi. I'll meet him at the entrance with the fare. But, if a woman answers—

CHARLIE: His wife, Perla?

WOMAN DOWNTOWN [*defiantly*]: Then just say that his men are having a birthday party and the candles can't be lighted till he gets here.

[*King enters the lighted area. The Mariachis go into a jubilant ranchero to greet him. He turns to the Woman Downtown as she crosses to him. She seizes his belt clasp and draws him to her.*]

WOMAN DOWNTOWN [*in his ear*]: We're honored tonight by the presence of a convention of Battery men; my husband's closed in on me with—henchmen! —And you're an hour late!

KING: You're surrounded by me. I told you I'd be later because it was Perla's late work day, and supper would be later.

WOMAN DOWNTOWN: Supper, Perla come first and I wait for a bus!??

MARIACHI: Come up and do a solo, King.

KING: No, no, *más tarde.* Perla can't understand that I come downtown ev'ry night. She sniffs at my clothes when I come home, sniffs them like a dog for you—perfume.

325

WOMAN DOWNTOWN: *Basta, basta, comprendo . . . [She drinks.]* Another, please. Have a beer.

[He doesn't move. She crosses to the bar for the drinks and brings them to him. She hands him the beer can and it slips from his hand. He looks, troubled, at his empty hand for a moment, then shrugs with a wry grin and picks up the can.]

KING: You don't drink down here, remember?

[She surrenders the cocktail to him, and he empties it on the floor.]

WOMAN DOWNTOWN: Yes, yes I—remember. Please, King, let's go upstairs. I have to talk to you. *¡URGENTE!*

[His attention is abruptly diverted by the appearance of a swarthily handsome young man, slick-haired, cat-like, leaping onto a platform above the Mariachis and at once beginning a fierce, sexually aggressive crescendo on drums. King stares for a moment in frozen outrage. Then he crosses slowly, menacingly, to the stand. The Mariachis avert their faces, shamed.]

KING: Julio!

[The oldest Mariachi descends from the stand and places a hand—propitiatory—on King's shoulder. King strikes it away. His speech should be interspersed with Spanish expletives.]

What is this? *Dios mío*, this *gato?* A drummer with Mariachis?

[The small, grizzled-haired man spreads his arms wide in a gesture of helplessness.]

Look! He stands shoving his *crotch* at—

JULIO: The manager insisted. *Yo no sé por qué.*

KING [*with desperate assertion of command*]: Management is *me!* Shit, I picked you all from little spick casinos; I build you to an outfit, King's Men, mine! Booked into Reforma, *México,* top-spot, Raleigh, Houston, Beverly-Wilshire, L. A.! Made, gave La Niña to star in East Ambassador Pump Room! And you spring on me a *maricón* in skin-tight satin pants, standing, jerking his crotch, and say to me "Management insist." *¡Escúchame! Management, me, insist OUT! Or am I OUT, have you counted me out now?*

[*The Woman Downtown holds him tight. He wrests himself free of her arms. At this point, King and Julio shout together: a scene of "presentation."*]

JULIO: Rey! King! We wait! But got to continue job here. Continue in Yellow Rose Lounge till you—

KING: I put you here.

JULIO: *Lo es.* But—

KING: What?

JULIO: We got to work till we know.

KING: Know what?

JULIO: If you come back or you don't; if La Niña comes back or not.

KING: Why do you ask if I come back with La Niña?

[*Julio shrugs, embarrassed. King turns downstage.*]

How can I keep control when I'm not active? Things slip out of my hand. Bring the manager here!

CHARLIE: He's—off!

[*King shouts to the Barman.*]

KING: *Charlie! Get me the desk!*

JULIO: King, why fight them now?

[*The Barman picks up the phone. King shoves Julio away from him, leaps onto the platform and hurls the Drummer off it. The Drummer lands nimbly on his feet with the smile of a cat, turns, and grins at the Woman Downtown.*]

KING [*to the Drummer*]: Git the fuck out of here, you *maricón!*

[*The Drummer goes off, laughing. The Woman Downtown draws King onto the stage apron.*]

WOMAN DOWNTOWN: No, now, love, you're sweating blood over nothing. He's gone. You threw him out and he's out! —May I request a number?

KING [*darkly*]: —Sí . . .

WOMAN DOWNTOWN: Julio! [*She calls to the Mariachis.*] "*Mujer*"!

[*They start immediately with the requested number. King is still breathing heavily. He moves a step and staggers, then grips her shoulders.*]

KING: —Yes . . . I was—*ha!*—lost—balance . . . [*He turns*

downstage again to appeal his case.] They know it was—benign—small growth, en-capsul—ated. . . . Just lifted right off the surface, like picking a—weed.

[*She kisses him. He turns to her.*]

No, no, wait till upstairs. *¡Hombres! Bésenme mucho para darme suerte.*

[*King stares raptly; he rubs his eyes.*]

La Niña!

WOMAN DOWNTOWN: *¿Qué pasa?*

KING: Singing, dancing! No—a—vision . . .

[*He tries to laugh, then rubs his eyes.*]

WOMAN DOWNTOWN [*sobered with concern*]: Let's go upstairs.

KING: You go on up from the lobby. I'll take the back elevator.

[*The Woman Downtown crosses unsteadily out of the light. The Mariachis are brought up. King crosses to them and shouts over the music.*]

¡Muchachos! ¡Mañana! La Niña comes home. Kid's coming home from Chicago! Tomorrow! How about that?

[*They respond with a jubilant "ranchero." King turns downstage and shouts.*]

Now we're living! *¡Hombres!* Sing it! La Niña tomorrow!

[*He turns to the Mariachis.*]

And today, this morning, I had my one-year check-up! The waiting period's over! Recovery is perfect! Doctor's sworn word today! Yeh, life is God, and good! —I'll see you all later . . .

[*The manager returns with the grinning Drummer.*]

GRIFFIN: *Julio!* —This drummer stays if you stay!

[*The Drummer springs nimbly onto the platform.*]

JULIO: King say no.

GRIFFIN: The president of the chain says *yes.*

JULIO: Why?

GRIFFIN [*contemptuously*]: You don't ask president why. You know why. Somebody's *money! Battery money. A lot!*

[*The Drummer begins; he builds to a crescendo as the forestage dims out. The crescendo continues through the set change, then halts abruptly.*]

SCENE TWO

The Penthouse bedroom of the Yellow Rose Hotel. The Woman Downtown enters with a vase of yellow roses. King is behind her as she enters the bedroom. He follows her, her eyes distant with brooding on the scene in the lounge.

WOMAN DOWNTOWN [*to King*]: You're still furious. Why don't you leave it downstairs where it happened?

KING: It didn't happen to you.

WOMAN DOWNTOWN: What you feel, I feel. I know what you feel, and I feel it.

[*She laughs, then she loosens her shoulder strap.*]

KING: —Don't strip now. It makes you like a stripper in Vegas. D'you take me for a pick-up, a stud, after all the—what?

WOMAN DOWNTOWN: —*What?*

[*There is a shocked look between them.*]

KING: I got a cyclone in my head. You feel that, too?

WOMAN DOWNTOWN: I feel it blowing down walls.

KING: You, you—haul me up here and I might as well enter the room of a hotel hooker—no name, no past, no future, a smell of liquor on your breath and peppermint Chiclets to take it off or sweeten it for tongue-kissing and a spray bottle of—

WOMAN DOWNTOWN: *Vol de Nuit*, night flight from—

331

[*She cries out and throws herself onto the bed.*]

KING: Stay off the bed. Sit in the chair. Sit in it.

[*She crosses to the chair and stands helplessly by it.*]

Sit in it, Downtown Woman!

WOMAN DOWNTOWN: You never called me that.

KING: You called *yourself* that.

WOMAN DOWNTOWN: *You* never did till just now, and in an ugly way, too. King, please let tonight be lovely. There's a reason.

[*His look turns abstracted.*]

KING: —There is—no limit to time—but for us, there's a limit, a short one.

WOMAN DOWNTOWN [*springing up*]: I won't, I refuse to take part in this scene—you've drawn up in your confused head.

KING: "Confused head?" You never said that to me before. So this is a night for saying things the first time?

WOMAN DOWNTOWN: I meant only the disturbance downstairs!

KING: You said confused head!

WOMAN DOWNTOWN: *Who in hell on earth doesn't have a confused head now?*

[*The music of the Mariachis is heard, quadraphonic, distorted.*]

KING: I stumbled. The beer can slipped from my fingers.

WOMAN DOWNTOWN: What of it? I drop glasses, spill drinks, stumble, too.

KING: When drunk; I wasn't drunk. And you didn't even notice.

WOMAN DOWNTOWN: I told you I did, I noticed. Why, I've spent years, years noticing, seeming not but noticing, hearing or overhearing, sensing, suspecting, pretending to ignore with a constant well-practiced smile, but—always alert like a hunted thing in the woods, preparing to run, run—with a pack at my heels.

KING: You know how to talk. Stay off the bed and talk.

WOMAN DOWNTOWN: Suppose I have nothing to tell you I haven't told you in bed?

KING: Tell me what makes you a woman that can't give her name?

WOMAN DOWNTOWN: You're back to that.

KING: We never got to that. Just sit there like a lady and tell me, tell me who it is that I love and make love to.

WOMAN DOWNTOWN: You want me to give you the sort of factual information about me that you put down on hospital record sheets or immigration papers. A beautiful way to spend our last night together.

KING: Last night together's more bullshit. Tell me.

WOMAN DOWNTOWN: All right. Specifics. Till you cry hush.

Father's position? State senator. Mother? Died at my birth—oh, yes, I was told that often, accusingly, as if I'd *deliberately* killed her by being born. Birthplace? Hugh ranch in West Texas. . . . Isolated as madness. . . . You sing ranchero. Ever been on a big ranch? Heard these sounds at night?

[*She throws back her head and imitates a wolf howl, then the barking of ranch dogs.*]

KING: *Sí, sí, ¡ya basta!* Go on.

WOMAN DOWNTOWN: Wolves' howls, ranch dogs' answer.

KING: Go on without animal noises; I know them; I've known them inside of me and outside.

WOMAN DOWNTOWN [*flinging hands to her face and rocking with desperation*]: I don't have breath to go on!

[*King drops before her, clutching her knees.*]

KING: *Por favor,* for me—*necessario, querida!* The huge ranch—why?

WOMAN DOWNTOWN: Had to be huge to hold secrets.

KING: *¿Secretos? ¿Qué secretos?*

WOMAN DOWNTOWN: Of my father's Indian mistress, their ill-ill-legitimate child, my half-sister called Running Spring. Not a political asset to a statesman. The mistress hated me, spoke to me only in Apache. Apache was the language besides the wolves' and the dogs' howls nights! For me? A spinster tutor all in black like a widow spider, the black beads clinking!

[*She is clasping his clothes, the ranch becoming a vision in her.*]

Hard black eyes—critical, despising. —Lessons, I couldn't—learn from her. I learned English from leatherbound books in my father's library. Yes, it had to be huge, the ranch, to contain my loneliness, the nights, the wolf howls—the secrets . . .

[*She extends a rigid arm.*]

KING: What are you—?

WOMAN DOWNTOWN: Drink, please. Or let me stop now.

KING [*handing her a tumbler of water*]: *Aquí.*

WOMAN DOWNTOWN: Water is not a drink, love.

[*He presses it to her lips; she swallows. He clasps her tight in his arms.*]

The Indian child and I were equally lonely. We lived by a—dry spring in an *arroyo*. In late April or May it would fill with clear water and we would wade in it on opposite sides of the *arroyo,* sometimes—smiling shyly across it.

Thank you for holding me. It's not so hard to tell now.

At twelve I first menstruated and didn't know what it was, thought that I was afflicted with some unique disease that couldn't be mentioned—to whom? The black-bead-clinking tutor? I locked myself in room, wouldn't come out for my solitary meals. Father returned that day; he was told I'd locked myself up. —He sent me to a private school for disturbed children, more like an institution.

This confirmed my feeling that I was afflicted with a dreadful, shaming disease. I ran away, not back to the huge, night-howling ranch, but to my godfather, the Judge. His wife explained the curse to me, but the nights of the ranch were rooted in me too deep, they had made me—strange . . .

A girl that talked like a book and was full of secrets . . .

335

Problems followed problems; they do that, once they are started.

KING: Your father, he make no effort to get you back to—?

WOMAN DOWNTOWN: Hardly! —Absence ideal resolution of conflicts. —Empty water, fill wine . . .

[*Stunned, King tosses the water out of the tumbler and fills it with wine.*]

I never saw him again except on political newscasts.

KING: He disappeared from your life?

WOMAN DOWNTOWN: The dead do that. However—well, I belonged to society as the great southern statesman's daughter. —I was presented to society in the state and the national capital, too! Oh, what lavish balls, as if for a girl infatuated with splendor! —The walls of the tall, mirrored halls were covered with white flowers! I would enter the rooms and freeze as if standing on blocks of ice! —And my lips would form that icy, perfect smile for such occasions. Photographs show that I was a beautiful mask of—what I still don't know. You see, in me something was wrong, invisibly but incurably twisted by those desolate nights, the wolf-howling and the woman's cries of ecstasy which I thought were—anguish . . .

Now this will amaze you! I was acclaimed the most popular debutante of the season, and all of the parties smelt the same to me, like important state funerals which I'd had to attend!

All of a sudden, a breakdown, carefully covered up, no mention made of it. Partial recovery at—Institute for Re-birth.

Released, but not from the ice. Returned to the dazzling arena with no apparent shadow on the lifelike face. Dancing, I didn't feel a floor under my feet or the arms of my partner. Kept my eyes on glitter of chandeliers to keep from screaming, which worked; it worked somehow . . .

No, no, stay with your music, it's no goddam business of yours.

KING: Tell me everything, all.

WOMAN DOWNTOWN: Oh, I don't think I could stop myself now if I stood before a direct hot-line to the center of La Hacienda, which I possibly am! Barefoot little rice-paddie and cane-field people, innocent-eyed, simple-hearted as water oxen, asking just rice in a hand or a bowl out of a day's or a night's work—set to war with each other in spite of their blood connection, religious and culture connection, because, *because!* —You see, the huge, secret investments had to be protected by—sympathetically corrupt regimes . . . Oh, fighting Asia's like fighting God and time, but they figured they could do just that, no big hassle, you see, genocide for profits undeclared. —Well? —Doesn't it blow your mind? Well, doesn't it? You look incredulous. Why should you believe things before they happened? Well, I know beforehand; I can predict it exactly because I've seen it in blueprints drawn up at La Hacienda. No. I'm not the oracle of Delphi or Dallas, but I had *access* to those blueprints, the design for surrendering a democracy to rule by power conspiracy. —It did blow my mind, it broke through my numbness. Me, I'd elected, chosen my connection and finally my knowledge—

KING: —You were in this!

WOMAN DOWNTOWN: In it! Yes, I was in it, I was married to it, not just walking wounded but walking dead which made me adaptable to it! —Fool that wanted "specifics," well, you've got them. Yes, *amigo, amor,* I was in it, bought, they thought, for a beautifully trained front, accepting the bouquets and official greetings with a smile that looked almost real on the ramps of the privately owned jets. Oh, I was transported widely, world over, and, you know, it was a—hypnosis, the motion.

KING: And him? You were with him?

WOMAN DOWNTOWN: I've told you about his—obscene whispers while—

KING: —I think you're a little girl that's had a bad dream and run to papa's bed to tell him about it . . .

WOMAN DOWNTOWN: Just a—bad dream, huh?

KING: Well—I believe in bad dreams . . .

[*He unconsciously touches the now invisible scar on his head.*]

WOMAN DOWNTOWN: There now, no more about it. I never told you these things. Let's play never heard of, forgotten.

KING: Like the scar on my head.

WOMAN DOWNTOWN: Yes, and I, here with you, human, in Penthouse B for beautiful in my life, begun one month ago when you came in and locked the door behind you. —Well? Say something!

KING: I don't know how we're going to work this out but some way will—with locked doors, God, magic—anyhow for a while.

WOMAN DOWNTOWN: Only a while?

[*He looks up as if listening to something, a reverberation, an ominous thing, still not too close—beyond the room and the Woman Downtown—a thing that gives his words a meaning deeper than their surface: a distant, warning trumpet.*]

KING: Life is only a while. Love—longer.

[*The Woman Downtown smiles and caresses him.*]

Now, now, honey, leggo, I'm supposed to get home early tonight.

WOMAN DOWNTOWN: Whose supposition is that?

KING: You heard of Perla, my wife.

WOMAN DOWNTOWN: Not as much as your daughter, La Niña.

KING: This involves La Niña.

WOMAN DOWNTOWN [*sitting up*]: How?

KING: I didn't tell you? She's comin' home tomorrow for a visit. I won't be downtown tomorrow . . .

WOMAN DOWNTOWN: Neither will I, King. Not down this town, anyhow . . .

KING: She's only comin' home for a short visit before she goes back to work.

WOMAN DOWNTOWN [*pouring herself a drink*]: I didn't mean I was leaving because of her. Actually her visit is very well-timed, coincides with a trip I'm obliged to make. Your friend Juan in the kitchen, can he still be trusted?

KING: *¡Sí! Amigo. Amigo fiel. ¿Por qué?*

WOMAN DOWNTOWN: The Judge and I have been using him as go-between, a messenger service. Tonight under a metal cover from room service he sent me this letter. It's from the Judge. Read it.

KING [*reading with some difficulty*]: "Congress which otherwise would—would . . ."

WOMAN DOWNTOWN [*assisting him*]: "—adjourn—adjourn this weekend, will hold special session . . ."

KING: How do you know this is from the Judge? Not fake?

WOMAN DOWNTOWN: Juan has called him for me frequently. From a pay phone in town. Last night a manservant of the Judge got on Juan's bus and passed him this. —It's not fake. [*She reads.*] "You will accompany me. Reservation made on Braniff Airlines, Flight 68, departing for Washington, D. C., 5:00 p.m. My car will pass service entrance at 4:15 exactly . . ."

[*King looks up. There is a pause.*]

KING: When?

WOMAN DOWNTOWN: Tomorrow.

[*He looks at her darkly.*]

—Originals of those photostat papers I mentioned once—remember?—have been decoded. Judge Collister and I are taking them to the capital and I—if I shouldn't be able, after I testify, to return to here, or anywhere near here—would it mean I'd never see you again?

[*She sits down very gravely and searches his face with her eyes.*]

KING: This trip you're taking is—*peligroso—muy peligroso.*

WOMAN DOWNTOWN: Dangerous yes, very yes, very—

[*She continues to stare at him gravely. He takes the drink from her hand and drains it. He pours another and returns the tumbler to her. She drinks; he drinks again. Sounds are heard: fireworks crackling and horns blowing below.*]

—Once you said, "Time has no limit for us."

KING: *Madre de Cristo*, forget it. The Judge is old, let him go! You? No.

WOMAN DOWNTOWN: No I'm going, it's an obligation, a, a—*my God, it sounds like all hell's broken out down there!*

[*She crosses abruptly to the window, raises the shade, then cries out repeatedly and wildly.*]

His sign, his sign, the Red Devil Battery sign, grinning at me through the window!

[*A red glare pulses in.*]

KING [*holding her*]: It's just an electric sign, honey. The building is being opened tonight by the Mayor. That's all, that's—

WOMAN DOWNTOWN: All? All? Battery Empire's devil-face grinning in at me?!

KING: Lie down, I'll—

[*He rushes to lower the shade.*]

WOMAN DOWNTOWN: *I can still see it; it pulses like blood through the shade!*

[*The red glare is extinguished. She crouches sobbing on the bed. He crosses to her. She plunges to him and starts tearing his clothes off.*]

341

KING: Now, now, love, you're—acting like a—

WOMAN DOWNTOWN: She-wolf? —Make love! Make love!

[*Pause.*]

KING: —After—all that?

[*She is undressing him. After a while she lets go of him and lies back on the pillows. He finally speaks huskily, shamed.*]

I'm sorry about that, but you know sometimes in a man it just don't work . . .

[*He sits on the edge of the bed.*]

—I want a cigarette.

WOMAN DOWNTOWN: I want a drink.

KING: Forget it. You don't need a drink.

[*They are both frustrated and angry.*]

WOMAN DOWNTOWN: I've got to have *something* tonight.

[*She reaches for the bottle.*]

KING: Put down the bottle.

[*She doesn't.*]

I don't like what you're doing; there's no future in it.

WOMAN DOWNTOWN: Just to wash down a pill, can't swallow it dry.

KING: You're going to wind up not young anymore, not beautiful, not elegant, but—

WOMAN DOWNTOWN: Yes, yes, *puta!*

KING: The kind that's picked up by any stranger and banged in alleys and back of trucks—I am—going to go home. How do I know what a wolf-howling woman might do or not do 'cause a—invalid man couldn't satisfy her one night out of a month.

[*Abruptly tender, she sits up, breasts exposed in the dim, aqueous light.*]

WOMAN DOWNTOWN: That was awful, forgive me! It made me vicious because I needed you so terribly this time that could be the last time.

KING: I guess a little of him was bound to rub off on you, love.

WOMAN DOWNTOWN: Moments, only moments. I turn to an animal.

[*Pause. He seems away.*]

—Am I with you or alone in space?

KING: —I think this Washington trip is—

WOMAN DOWNTOWN: I know what you think. You're right. Maybe just a gesture, and maybe—fatal. But doesn't it make a sort of dignified monument to mark where I was, a woman without a name, inclined to wolf-howls at night? Are you still on the bed?

[*He nods, silent.*]

343

Just seated beside me, not touching?

[*He slowly turns to look at her, then throws himself into her arms. The room is dimmed out. Music. When the room is lighted again, he is beside the bed, nearly dressed. She is watching him from the bed.*]

You know, there's somewhere beyond, and that time I think we went there.

KING: —Sleep, now?

WOMAN DOWNTOWN: Yes, now, quickly. This kind of exhaustion's a comfort, all the truth and then love.

[*He crosses to the window and opens the drapes.*]

Don't!

KING: I think it's daybreak.

[*He raises the shade to the pulsing red glare. She stares at it unblinking. He raises his right forearm and strikes it with his left palm.*]

Battery Man, here is to you, my salute!

WOMAN DOWNTOWN: Again, for me!

KING: Yeah, again, for us both!

THE SCENE DIMS OUT AND FAST CURTAIN

ACT THREE

We see the city in profile, many windows of tall buildings are catching the light of sunset; they are like myriad candles and they change color during the phone conversation, turning from gold to flame and to ashes of flame and, finally, to dark, with here and there a point of electric light or a touch of neon. On top of the highest tower is the only neon sign which is now visible. It is the Red Devil Battery Sign. It should not be consistently vivid; it should fade during episodes of the play from which it might distract. King is seated, naked to the waist, at a small kitchen table; beside him is a standing, revolving fan; his sweat-drenched shirt billows like a white signal of surrender before the fan which revolves with a low humming sound. Since King was last seen, he has suffered an accident: a gauze bandage about an inch and a half square, neatly secured by tape, makes it apparent that he has received an injury to his forehead. But what is most noticeable although not always present are odd hesitations and mistakes in his speech and inaccuracies in his reach for things. He may not be as mobile during the phone talk as the Woman Downtown, but he should remain by no means static. . . . As the scene begins there is a spot on the Woman Downtown, speaking in a voice strangulated by shock.

|||||||||||||||||||||||||||||||||||||||||||||||||||||||||||||||||||||||||||||||||||||||||||||||||||||||

KING: Hello? Yes?

WOMAN DOWNTOWN: King! I'm calling from hotel kitchen; Juan is guarding the doors. Can't you speak? Am I Charlie the barman?

KING: No. . . . Perla meeting La Niña. At airport.

WOMAN DOWNTOWN: Had to call you even if they were there. King, King, they've killed him! They've killed him!

KING: *Cálmate, cálmate.* —Who? Killed?

WOMAN DOWNTOWN: Guardian! Judge Collister. Raided downtown office. Shot guards, entered and killed him. Looted the files, got decoded documents. But I'm . . . telling it backwards. King, I got this phone call today from some anonymous caller in the Battery Empire's legal department.

KING: The call a threat?

WOMAN DOWNTOWN: Yes, threat. Anonymous voice said: I speak for man from whom you stole documents. You make no move that's unknown. All is monitored. So be careful if you value your . . .

KING: Life?

WOMAN DOWNTOWN: Yes. Life. Voice continued: This eminent, unreachable, unimpeachable man has authorized us to advise you to leave country at once, leave continent. Go to Europe or Asia and stay there, passport and passage provided under false name, surrender all claim of connection as if you had never existed in his life or you won't exist in his life because you will *not exist!*

KING: I think they could do that with that much money, love, because that much money talks and when it talks there is no answer.

WOMAN DOWNTOWN: Oh, yes, it talks, money talks, not heads, not hearts, not tongues of prophets or angels, but money does, oh money hollers, love.

KING: —I think your master of Hacienda with his battery sign and his secrets has money enough and power enough to obliterate all life on earth, generals, rulers, presidents—and yours, Downtown Woman—

WOMAN DOWNTOWN: —King, what's wrong with your voice, you talk so slow and you—you—

KING [*looking slowly into space*]: —Something happened to me today—

WOMAN DOWNTOWN: *What?*

KING [*now speaking with a toneless deliberation again*]: —I started to walk to a store. All of a sudden I could see two sidewalks. I took the wrong one. [*He chuckles darkly.*] I came to in a—in a—drugstore with a cut on my forehead—

[*A door slamming is heard.*]

No, no, Charlie, no game of cards tonight.

[*Perla appears in her black straw hat with the plastic cherries.*]

WOMAN DOWNTOWN: Oh, I get it, they're home! Call me back in the bar!

KING: Yep. Maybe tomorrow.

[*King hangs up the phone. The Woman Downtown retreats into the shadow upstage.*]

PERLA: "Downtown Charlie" again, huh? Ev'ry time I, ev'ry night I—

KING: Where's the kid, Perla?

PERLA: They went to pick up some stuff for supper.

KING [*carefully, darkly*]: —They, did you say "they"? —She arrived with the Trio?

PERLA: —What's wrong with your forehead?

KING: That, nothing, a—little bump. I knew something was wrong. Is Niña married?

PERLA: What's wrong is that she *ain't*.

KING: She's—going—with—some man?

PERLA: Yeah, and the man is married.

KING: You just said she wasn't married.

PERLA [*shouting, shaking*]: I said *SHE* ain't, but *HE* is!

KING: Oh. Separate. No. Let me—get this—straight.

PERLA: Yeah, do that. Try! How did you get that bump?

KING: —Bump? Oh, nothing—important.

[*He grins at her savagely.*]

PERLA: Important enough to put a bandage on you big as that?

KING: We're talking on diff'rent subjects. Will you stick to one?

PERLA: Yes. The bandage.

[*She reaches to touch it, and he slaps her hand violently away.*]

AHH!

KING: That is not the subject. Will you take off that goddam hat with fake cherries on it? An' wipe the sweat off your face; you look like a spick chambermaid at The Yellow Rose Hotel with that shiny piece of straw like a chocolate sundae with cherries on it!

[*He snatches off the hat and rips it in two.*]

PERLA: *My hat!*

KING: *Donate it!* —To the *dump yard!* Now set down and draw a natural breath.

[*She snatches at a pencil and paper.*]

Don't snatch nothing from me! Remember I drove a car. A Mercedes limousine, before an accident made me your—*invalid—dependent!*

PERLA: —King . . .

[*She half-extends a hand to his head. He knocks it away.*]

KING: Yes, I lived like a king with King's Men and drove all night between gigs in a—limousine, not a trolley, before I became your—*invalid—dependent!*

PERLA [*suddenly in tears*]: —Your mother named you Rey. When you were a little boy they called you Reyecito, the little King.

KING: *Explícame,* La Niña, *¿dónde* . . . ?

PERLA: *Atiende, cállate.* She's been living almost a year with

349

a married man in Chicago and—he's here! —Now are you satisfied with the explanation? Be prepared for a shock—she looks like a tramp!

KING: Cancelled? Out of her jobs?

PERLA: She ask me to go with her to the ladies' room at the airport. Soon's we got in, she grabbed my arm and said, "Mama, he's got a pistol on him!"

KING [*slowly*]: Looks like a tramp and is living with a—hood?

PERLA: *Shut up! They're coming in!*

[*La Niña enters the kitchen area, nervously meeting the cold scrutiny of her father. She is still beautiful but the fresh, young being which King remembers has been lost and he regards her as if she had criminally robbed him of it now as he faces his death. During the several beats of silence as they regard each other almost as if the scene were frozen into a tableau, we hear the ghostly Mariachis singing, just audibly.*]

KING [*finally*]: Well, kid?

LA NIÑA [*with a sobbing catch of breath*]: Hi, Daddy.

KING: I guess you were cancelled out. Makes two.

PERLA: What kind of way is that to receive your daughter?

LA NIÑA: —How did you hurt your—?

[*Perla gestures to La Niña to introduce McCabe.*]

Papa, this is Mr. Terrence McCabe.

[*There is another moment of silence. McCabe deposits groceries awkwardly, shuffles forward and extends a shaky hand to King.*]

MCCABE [*in a hollow, pleading voice*]: Hi, Pop.

KING: —Who the fuck is this man calling me "Pop"?

LA NIÑA: —Daddy, he's a—friend of—[*Her voice expires.*]

PERLA: He's the man that followed her down here . . .

LA NIÑA: We stayed outside; we thought you'd prepare him for—

KING: —Words—don't prepare—for appearance. Christ, you do look like a tramp.

[*McCabe circles La Niña into his arms. A great emotional violence rises in King.*]

Things have slipped from control! Money, Battery money!

LA NIÑA: King, what are you, what is he—?

PERLA: He hurt his head.

KING: *¡Cállate!* —The outfit, King's Men, is not managed by me. Now. . . . *Dig?* No more than you're in the Pump Room. *Why?* You put no value on nothing but fucking? Booze, you're on that, too? Booze and bed with—this prick?

MCCABE [*arm about La Niña*]: King she's shaking.

KING: Let her shake your hand off her!

351

[He staggers to his feet and falls back into the chair, nearly throwing it over. McCabe catches the chair back.]

—You prick of a mick come here with—unlicensed firearm and my daughter a slob!

[King suddenly drops the pencil, jerks open the table drawer and pulls a carving knife out and points it at McCabe's groin. McCabe covers the threatened area with a hand.]

Now we are both armed, but I have an advantage. My weapon's in my hand, ready for surgery on you if you don't surrender to me this unlicensed firearm right now.

LA NIÑA: King, we've got to work it out quietly, not this way.

MCCABE: Niña and me, we've been through a lot together; we can't explain all at once.

PERLA: King, King I think—

KING *[without looking at her]*: Think, do you, you think? I never thought you thought!

MCCABE: If we could all sit down without the knife pointed at me. Can't we? All? Sit down?

KING: Naw, naw, no room in the room, just, just standing room only! With La Niña singing!

[He gulps a rasping breath. La Niña leans toward him, hands resting on the table, and sings.]

LA NIÑA: . . . *Amor, amor, amor.*

[His eyes focus on her slowly.]

KING: —Yes, presenting—the star . . .

PERLA: Sing in the kitchen and put the food on plates; we can't have supper out of the boxes.

LA NIÑA [*breaking away*]: Who wants supper?

KING: Supper? They come for *supper?*

PERLA: Yes, it's time for—

KING: *Supper?*

PERLA: *¡Ayúdame en la cocina!*

[*She seizes the girl's arm again and draws her into the kitchenette, then returns for the bags. McCabe, assisting her, spills them. King sways forward.*]

MCCABE [*rushing to catch his shoulder*]: Watch it!

LA NIÑA [*in kitchenette*]: You never said a thing to me.

PERLA: I said wait till I call you.

LA NIÑA: Till *now,* for *this,* the *end?*

PERLA: *Here!*

[*Perla slams a plate on the table.*]

LA NIÑA: Supper off broken plates, Mama?

PERLA: Yeh, ain't everything broke?

[*There is a moment of silence. They turn opposite ways, sobbing. The Mariachis sing, offstage.*]

MARIACHIS [*offstage, softly*]: . . . *Amor, amor.*

[*There is another moment of silence. Then the phone rings on the table between the two men. King slowly picks up the receiver. Spotlight on the Woman Downtown.*]

KING [*speech slurred or gasping*]: Charlie? —Y'know I told you I can't come downtown tonight. My girl, my daughter's just come back from Chicago, with a serious problem—no game for tonight, cancelled.

[*King hangs up. The spot goes out on the Woman Downtown. Perla appears in the doorway.*]

PERLA: Downtown Charlie calling back so quick? —How stupid am I, King, in your opinion of me?

KING [*fiercely*]: Perla, give me time to think over this question.

PERLA: Oh, have I got some things to speak to you later.

[*She turns and leaves, beginning to cry.*]

MCCABE: Niña's been homesick, depressed since—she lost a— baby we were expecting . . .

KING: Expecting? A baby? By you? Baby face?

MCCABE: There was—no one but me.

KING: And your wife? Don't exist in the picture, not inside the frame of it? You're married but slept with my daughter and—!

[*He springs up and strikes McCabe. The blow is hard, but McCabe seems not to feel it.*]

—Did I hit you?

MCCABE [*quietly*]: Yeah. —Why not?

KING: —You rented a car. Get back in it and go.

MCCABE: Where? Without Niña. There's only two ways out. I stay with Niña or check out of my life.

KING: —Hysteria's for women. You've got a gun? —I have some trouble walking and I want to talk to you, private, in the yard. Help me. Don't make it noticeable to them. I'll hang on your arm like a—close buddy and we'll—make it slow . . . slow . . .

MCCABE: Yes, the talk should be private. Between us. —Ready? —*¿Pronto?*

KING: Wait till—I see better. [*He grasps McCabe's arm.*] All right. Ready. Start now.

[*Very slowly they advance toward the yard. The crossing is bizarre, the women watching in shocked silence. King and McCabe enter the kitchen. King tries desperately to move and speak naturally, but the walk and staring eyes betray his condition.*]

PERLA: *Hace frío afuera.*

[*She snatches up a shawl and puts it about him.*]

KING [*tearing it off*]: *For Christ's sake, bitch, don't put a mantilla on me!*

LA NIÑA: Papa!

KING: You know I got up with the men and I sang.

LA NIÑA: *Bueno*, Papa.

MCCABE: Take my jacket.

KING: Naw, naw, will you go in the goddam yard? It's cooler in the yard for—conversation that's—necessary.

MCCABE: There's two steps down.

KING: Yes, I remember the number.

MCCABE: Yes, it's cooler out. I feel a breeze.

KING: Yes—it's—cooler out. You feel—?

MCCABE: —A breeze. I've been sweating all day, very—profusely like I had a—fever. I guess—anxiety, Pop.

KING: —I have—limit of—vision. Chairs?

MCCABE: Yes, this way, no hurry.

KING: That's—your opinion, not—mine.

[*They advance downstage to the yard as formally as a pair of pallbearers.*]

I think—there is—a hurry.

MCCABE: Here they are. Take a seat.

[*Perla moves back into the house.*]

KING: Take your hands off me!

[*He falls, gasping, into one of the chairs. McCabe puts the shirt about him. He fastens one button and King tears the shirt open.*]

I will—not be—buttoned!

MCCABE: —I—understand. A man—

KING: Is not a man if—supported and limited and—buttoned. A Chinaman—said to me once—in next bed at—hospital—"Death is not big enough to hold life and life is not big enough to hold death"—and yet that morning the problem—solved itself very simple with a white canvas curtain to—

MCCABE: —Conceal the—?

KING: *Solution!* Your name is?

MCCABE: My name's—Terry McCabe.

KING: Sorry I . . . forgot. Such a nice Irish name. You run out of potatoes too fucking quick and you come here too many and you decided it wasn't potatoes you wanted but liquor and parades and wakes and political power. Bosses and corruption. Oh, back home you're into revolution but here you're into—ripoff. . . . Christ, you babyface mother! —My head aches. Go in. Go in the bathroom and get me—

MCCABE: What?

KING: Something begins with a "D" they use to give me for killing the head pain—Demerol! —Don't say nothing about it, just bring it out.

MCCABE: Right. [*He crosses to the house interior.*] Excuse me. Where is the bathroom?

[*La Niña points.*]

LA NIÑA: Mama, you are lying. *¡Mama, estás mintiendo!* There had to be signs first, something you noticed!

[*Perla is both guilty and defiant.*]

Stop messing with delicatessen stuff.

PERLA: I worked, didn't I work?

LA NIÑA: Never till he fell!

PERLA: You think it was not work for me, too, the travel, the packing, and I got no applause for it, nobody shouted me bravo, nobody called me *olé!* But when—

LA NIÑA: Yes, now you are admitting it now.

PERLA: I tell you like it was, yes!

LA NIÑA: Not facing me with your eyes, but—

[*She seizes a carton of salad and hurls it at her mother. Perla turns on her with a blaze of fury.*]

PERLA: Now with eyes I face you! Signs, there were signs. While I worked, he worked a crossword puzzle, and when I came home to make supper, he still worked on the puzzle, and at supper the fork would slip from his fingers and he would look at nothing like he saw something in nothing!

[*McCabe reappears in the doorway.*]

LA NIÑA: But you never, never did you call me except to say,

"Stay in Chicago," and to make sure that I stayed and to call me "*Puta!*"

PERLA: It was not you but me that my husband belongs to, I thought, I believed, till he come home with perfume-of-women smell on him and sat out there in the yard chair till I went sleepless to bed, all hell out there exploding like in my heart! While the warning, the signals begun to grow.

LA NIÑA: —Mama, I think it's too late to fight over what's left of him.

PERLA: You got something in your hand.

MCCABE: Just—

PERLA: *What?*

MCCABE: Something he asked for from the medicine cabinet.

[*Automatically he reaches out for La Niña and draws her to him. In the yard, King stands facing the house, fists clenched.*]

I like him, I respect him, I bring him what he needs for his pain. Oh, the beer, the six-pack . . .

[*He picks it up and goes into the yard.*]

KING [*as McCabe crosses to him*]: *Dos Gatos* . . . two cats.

MCCABE: I got the, here's the— [*He hands King the Demerol bottle.*] —and beer.

KING: Open for me. —Shit, not the beer, the—

MCCABE [*very gently*]: Sorry, yes. [*He gives King a capsule.*]

KING: Now to wash down the—

[*McCabe extends the beer can to him, but King seems not to see it. Very gently, McCabe thrusts the capsule in King's mouth and then lifts the opened can to his lips.*]

—yes, turning to—dummy, situated by—dump heap . . .

[*There is an explosion in the Hollow. King shouts toward it as if a last cry of defiance. McCabe assists him into the chair.*]

Now. Tell me how did it happen.

MCCABE: I could tell you better if you dropped the knife from your hand, Pop.

KING: One lie out of your mouth and it goes in you, "Son!" So it stays in hand!

MCCABE: My life before I met Niña was—*vacant* as that . . . vacant . . .

[*He gestures toward the Wasteland.*]

KING: —Dump heap?

MCCABE: Yes, empty, empty. Emptiness filled with violence! Oh, I tried to occupy, to satisfy myself with statistics . . .

KING: Occupy with stat? Lift your goddam crybaby head and speak plain to me! *¡Chico!*

MCCABE: Statistics on buyer-consumption—response to—promotion—commercials.

KING: Don't know what you're—

MCCABE: *I said that I'm a trained, well-trained, computer is what I said! Programmed to be not human! But—I am! Human!*

[*Perla throws open the door.*]

KING: Don't—shout at—my head—"Son!" —There is a *pressure*—in it.

MCCABE: You said "speak plain." [*He rises abruptly.*] What more do you want to know? I went out nights alone. Sat alone at bars. Then once—the room where Nina, to this place on the lakefront, where she worked with a trio. I saw what was *not empty.* Stayed and stayed till they shut the place each night. Finally one night at closing I worked up the courage to send a note to her: "Let me buy you a drink, please."

KING: She answered this—*proposition?*

MCCABE: Don't—don't call it that!

KING: Then call it *what?*

MCCABE: —It was no proposition. It was an—appeal. She granted. I could talk, just held her arm close against me. And we didn't talk at the table. Very little, very difficult till—

KING: What?

MCCABE: My eyes blurred—over with—

KING: *¡Lágrimas! Tears!*

MCCABE: I seemed to be looking at her through—tears. Then she took hold of my hand. And what she said to me then was: "—You—are in pain like—my father." Then— "Wait here a

361

moment." —She—booked a room and came back and said, "I will hold you tonight, I will just hold you," she said.

KING: "Hold you?" That was all?

MCCABE: *Then.* But the next night—*all* . . .

[*A distant explosion is heard.*]

What was . . . ?

KING: Shots between gangs in the Hollow. —Between here and downtown is this hollow for dumping. Fog collects in it. It is—playground for—kids, yeah, they dig caves in that hollow out there in that—rubble, heaving rocks at each other, some nights, shots, explosions, soft drink bottles with nitro. Oh, it's not—not—put in headlines but—is going on all the time and people don't dare admit—how far it has—gone, no, not yet, but soon it will blast too big for—city—denies. I'm expected downtown.

[*He is standing, gripping McCabe's shoulder for support.*]

MCCABE: I will drive you there, King.

KING: Not downtown, just—is she watching? List'ning?

MCCABE: No.

KING: What are you? Baby-face *boy* or *man?*

MCCABE: La Niña is pregnant, again.

[*King stares at him silently for a moment; then drops the knife.*]

KING: Now. Give—firearm.

MCCABE: That—subject we'd—covered.

KING: Not cover till firearm surrender. Give me the . . .

MCCABE: If you say "stay." I can't until you say "stay."

KING [*shouting*]: *STAY*. My child bearing your child?

MCCABE [*urgently, with love*]: My child growing in yours.
Life is continued that way, a child of a man bears a child of a
man—

KING: And the man—dies.

MCCABE: But the life of him is continued.

[*Another explosion is heard in the Hollow.*]

KING: I taste—blood in my—mouth . . .

[*He staggers; McCabe holds him tight again.*]

Gracias. Yes. Stay. But then, what? For La Niña? To turn to a
slob, gradual, like her *madre*, not singing but remembering singing? Too tired to dance flamenco, but remembering flamenco?
This girl I made and gave to the world, she what could have
stood higher than the new sign on the new skyscraper, tallest in
Corona, one you see nights miles away. *That!* —That—height—
for her was my dream, the dream of a man with quick death in
his skull, this flowerpot of a skull with a flower in it that is
cracking the pot. I think you want just your comfort, not her—
glory.

MCCABE: No—no.

KING: Aw, don't say no, just "no" like a kid asked if he stole
something. No is too easy to say to a question that big.

MCCABE: I want her to be again the way that she was—the way you remember and I give you my word.

KING: —When a man gives his word he gives a—guarantee of it, a pledge, a thing for, for security on his word, if he's a stranger. And you're still a stranger to me.

MCCABE: What do you want?

KING: I want the—firearm you got on you.

MCCABE: Here. Take it. It's yours. I have no use for it now. She will deliver the child and she will go back to what she was made for, by you. I want her to be the—

KING: —Highest?

MCCABE: The girl I first knew—

[*He has surrendered his revolver to King.*]

I may be a stranger to you. You're not to me.

KING: Just tell me which way is the gate because I'm leaving now. I have a date with a downtown woman, downtown.

MCCABE: Let me take you there to her.

KING: No, no, just where's the gate.

MCCABE: Let me walk you to it.

KING: I told you I want no more assistance. I just wanted your word and the pledge in my pocket. I see it now, I'll make it.

[*He stumbles rapidly forward but encounters the fence, not*

the gate, and crashes fiercely through it. He stands by the
broken fence as King's Men appear at either side of the stage.
McCabe clings to the back of a yard chair for a moment. His
eyes are tightly shut, then he looks into the sky. There is a
muted clash in the Hollow.]

MCCABE [whirling toward the house]: Niña! Niña!

[Perla rushes to the kitchen door; she makes a disgusted gesture and turns to the girl.]

PERLA: *¡Tu caballero loco te llama afuera!*

[La Niña descends into the yard. McCabe extends his arms
to her.]

MCCABE: It is settled between us.

LA NIÑA: How?

MCCABE: *I stay!* —He wants it.

LA NIÑA: Where is King?

[Perla approaches behind them. The following dialogue is fast
with some overlaps.]

PERLA: Supper is set if anybody wants food.

LA NIÑA [clinging to McCabe]: Where is the pistol?

MCCABE: He made me surrender it to him for permission to
stay.

PERLA [hearing this, crying out]: You surrender death to
him! *King!*

365

MCCABE: A King can die like a king.

PERLA: *Where is he? Look! The fence is broken!*

MCCABE: That is a man's right if he wants it.

PERLA [*rushing to the broken fence*]: A crowd is on corner. *King!*

[*She collapses to her knees, clinging to the fence post. The house and yard begin to dim. McCabe catches hold of La Niña as she rushes toward the fence.*]

MCCABE: Stay here, be calm, think just of our child in your body; for King and for me, keep it safe in you . . . safe.

THE YARD DIMS OUT COMPLETELY

SCENE TWO

The Mariachis sing as a section of the lounge is lighted. There is a spot on the Woman Downtown.

DRUMMER: *¿Qué tal, Chiquita?*

WOMAN DOWNTOWN [*fiercely*]: Intimate form of address like to *puta*. Translates to "How'm I doing." *Bueno, muy bueno,* like the best in hell ever.

[*The Drummer, giving a quick look about, circles her low with an arm.*]

Your hand is presumptuous, Drummer, I'm still in King's kingdom.

DRUMMER: King's lost his kingdom.

WOMAN DOWNTOWN: *¡Disputable!*

DRUMMER: *Por favor.*

[*He circles her unsteady body again.*]

WOMAN DOWNTOWN: Snake arm, quick as rattler from desert rock.

[*The bar phone rings. King appears on the forestage, opposite side.*]

Phone!

[*The Barman touches the phone to establish it. The profile of the city is dimly visible between King and the Woman Downtown. The Woman speaks furiously to the Barman.*]

He's hung up! You took so long to call me, he's hung up!

KING: No, love, I—try to—spe—I am—trying to—speak.

WOMAN DOWNTOWN: I can hear you breathing.

KING: Yeh. Still breathing. I started to come downtown but only got to the drugstore on the corner.

WOMAN DOWNTOWN [*controlled*]: That's all right. I'll come there in a cab. Barman, call me a cab, quick. See, I've called a cab. Now give me the address. I will come and get you.

KING: No, just listen. I called to tell you good-bye.

WOMAN DOWNTOWN: Hold on a minute. Barman, have this call traced. Have a phone operator trace where it's from, please hurry, it's—emergency! [*She has covered the mouth of the phone.*]

KING: I heard you, there's no time.

WOMAN DOWNTOWN: Oh, yes, there is, there's always more time than you think. And listen, you great son of a bitch, you owe it to me. Give it to me or I'll—

KING: Yes, I know what you'll do and I can't stop you.

WOMAN DOWNTOWN [*turning from him to cry out to the Barman*]: Have you traced it, have you got the address—drugstore—Crestview.

[*The Mariachis fade in.*]

King? Love? It's all right, you know. King. King, I've moved
to a room with no Red Devil grinning through the window, a
room the opposite from it but with a bed king-size for you to lie
with me once more and I've prepared the room for you. I knew
you were coming downtown. There are—roses, fresh linen, clean
air! Mariachi. I will undress you. I'll hold you.

[*She is crossing the stage, imploringly, toward him.*]

Now, just give me the address of the drugstore to bring you
where we can go together as it's meant to be, King. Listen. Do
you remember the night I first saw you? My life began that
night and is going to end this one. Can you hear me, King? All
I hear is your breath. Tonight I won't say a word that isn't right
for a lady to say, I swear. We have to go but we have to go
together.

KING: Honey, I told you—I can't make it downtown.

WOMAN DOWNTOWN: Oh, but you can and you will.

KING: —Good-bye, love. I think the drugstoreman has called
an ambulance to take me away and they'd drill through my
skull to cut at the flower, to prune it. What would be left? A—
imbecile?! No! I have to go quick, now.

WOMAN DOWNTOWN: I dare you to hang up on me, don't you
dare hang up on me. I will stop the ambulance at the drugstore.
I'll take you to my room at the Yellow Rose or be—an uniden-
tified—female body—mutilated past recognition back of a truck
in an alley if you don't tell me where—

KING: Good—bye—love . . . *much* . . . *loved!*

[*He staggers to his knees and in the fall the revolver slides
out of his reach. The Pharmacist, an elderly man, gentle, anxious, stoops to pick it up.*]

369

That's—mine, return, please.

OLD MAN: *Son*, they're coming for you. Hang on, just—hang on . . .

[*King tries to rise; the Old Man helps him into a chair but stands back as King reaches for the revolver now in the man's jacket pocket.*]

KING: Christ, it's all I got left, Pop. She said she is coming.

[*The Drummer is in whispered colloquy with Charlie. As the Woman Downtown staggers, near collapse, back to the bar, Charlie, face impassive as stone, jerks his head toward the shadowy upstage, a signal to the Drummer who exits that way.*]

WOMAN DOWNTOWN [*to the Barman*]: Traced it, did you trace it?

CHARLIE: Wasn't time.

[*She turns about frantically and sees Crewcut at the entrance.*]

WOMAN DOWNTOWN: Get "Crewcut" away from that door. I'm coming out that door, and it's worth this and this and this and this to me to get to the taxi rank on the curb!

[*She has thrust bills across the bar.*]

CHARLIE: Know the way?

WOMAN DOWNTOWN: Will find it if not obstructed.

[*There is a vertiginous swirl of color on the cyclorama as she*

*sways, extends her arms sideways for balance, staggers for-
ward. Crewcut calls to Charlie.*]

CREWCUT: Where's she going?

CHARLIE: To the Drummer Boy in the alley. Don't follow; the
Drummer can handle this better alone out there.

[*As the bar dims out, the dark menacing towers of the night
city appear, projected on the cyclorama. In a very dim circle
of light the Drummer is seen, waiting. A door slams and the
Woman Downtown enters the dim light.*]

WOMAN DOWNTOWN: Drummer!

DRUMMER: *Sí, tamborilero* that King don't like but you do.

WOMAN DOWNTOWN: *Cab, cab!*

[*The Drummer seizes her and pulls her out of the light. He
pulls open her coat, touches her brutally, roughs her up. He
takes a picture; the light of a flash-photo is seen. The Woman
Downtown scratches the Drummer's face.*]

Cab, cab!

[*The Woman Downtown breaks free and exits. The Drummer
puts a handkerchief to his face. As the Woman Downtown
exits, calling for a cab, Charlie and Crewcut re-enter.*]

CAB DRIVER [*offstage*]: Okay, lady, no screamin' is necessary!

CREWCUT [*entering*]: You let her go loose, you goddam—

DRUMMER: Clawed my face bloody!

371

CHARLIE: Follow! Crestview Pharmacy. Move!

[*The Drummer—watched by Charlie and Crewcut—runs off-stage after the Woman Downtown.*]

CROSS FADE LIGHTS

SCENE THREE

<hr>

The pharmacy section of the stage is lighted.

<hr>

KING [*to the Old Man*]: She—said she is coming. Old Man, Pop, don't move. I go to lock door against all that could come to attend—this necessary finish but the lady—nameless—with eyes I want to look into—a last time . . .

[*He stumbles forward slowly, revolver in hand. The Woman Downtown, disheveled, dress torn, appears before him. Slowly, she lifts her hand, meaning "Wait!"*]

WOMAN DOWNTOWN: Wait!

KING [*hoarse, tender*]: You did find without address. Should have stayed where we live, but—

WOMAN DOWNTOWN: I never lived there with anyone but you.

KING: Here—is dangerous—for you. Outside on corner they gather, the—gangs from—

OLD MAN: *Lady, call police. I know those voices out there, bombers, young hoods from the Hollow!*

[*Four apparitional Mariachis appear and advance in their silver-embossed black velvet suits and wide sombreros.*]

KING [*going into fantasy, attempting to stand straight and salute*]: ¡HOMBRES! [*He smiles reassuringly at the Woman Downtown.*] Now you are—protected! —By my men.

WOMAN DOWNTOWN: King, there's no one but you and me and the Old Man.

373

[*In a formal, dance-like fashion, his visionary Mariachis divide about King and the Woman Downtown to form a line between them and the Old Man crouched near the wings, downstage left. The Old Man's quavering voice keeps up a continuous, barely heard, threnody of despair.*]

OLD MAN: Can't sell out, but got to quit.

KING: —Love—request number.

OLD MAN: Got to leave . . .

WOMAN DOWNTOWN: King, oh, King, you're dreaming!

OLD MAN: Got to close . . .

KING: *Sí, sueño.* Dreams necessary.

OLD MAN: Gangs raid houses, stores . . .

KING: "Life is—too big for death?" [*He shakes his head with a savage grin.*] No! *Al contrario.*

OLD MAN: Police don't come . . .

KING: *Solicita el número.*

WOMAN DOWNTOWN: Can't—think! Please! We knew it was coming! Our last time but not here, *¡por favor, no aquí!*

OLD MAN: Don't even pray for help now . . . [*He kneels, covering his face.*]

KING [*oblivious, almost exalted*]: *La señorita solicita una canción, un vals, hombres.*

[*They play softly. King speaks to the Woman Downtown.*]

Don't move. Look me in the eyes.

WOMAN DOWNTOWN: You? Too?

[*He nods. They take opposite chairs, their eyes fixed intensely on each other. Pause.*]

KING: I love—a lady.

WOMAN DOWNTOWN: King, do you respect me, now?

KING: —You? Respect? —Yes! *¡La verdad!* Truth. I give you that name, now.

WOMAN DOWNTOWN [*in a last anguished appeal*]: Then come downtown with me now?

KING: Hospital called, ambulance coming. No time.

WOMAN DOWNTOWN: A cab, my new room are waiting; believe me, I know the best way.

KING: —Your clothes are torn?

WOMAN DOWNTOWN: Just that?

KING: Keep looking in eyes.

[*He lifts the revolver slightly toward his head. She gasps and half rises.*]

Don't move.

[*The door is forced open with a crash and the Drummer*

enters. He flashes a photo. King blinks, then speaks, articulating slowly, fiercely.]

—Oh. Drummer! You—got acquaintance!

[*The revolver has swung toward the Drummer.*]

WOMAN DOWNTOWN: Yes, he followed me.

DRUMMER [*retreating, cat-like*]: If you fire, you hit her, not me.

KING: No, not her! [*He staggers rapidly forward, thrusting her back into the chair.*] I see narrow but straight. First, tell me who pays you, employed by, for what?

[*The Drummer makes a sudden dash for the door. As he flings it open, King fires. The Drummer falls. The Woman Downtown screams. King crashes to the floor with the Woman Downtown clinging to him. The pharmacy door hangs open and a fantastic group enters. These are the wild young denizens of the Hollow. They seem to explode from a dream—and the scene with them. The play stylistically makes its final break with realism. This break must be accomplished as if predetermined in the* mise en scene *from the beginning, as if naturally led up to, startlingly but credibly. The kids, adolescents, some pre-adolescents—they could be as few as four or as many as seven—are outlaws in appearance and dress. The Hollow marks them with streaks of dirt on their faces, bloodied bandages, scant and makeshift garments. Among gangs of this kind there is always an individual who stands out, not as leader with such warring factions, but as the most powerful, the pre-eminent one. In this case, one older than the others, totally fearless, a boy-man with a sense of command and an intelligence that isn't morally nihilistic. His speech is almost more like gutteral explosions of sound with*]

376

gestures. At the entrance of the gang members, the Old Man has rushed to his cash box and thrown himself despairingly across it. A couple of kids, screeching like monkeys, rush at him, but the dominant youth shouts a gutteral command to them. This dominant one has on his singlet, crudely red-lettered, the word, "WOLF"—significantly not "WOLVES."]

WOLF: *Ahgah, nada! Leddum lone wid is nigguls!*

[*Something in his harsh voice rouses the Woman Downtown from her crouched moaning position over King's dead body. Wolf's eyes are on her face, demented with grief. Her eyes meet Wolf's. Her head is thrown back, teeth exposed as a she-wolf snarling. A moment passes. The Wolf nods and advances to her, lifts her to her feet; she offers no resistance. In his supporting hold, she recognizes or senses something rightly appointed as her final fate.*]

WOMAN DOWNTOWN: Yes, you. Take me. Away . . .

[*A savage little hood rushes at her to tear the watch-bracelet from her wrist. Wolf strikes the kid aside and awkwardly but strongly encircles the Woman Downtown's waist with his wire-torn arm.*]

WOLF [*beyond dispute*]: She goes wid us. This is—

WOMAN DOWNTOWN: Woman. [*Gasp.*] Down. [*Gasp.*] Town . . .

WOLF: It's enough, for me and for all. Listen! This woman. Ya mother.

BOY [*with a touch of challenge*]: Motha of—

WOLF: Yes. Mother of all.

377

BOY: Why?

WOLF: Because she is Sister of Wolf!

[*A flare goes off behind them and a muted sound of explosion is heard in the Hollow. Against its lingering, warning glow, the denizens of the Hollow all advance, eyes wide, looking out at us who have failed or betrayed them. The Woman Downtown advances furthest to where King's body has fallen. She throws back her head and utters the lost but defiant outcry of the she-wolf. The cry is awesome. There is a second explosion and a greater, whiter flare, exposing more desolation. Wolf takes her hand. All are standing motionless.*]

THE SCENE DIMS OUT

THE END